THE
TRUTH
About
BREAST
CANCER

CLAIRE HOY

First published in 1995 by
Stoddart Publishing Co. Limited
34 Lesmill Road
Toronto, Canada
M3B 2T6
(416) 445-3333

Canadian Cataloguing in Publication Data

Hoy, Claire
The truth about breast cancer

ISBN 0-7737-2833-3

1. Breast — Cancer — Political aspects.
2. Breast — Cancer — Treatment.   3. Women —
Diseases.   I. Title.

RC280.B8H6 1994   362.1'96994490082
C94-931322-X

Cover Design: Bill Douglas/The Bang

Printed and bound in Canada

"Please Forgive Me If I Cry" reprinted with
permission of the *Toronto Sun*.

*Stoddart Publishing gratefully acknowledges the
support of the Canada Council, the Ontario Ministry
of Culture, Tourism, and Recreation, Ontario Arts
Council, and Ontario Publishing Centre in the
development of writing and publishing in Canada.*

To Beverley,
in loving memory

Contents

Preface

I WAS SITTING IN THE WEST BLOCK cafeteria on Parliament Hill in December 1992 eating the soup of the day and grousing about the heavy publicity given to Canada's health minister, Benoit Bouchard, who had just announced in Toronto that the federal government was giving $25 million to breast-cancer research over the next five years.

Like most people, I became acutely aware of this dreaded disease only when it hit close to home, when my wife was diagnosed with it in 1974, two years before she died at age 33.

Over the years, I had often wondered why the women's organizations didn't raise more of a stink about the lack of breast-cancer research and why the formal cancer societies love to put such a happy face on the disease despite its ever-increasing toll.

But Bouchard's smug pronouncement, and the resulting congratulatory reaction, really burned me. Big deal, I thought.

Veteran journalist Judy Morrison, then with CBC radio, one of several people at the table with me, said simply, "Why don't you write a book about it? You obviously have your strong personal experiences and nobody could accuse you of writing a feminist tract."

So I did. But not without considerable help.

As usual, the Parliamentary Library went out of its way to be helpful, not only the staff in the main library, but the clipping service and reading room as well.

My two researchers, Tom Korski in Ottawa and Charlotte Montgomery in Toronto, were fantastic. Without their impressive legwork, the book would not be as complete as it is. And many of my other journalistic colleagues chipped in voluntarily by sending me clippings and suggestions for interviews on a regular basis. And my son Paul used his computer skills to research the electronic highway.

I also want to thank my wife Lydia for her constant encouragement, and my publisher and editors for their invaluable contributions.

Claire Hoy
Toronto, Ontario
August 1994

Prologue:
Please Forgive Me
If I Cry

WHERE TO BEGIN? WHAT TO SAY?

*

Memories. Late fall in 1956 when I stood her up on a blind date to flip around with a gang of friends.

Or two weeks later when I met her formally after shooting her in the behind with a pellet gun as she skated by.

And 1963. Marriage. Able to rent and furnish an apartment because she had worked and saved her money. She liked to plan.

1966. Our son, Paul, is born. 1968, Kathy is born. Good years. Good times.

Now she is dead.

What do you say about someone you knew and loved for 20 of her 33 years? How do you put your heart into words?

This column is not really meant for people to read. I shouldn't be writing it. It is too personal, too intense. It is a way for me to ease the pain, to commit to paper the life I spent, we spent, before cancer killed her June 2, the day after our 13th anniversary.

Please forgive me for becoming personal. Normally I write political stuff. I suppose all columns are personal. That's what makes them columns. But now I am not an observer. I am a participant.

I remember March 4, her last birthday. She had just finished a long series of radiation treatments. As we were going to bed she sat up, tears running down her cheeks, turned to me, kissed me gently and whispered, "I guess I'm losing aren't I?"

She faced it better than I did.

When famous people die it is big news. We list their accomplishments; quote other famous people saying nice things about them.

When ordinary people die, like my Beverley, it is more private. Those who knew her suffered pain. Those who loved her lost a vital chunk of themselves.

Please forgive me if I cry.

Our . . . my . . . children, what of them? She asked of them up to the end. Let them remember me; let them know how much I loved them, how I'll miss them, how I'll be waiting for them.

They know that, but they ask: Why Mommy?

Kathy coming home from school, eight years old, asking, "Daddy, what is cancer?" I try to answer but they change the subject. They don't want to know for sure what they already know in their hearts.

What is appropriate to say for your wife, the mother of your children; a warm, compassionate, witty woman, who now is gone?

I'm sure most of you have suffered the kind of wrench, the pain that right now drags me and my children down. I'm sure, like us, you ask, Why?

Death was no surprise. We'd known since November. But that doesn't make you ready. It makes you think you're ready, but when stillness came, it tore out a chunk of my gut, a piece of my brain. We are not as strong as we think we are. Even if I am the original rock.

For a few days the activity comforts you. Help the children, make funeral arrangements, greet friends who come to pay respects, cry gently at the funeral, watch them bury her, go with friends, acquaintances, relatives you only see at weddings and funerals, for a sandwich and drink. You must be strong.

That night you and the children drive home. Alone. You walk into the house you've shared and you know, for the first time you really know, that she is not home and not coming home. The children know it too.

"Now I lay me down to sleep . . ." you repeat with them, as Mommy often did, but you can't get by the part which says "God bless Mommy . . ."

Why, the children ask again, crying? How can you explain when that's all you've been asking yourself? Why? Why her? Why a young, vibrant mother, a beautiful woman with everything to live for? Why?

You rationalize at least her suffering is over. You find some comfort, not much, telling the children that because of her we have each other; we have the memories, the knowledge we loved her. "I don't want the memories, I want my mother," Paul says. There is no answer for that.

We have a million pictures, the last one our boy took Easter Sunday, the last day she spent at home. She is smiling. I am not.

We are packing now to move. My daughter told a neighbor she did not like this house because "it made my Mommy sick."

Time to start again, to pick up the pieces, to carry on.

I know I should be thankful for the time we shared, the children, the 20 years, the treasury of memories.

In time, it will be easier to convince ourselves of that, to remember the joy without feeling the pain. In time, we will join her again, a belief which, despite being so out of fashion, offers the strength to carry us through.

I cherish memories; I cling to faith. I'll remember her smile when I showed her the yellow roses on our anniversary. She loved yellow roses. She whispered "anniversary," then drifted off to sleep.

Last week, I had to throw the roses out. I'll remember them, and her, always.

I'll see her in the faces of the children.

You would have liked her too. And you would have wondered why it happened.

1 The Politics of Breast Cancer

ON AUGUST 15, 1993, NEW YORK MODEL Matuschka published a startling portrait of herself on the cover of the *New York Times Magazine*, her white dress cut dramatically away to reveal a mastectomy-scarred chest where her right breast used to be.

For most readers, it was their first horrifying glimpse at the ravages of breast cancer on a woman's body. Many readers reacted with outrage; others with praise. A *Times* spokeswoman was quoted as saying the calls were "about 50-50 pro and con . . ."

The headline on the magazine declared: "You Can't Look Away Anymore."

Matuschka certainly hasn't been looking away. A former lingerie model whose mother died of breast cancer, she lost her own breast in 1991. Before that she regularly displayed photos of her breasts in her work. Now, as part of a group called WHAM (Women's Health Action and

Mobilization), she distributes poster-sized, one-breasted portraits of herself.

To a large extent, however, this disease, which kills one North American woman every 12 minutes, has been spirited away in its own little closet, hidden from constant view, whispered about as one of those "women's problems" and widely ignored by politicians, medical researchers and lobbyists — including women's lobby groups, who spend most of their time on more politically in-tune causes.

Graphic photographs of dying AIDS victims are not unusual on our TV screens or newspapers and magazines. Nor are poignant pictures of the bloated bellies and emaciated limbs of starving Third World children, or the bullet-riddled corpses and bloody, mutilated victims of wars the world over.

But who wants to see a 60-year-old one-breasted woman filling their TV screen? And they're the lucky ones: those who survive breast cancer.

Breasts, of course, are an integral part of the Western conception of beauty. Many women who have lost one or both breasts can't bear to look at themselves any longer and dress and undress in the dark. Everywhere we look in society, we see breasts — in men's and women's magazines, in advertisements, on the beach. To some extent women have grown up measuring their self-worth by the size and shape of their breasts.

Despite the frightening incidence of this form of cancer in our society, few have actually seen what a mastectomy can do.

Artist Linda Robinson Walker, writing in the *Washington Post* about witnessing the "still-raw mastectomy wound" of her friend, wrote: "I had never seen a mastectomy scar before, either in a picture or in person. That this could be true, that I could have reached my 50th year so protected and insulated, sent me on a search for images and understanding. It was a frustrating search. A pall of silence, denial and distraction has hidden from us what it means and looks like to lose a breast."

Breast cancer is truly a universal disease. It has been estimated that in 1993 the number of new cases worldwide would pass the 1-million mark for the first time. It's the most frequent tumor for females worldwide, usually by a large margin in the more developed countries. But even in countries where the numbers have been traditionally small, the incidence is growing. And the deaths are mounting. In Osaka, Japan, for example, the world-standardized rate per 100,000 per year (aged 30 to

74) shot up from 26.9 in 1970 to 48.8 in 1985. Over the next five years, the incidence rate shot up another 55.1 percent. Between 1965 and 1985, the death rate in Japan from breast cancer jumped from 8.1 to 12.6. In South Australia the incidence rate remained stable at 116.7 between 1970 and 1985, and the rate in New South Wales dropped slightly. Even so, the death rate overall in Australia increased from 38.3 to 40.7 during the 20-year period ending in 1985.

Between 1965 and 1985, the death rate also increased, often dramatically, in Chile, Costa Rica, Panama, Puerto Rico, Uruguay, Venezuela, New Zealand, Singapore, Belgium, Denmark, France, Germany, Greece, Ireland, Italy, the Netherlands, Portugal, Spain, Scotland, England, Wales, Austria, Czechoslovakia, Finland, Hungary, Norway, Poland, Romania, Switzerland, the former Yugoslavia, Spain, Israel and many other countries.

Right now — today — some 2.6 million American women may have breast cancer. Many of them don't even know it yet. The United States and Canada have the highest rates of breast cancer in the world. This year, for example, some 183,000 American women will be diagnosed with the disease and 46,000 will die. In Canada, more than 16,300 women will get breast cancer and 5,300 will die.

In the United Kingdom, which has the world's highest breast-cancer mortality rate, there will be 24,000 new cases and 15,000 deaths, one every 30 minutes. Breast cancer is the most common single cause of all deaths for U.K. women aged 35 to 54.

Current mortality rates per 100,000 women range from the high of 28.4 in England and Wales, to 27.7 in Scotland and Northern Ireland, 26.4 in the Netherlands, 22.1 in the United States, 19.9 in Iceland, 19.2 in France, 18.6 in Sweden, 16.8 in Finland, 13 in the former Yugoslavia, 9.2 in Venezuela and 5.8 in Japan.

Breast cancer — cause unknown, cure uncertain — fits any objective definition of an epidemic. But it is generally not seen that way. In fact, it is often unseen outside the immediate circle of the women — and yes, some men — who have it.

A number of women want to change that. Taking their cue from AIDS activists, many breast-cancer survivors are now beginning to mobilize, to demand a share of research and treatment money more in keeping with the magnitude of the scourge.

The Truth About Breast Cancer

In Canada, the federal government, with much fanfare and considerable media and public applause, increased its spending on breast cancer research in late 1992 to $2.8 million. By comparison, the federal government contributed $33 million to AIDS research in 1991. Breast cancer killed 5,000 Canadians that year. AIDS killed 72.

A year later, the government dramatically increased AIDS spending in Canada to over $40 million, yet AIDS activists bitterly complained that it wasn't enough. A February 1993 public opinion poll showed how successful their lobby efforts have been; 72 percent of the 1,507 Canadians polled said spending on AIDS should be a higher priority for the government. They weren't asked about breast cancer.

In the United States, where 46,000 women will die of breast cancer this year, the Public Health Service spent $1.878 billion on all types of cancer and $1.262 billion on AIDS/HIV research. Yet, since 1980, 194,000 Americans have died of AIDS, while 450,000 (more than twice as many) have died of breast cancer alone. In the States, a new breast cancer will be diagnosed every three minutes.

As television commentator and now breast-cancer activist Linda Ellerbee recently explained, the difference is that AIDS is always fatal, while "some of us survive."

About one-third don't, however.

Breast-cancer activists point to relative statistics not to argue that AIDS is overfunded, but to say that breast cancer is tragically underfunded.

It has been 17 years since my first wife Beverley died of breast cancer. She was 33, mother of our two young children. Despite the money spent, the changes in treatment methods and the development of alternative medicines, survival rates haven't improved since then. In fact, they're slightly worse now, and the incidence of breast cancer has increased dramatically.

What remains, however, is many built-in barriers for women, particularly in medical research, where men's diseases have historically been taken more seriously than women's. There also remains an attitude in medicine that if a woman complains, give her a pill. It's all in her head anyway. That accounts for the fact that women are prescribed tranquilizers twice as often as men.

My wife, for example, was told she was imagining a problem. She was too young for breast cancer. Well, she wasn't, and many younger women are still being dismissed in this way today.

On December 23, 1971, then President Richard Nixon launched what was grandly called the "war on cancer" by signing the National Cancer Act. Over the next 20 years, the number of new cases nearly doubled, jumping from 73,000 to 135,000. Even after factoring in population growth, the rate of breast cancer in the United States increased from 82 to 110 cases for every 100,000 women, a jump of 34 percent.

In 1984, the National Cancer Institute (NCI) in the States launched its cancer prevention awareness program as part of an overall effort to reduce the rate of cancer mortality to one-half the 1980 rate — from 168 per 100,000 to 84 per 100,000, by the year 2000.

Within a few years, however, the NCI conceded that its targets were totally unrealistic. Worse, instead of cutting the cancer mortality rate, they admitted they expected it to increase from 171 in 1984 to 175 per 100,000 by the year 2000.

A December 1991 report from the U.S. General Accounting Office to the Subcommittee on Human Resources and Intergovernmental Relations concluded that "many breast cancer patients live longer and better lives than their predecessors . . . [but] we do not seem to be winning the war against breast cancer."

On February 4, 1992, 68 prominent U.S. national health experts called a news conference in Washington and accused the NCI of having "misled and confused the public by repeated claims of winning the war against cancer."

While there has been clear progress in extending the lives of breast-cancer victims, through better drug treatments and/or earlier detection by mammography, the current overall prognosis remains bleak. Even so, the breast-cancer establishment has opted to present a happy face to the public — a position not warranted by the actual results. Slogans such as "Cancer Can Be Beaten," and constant news stories about scientists on the verge of new and exciting cures, distort the grim reality. But they serve to ward off some of the political heat that would likely be generated if more people understood the gravity of the situation.

The Truth About Breast Cancer

A January 1994 article in *Scientific American* offered an unsettling quote from the well-known McGill University professor of epidemiology and biostatistics John C. Bailar III, who created a storm in 1986 by publishing a damning lack-of-progress report on the "war on cancer." He said he had come to the same disturbing conclusion now.

"In the end, any claim of major success against cancer must be reconciled with this figure," he said, pointing to a simple graph that showed a stark continuing increase in U.S. death rates from cancer between 1950 and 1990. "I do not think such reconciliation is possible and again conclude, as I did seven years ago, that our decades of war against cancer have been a qualified failure. Thank you."

He was not just speaking of breast cancer, of course, but of all cancers, the second leading cause of death in the United States behind heart disease, with an expected 526,000 U.S. deaths in 1993.

Breast-cancer deaths have conformed to a pattern found in other cancers: the death and incidence rates have stayed relatively constant or are decreasing in young people, while they are increasing in older people. In women under 50, breast-cancer deaths have decreased slightly. But in women over that age, they have become more common.

Scientific American points out that the National Heart, Lung and Blood Institute in the United States, which has the second-largest budget of the national health institutes — behind the National Cancer Institute's $2 billion — can boast of a 30 percent reduction in deaths from heart disease since 1975 "as evidence of its success in pioneering treatments and, significantly, in promoting exercise and healthy diet. The NCI can report no victories on that scale. . . . The critics accuse it of having neglected research aimed at prevention in favor of the search for cures. There has been little to show for the $25 billion spent on the war on cancer, they charge: oncologists still mainly cut, poison, burn and hope."

Bailar is quoted as saying he is fed up with the "constant procession of hopeful news stories" suggesting a cure is just around the corner.

He believes the NCI should spend more money on prevention.

"We've come to the point where we must face a really serious problem square in the face. What if there aren't any major advances to be obtained in chemotherapy? For a lot of years now, we've been tinkering. It's not going to solve the big problem of cancer, and we need a major advance. [Prevention] is going to involve everybody over their whole lives.

"It's going to involve cleaning up the workplace and the environment, it's going to involve changing our diets, and it's certainly going to be a bigger hassle and more expensive than our ideal treatments would be," Bailar said.

Throughout the years some prominent women have come forward to focus more attention on breast cancer. Shirley Temple Black spoke out in 1972, for example. In 1974, then First Lady Betty Ford, 56, underwent a radical mastectomy. Shortly after that, vice-president-designate Nelson Rockefeller's wife, Margaretta (Happy), 48, underwent surgery to remove her left breast, sparking widespread public discussion of the disease. Rockefeller had a second mastectomy five weeks later. During 1993, President Bill Clinton's mother, Virginia Dell Kelley, fought a highly public and inspirational battle against the disease, again helping to focus national attention on the issue before she died from it on January 6, 1994.

Even so, breast cancer has yet to attain the prominence and media exposure of AIDS. Just turn on your television to any awards show from Hollywood, New York or Nashville. Performers routinely don the red-ribbon AIDS symbol. There's so much peer pressure in the industry that most people dare not be seen at public events without their ribbon. American icon Elizabeth Taylor works tirelessly and with considerable effectiveness raising money and awareness for AIDS.

A few Hollywood celebrities have joined the fight for breast cancer, but their voices are often drowned out in the hoopla over AIDS.

This book attempts to explain why this is so. It explores the reluctance of the medical fraternity to try new techniques, the historical bias of medical research against women, the stunning silence from traditional women's rights groups.

It will take a hard look at the controversies surrounding breast implants and reconstruction, and at the dispute even among mastectomy patients over whether prostheses are a blessing or an evil.

There are studies examining the risks and benefits and the cost of regular mammograms.

The book also offers a critical examination of the massive tamoxifen "prevention" test currently being conducted in the United States, Canada, the United Kingdom, Italy, Australia and elsewhere. And it will delve into the search for other new "cures," such as taxol, as well as the highly controversial genetic research — the race for the breast-cancer gene — which may create as many problems as it solves.

In many smaller communities, women are still given mastectomies when a more simple lumpectomy would do just as well. Even in Canada, where the state medicare system is envied around the world, many breast-cancer patients are forced to undergo surgical procedures or are placed in real danger on lengthy waiting lists, because there is a shortage of hospital staff to operate the radiation equipment.

From 1940 to 1982, breast-cancer incidence in the United States rose by 1.2 percent a year. For the next four years, however, the rate sky-rocketed to about 4 percent a year. Between 1980 and 1985, it increased by 15 percent in Canadian women and 21 percent in American women. Despite the claims of progress from the cancer establishment, that trend continues today.

Indeed, breast-cancer incidence continues to grow rapidly throughout the industrialized world. A 1990 report from the German Federal Health Office concluded that "time trends in the mortality rate of breast cancer indicate an epidemic." By the year 2000, more than 1 million women, mostly in the industrialized world, are expected to die each year from the disease.

A November 1992 study by the environmental group Greenpeace sets out at least a prima facie case of a deadly link between breast cancer and pollution from industrial organochlorines. Yet, unlike most of Greenpeace's work, it has been met generally with a deafening silence from the political establishment, the women's movement and the media.

Among other things, Greenpeace found that the one country that banned organochlorine pesticides — Israel — quickly went from breast-cancer rates that were among the highest in the world to rates in keeping with those of other industrialized nations. It also found that U.S. counties with waste sites were 6.5 times more likely to have elevated breast-cancer rates than counties without waste sites, and that women with breast cancer tend to have higher levels of organochlorine pesticides and PCBs in their tissue than women without breast cancer. Slowly, the message is beginning to sink in. In 1994, for example, the International Joint Commission issued a toughly worded report attacking the continued dumping of chemicals into the Great Lakes. This and other environmental factors are also explored in detail.

There are hundreds of women across North America who are frightened by the prospects of breast cancer because their mothers or other close family members have died of it. Some are so concerned that they've had both breasts removed, even though they have not been diagnosed with the disease — stunning testimony to the fact that of all the diseases women face, breast cancer is one they fear more than many others.

The personal stories of these and other women are told in this book. Some turn to medical quacks and religious "faith healers" to "cure" their breast cancer. Others encounter the unconscionable suppression of legitimate unorthodox medicine by the medical establishment.

Breast cancer, of course, can strike any woman. Class, social status, education and color don't seem to matter in the incidence rates, but there is strong evidence that these factors greatly influence the availability and success of treatment. This book takes a critical look at that too.

The really frightening discovery is that medical science still doesn't know why, let alone what to do about breast cancer. Often, by the time it's detected, it's already too late.

I remember when my wife Beverley first discovered a lump, she went to a doctor who told her it was nothing to worry about. She was a nurse, so she worried. She went to another doctor, who said it would be fine. But the pain grew, and finally she found a doctor who took her seriously. Too often, even today, this pattern is repeated.

I remember her trauma upon waking up from exploratory surgery to find her right breast and lymph glands gone. I remember her pain and suffering through the treatments, her agony of losing her hair and dignity.

Most of all, I remember her, one day in her hospital bed shortly before she died, looking up at me and saying: "I know it's too late for me, but I hope they do something so Kathy [our daughter] won't go through this hell."

I hope so too. And maybe, just maybe, this book will help nudge society along the road to giving this dreadful disease the attention it and its victims deserve.

2 Tamoxifen: Panacea or Pandora's Box?

MILL VALLEY IS CLASSIC CALIFORNIA dreamin'.

A bustling New Age town of 14,000 perched on the eastern slope of the 2,600-foot Mount Tamalpais overlooking beautiful Richardson Bay, it is one of a string of elegant San Francisco suburbs neatly nestled in the hills just a few miles north of the world-renowned Golden Gate Bridge.

The locals boast of its mild climate, its eclectic mix of old and new, its narrow hillside streets, spectacular, forested canyons, and its sophisticated boutiques set along downtown streets lined with majestic redwood trees.

This is where the rainbow ends.

With a "typical" house averaging US $430,000, median household income of $55,748 and just 2.9 percent unemployment (the lowest in California), this former logging town is among the most affluent communities in Marin County, a county with the highest average household incomes in the entire state.

Fifty-four-year-old Bobbe Rigler lives here. But her California dream has developed an edge.

It's not because Mill Valley sits virtually on top of the San Andreas Fault, a major earthquake waiting to happen. Occasional tremors, and the inevitable predictions that the end is near, are everyday realities in and around Marin County.

No, what bothers Rigler, and untold thousands of "healthy" women just like her, is her family's troubled medical history. She is considered "high risk" for a disease that public opinion polls show women fear more than any other — breast cancer.

First, she watched her mother lose her courageous five-year battle against this relentless killer. Then her sister was diagnosed with it and had a mastectomy. So too did a first cousin. Even her 30-year-old daughter discovered a lump in her breast. It turned out to be non-cancerous, "but it scared the shit out of her, if you'll pardon the expression.

"I think I'm surrounded by breast cancer. I think I'm high risk. I'm going to do anything I can to beat this. . . . I was living in fear all the time," says Rigler. "It was becoming an obsession."

And so, two years ago Rigler became one of 16 women in Marin County, and up to 16,000 in Canada and the United States (plus thousands more in Australia, Italy and the United Kingdom) — up to 40,000 women worldwide — to sign up for a series of separate but similar five-year research projects testing the long-term impact of the synthetic anti-estrogren drug called tamoxifen.

In addition, organizers of the U.K. study hope to sign up women in Switzerland, France, Holland, Germany and New Zealand.

The tamoxifen trial, formally called the Breast Cancer Prevention Trial (BCPT) in the United States and Canada — and similar names in the separate tamoxifen trials in England, Australia and Italy — is the clinical equivalent of the World Cup of breast-cancer prevention research. It is a massive experiment using a powerful drug on healthy women, some of whom will die as a direct result. While its boosters claim it may eventually help stop the spread of breast cancer, and the test may save some women who would otherwise get it, it will also end up killing some women who would otherwise be alive and cancer-free had they not volunteered for the trial.

To some extent, the trials are the cancer establishment's political response to the emerging activism of breast-cancer organizations and individuals. They are agitating for a swing in emphasis, from the traditional approach of looking for ways to treat the disease, to researching ways to prevent it.

After all, the current approach isn't working that well. The United Kingdom, for example, has the highest mortality rate in the world for breast cancer: 52 deaths per 100,000 women, or about 15,000 deaths a year. Canada and the States are not much better off: they have the highest incidence rates. In Canada, about 16,300 women get the disease each year, and 5,300 die — approximately one death every 90 minutes. In the United States, more than 180,000 women contract breast cancer each year, and 46,000 die — about one woman every 12 minutes. Worse, both the incidence rate and the mortality rate are growing. By the turn of the century, about one American woman in seven can expect to get breast cancer during her lifetime if she lives to the age of 85.

But the study has raised major ethical concerns for many others. They are worried about the wisdom and morality of giving otherwise healthy women a pill that may cause serious side effects, including death in some cases, and may or may not prove effective in fighting breast cancer in the long run.

If it works, those promoting it will be heroes. If it doesn't, many women could pay a terrible price.

Cindy Pearson, program director for the National Women's Health Network in Washington, D.C., has no doubts about the politics behind the trials. She says that while she can't prove it, and nobody ever said it to her directly, she believes she knows why the NCI is so anxious to complete the BCPT. "My opinion is they were really starting to feel the heat." She said the NCI was being blasted for not doing something on prevention, and this political motive led "almost subconsciously" to this trial.

In 1992, Professor Gordon McVie of the United Kingdom's Cancer Research Campaign admitted as much in a press statement defending the trial from serious medical criticism there. "For a long time," he said, "we've been under pressure to shift the emphasis from treatment to prevention. Now we have a real chance to do something positive to help reduce the incidence of breast cancer which currently claims the lives of 15,000 women in Britain each year."

And the May-June 1993 edition of *Ms* magazine details how the BCPT became the NCI's "showpiece trial" based on "highly speculative scientific rationale," after the cancellation of an even larger test, the Women's Health Trial. That test would have monitored the impact on breast cancer of eating less fat for 32,000 American women at a cost of $100 million. *Ms* argues, "The clinicians who dominate NCI were simply not going to give ground to research that emphasized such public strategies as dietary change at the expense of their research priorities. If the NCI were to back prevention studies, this group believed the research should emphasize disease control through medical intervention and technology — keeping the funding pipelines flowing along their customary routes."

In addition, the need for a study on whether tamoxifen can prevent cancer has become even more urgent because more and more doctors are prescribing the drug in women at high risk for getting breast cancer, even though the Food and Drug Administration (FDA) hasn't approved it for that use. Obviously, doctors should not be doing this. But rather than using this as an excuse to justify the experiment, surely doctors would be better advised to wait until tamoxifen is proven scientifically to be a useful preventative for women without breast cancer before prescribing it to them and handing them an uncertain fate.

Even the trial's most enthusiastic organizers admit they expect the experiment will cause 50 to 60 cases of uterine cancer, which is nearly double their original estimates, to say nothing of possible liver cancers, lethal blood clots, severe depression and other side effects. They counter, however, that tamoxifen will also prevent considerably more breast cancers, a claim several leading research scientists hotly dispute.

Dr. Leslie Ford, who oversees the BCPT for the National Cancer Institute in the United States, says that even with a recently announced increase in uterine cancer risk, "the risk-benefit calculations [of the BCPT] are still clearly in favor of testing tamoxifen as a breast cancer preventative."

But Dr. Trudy Bush, an epidemiologist at Johns Hopkins University in Baltimore, who examined the data upon which this critical risk-benefit analysis is based, said on Canadian Broadcasting Corporation (CBC) television that "the overall risk of participating in the trial is greater than any overall derived benefit."

Dr. Adriane Fugh-Berman of the National Women's Health Network in Washington is even more direct. She says tamoxifen is "a decent breast cancer treatment, but it has no place in healthy women . . . tamoxifen is way more dangerous than anything we've ever considered as a public health intervention. Starting this trial was unethical. I think continuing it is unconscionable. Disease substitution is acceptable in a treatment trial. It's not acceptable at all in a prevention trial."

One of the more troubling aspects of the trial is that its organizers often fend off the critics in terms that sound more like a carnival huckster singing the praises of a cheap Kewpie doll than a serious clinician relying on sound scientific rationale.

In March 1994, for example, the *Chicago Tribune* reported that a Canadian researcher, Dr. Roger Poisson of St. Luc's Hospital in Montreal, had been involved in what he cavalierly described as "silly little mistakes" and "white lies." In fact, he had been involved in falsifying data on breast-cancer research for several years on more than 100 of the 1,511 patients he had enrolled in his part of 22 studies from 1975 to 1991. One of these "white lies" was telling a woman who had developed cancer in both breasts that she had it in only one. Another woman died, but Poisson continued to report on her for two years more as if she were still alive. Poisson even kept two sets of patient records, one marked "true," the other "false."

Poisson had been a major contributor to landmark studies conducted by Dr. Bernard Fisher of the University of Pittsburgh, a respected surgeon and senior cancer researcher in charge of a giant U.S.-Canada medical research consortium called the National Surgical Adjuvant Breast and Bowel Project (NSABP) — a group formed in 1958 and involving some 6,000 doctors, nurses and other medical professionals at 484 academic centers and hospitals in Canada and the United States. These studies, among the most frequently cited in modern medical literature, had virtually revolutionized the treatment of breast cancer, particularly for the disease in its early stages, changing the preferred treatment from a complete mastectomy to a breast-saving lumpectomy.

It did not help to inspire public confidence in the current tamoxifen trial to learn that the Pittsburgh researchers first discovered serious irregularities in Poisson's work in June 1990, when two reports of a breast-cancer operation for one patient at St. Luc's Hospital appeared to be identical, except for different dates of surgery — a discrepancy which determined whether they were or were not eligible for the study.

It took Fisher eight months to even report the problem to Washington authorities. Federal officials from the U.S. Office of Research Integrity then conducted four audits involving some samples and discovered more irregularities. So they eventually reviewed all 1,511 of Poisson's cases.

Still, Fisher refused to let the public in on the scandal. But on January 7, 1993, an NCI official wrote Fisher urging him to review the audit procedures and case selection method because data irregularities "went undetected for more than a decade." Two days earlier, the NCI had written Fisher a letter asking him to publish the results soon, saying the NCI's journal was willing to expedite the review process.

While this extraordinary coverup was going on within the cancer establishment, however, Fisher and the NSABP put the finishing touches on the BCPT study, launched the $68 million trial and began to recruit the thousands of "healthy" women needed to test their controversial hypothesis.

Had it not been for the *Chicago Tribune*'s article on Dr. Poisson, nearly four years after Fisher's group first discovered the clinical fraud, the public would still be in the dark.

Dr. Paul Myer, chairman of the department of biostatistics at Columbia University in New York, told the CBC he found it "very disturbing" that a "major failure" occurred in the management of the trial. "Even more disturbing I found was the long time that has passed since that information was found and the failure to make it all public in the way that I think it should be made.

". . . It is not appropriate for us to take a lordly view and 'we will figure out what's right and we will tell you about it.' The patient has very much the right and the reason to say, 'I want a hand in the choice myself.'"

The soothing assurances from trial officials that the false data changed nothing are hard to accept. They are the same ones who downplayed the risks of tamoxifen to trial volunteers and who mishandled the Poisson affair, including Fisher's long refusal to order an outside audit. Sadly, this systemic, paternalistic, doctor-knows-best-so-don't-bother-your-sweet-little-head-about-it-dearie attitude still prevails, and women are routinely denied the full information they need to make an informed decision about whether to enter the test or not.

Even though many of his colleagues still hotly defend Fisher, the public and political fall-out from the false results — and Fisher's handling of them — ultimately cost him his job. But the NCI and the National Institutes of Health (NIH) didn't cover themselves in glory either. They too knew long before they did anything, and only took action after the fraud was exposed by the media.

Doctors aren't entirely sure why tamoxifen reacts the way it does, but one way they believe it works in breast cancer is to interfere with the activity of estrogen, a female hormone that promotes the growth of cancer cells in the breast. Tamoxifen is called an anti-estrogen because it works against the effects of estrogen on breast-cancer cells, slowing or stopping the growth of those cells. It is, however, only effective on hormone-dependent tumors, those that need estrogen, a natural hormone, to grow. That represents about one-third of breast tumors. Critics of the test say that tamoxifen stimulates the growth of a class of aggressive breast-cancer tumors that lack estrogen receptors and so are resistant to tamoxifen.

Nevertheless, tamoxifen has been used in pill form for about 20 years to treat patients with advanced breast cancer. Since 1985 it has also been used for "adjuvant," or additional therapy, following radiation and/or surgery in early-stage breast cancer. In some types of breast cancer, it has reduced the development of contralateral cancer (cancer in the opposite breast) by up to 40 percent. It has also been helpful as a treatment for postmenopausal women with breast cancer, but not as a cure. And it has not been particularly helpful for premenopausal women. In fact, it has led to serious problems in that group. Yet almost half the women entering the BCPT are premenopausal.

The stated aim of the trials is breast-cancer prevention, but there's more at stake than clinical efficacy.

Some 60 percent of women diagnosed with breast cancer today — more than 1 million in total — are taking tamoxifen. At a cost to each of about $900 a year, think of the future market should the test end with a recommendation that all women from their 30s and older use tamoxifen as a prevention tactic. Granted, if it worked, it would also save hundreds or thousands of lives and untold millions in hospital and other medical costs. But the potential payoff for the manufacturers and the prestige for the study's founders are enormous. It's no wonder the manufacturer provides tamoxifen free for the trials.

With well over $100 million invested in the trials, the bulk of the medical and cancer establishments enthusiastically supporting them and several national governments deeply committed, the tamoxifen trials have become the single largest breast-cancer-prevention experiment ever attempted.

They've also become the most controversial.

In September 1990, the U.K. Coordinating Committee on Cancer Research met at Oxford with researchers from Canada, the United States, Australia and Holland, all of whom, except Holland, have subsequently begun trials using tamoxifen as a preventative experiment on "healthy" women. They agreed at that meeting that "the rationale for doing a tamoxifen chemoprevention trial is no longer controversial." But like many subsequent claims concerning the benefits of this trial, that prediction was wildly premature. The tamoxifen trials are now more controversial than ever.

The NCI, one of the major sponsors of the BCPT, raised considerable expectations by asserting at the outset of the trial that tamoxifen "may be able to reduce by one-third or more the number of breast cancers that occur in women at increased risk. In addition, tamoxifen may decrease the risk of heart attacks by lowering blood cholesterol." They also claim it can prevent osteoporosis (brittle bones) in older women.

Then again, it may not do these things. Who can really say? What we can say, however, is that both the NCI and the NSABP's scientific rationale for predicting such startling results is weak.

This tendency of the sponsors of these trials to exaggerate the possible benefits and downplay the risks, which is tantamount to claiming victory before the opening whistle of the game, has led to a growing chorus of critics countering such rosy predictions by arguing that they are not supported by known scientific data, and the clinical trials, in

17

fact, will undoubtedly cost the lives of many women who wouldn't have contracted cancer in the first place if they hadn't joined the trial.

As things stand, the critics have a point.

For one thing, the BCPT in the United States and Canada — and the International Breast Cancer Intervention Study (IBCIS) in the United Kingdom, Australia and several other European countries — is not recruiting women who have breast cancer, whose treatment tamoxifen is designed to combat. Nor are they restricting their recruitment to postmenopausal women, in whom the drug has shown better success. Instead they are testing the drug as if it were a preventative, on women who do not have breast cancer. They aren't sick. They are simply deemed to be at a higher risk than the average female population, which means, of course, they are more frightened of getting breast cancer and generally more desperate to try anything that offers to spare them from it. But the drug itself, even if it does prove effective in stopping breast cancer, increases the risks of other cancers, and several other potential side effects, some serious, others not so serious. This makes it a bit of a crap shoot, which has led to charges that the organizers are preying on women's growing fears about this dreaded disease.

Risks, of course, are always relative. While all of the women who meet the "high risk" definition to join the clinical trials are afraid they'll get breast cancer, the vast majority of them won't. Indeed, about 75 percent of all women who do get breast cancer do not have any of the known "risk" factors, other than the fact that they're women.

However, all of the women in these trials who are taking the tamoxifen pill itself rather than just a placebo will suffer side effects ranging from uterine cancer to vaginal dryness or discharge, mild or severe depression, weight gain, or moderate to crushing hot and cold flashes. Studies have also shown that in rare instances, tamoxifen use is associated with blindness, and there is growing concern from laboratory experiments with rats that prolonged use of the drug may cause deadly liver cancer as well. It can also lead to lethal blood clots in some circumstances. Another recent study showed that women who get endometrial cancer (cancer of the lining of the womb) from tamoxifen have more chance of dying from it than those who develop uterine cancer naturally. Tamoxifen-induced uterine cancer is far more aggressive, and because of that, these women are more likely to die.

To join the U.K.-Australian study, women must be aged 45 to 64 with either a mother or sister who has had breast cancer, two close relatives who had it, or a previous breast lump that was abnormal. Or they can be 35 to 44 with a strong family history or a previous abnormal breast lump.

The BCPT threshold in the United States and Canada is that women, whatever their age, should have the same "risk" of breast cancer — one chance in 24 — as a 60-year-old woman. Any woman aged 60 or more qualifies on the basis of age alone. Women aged 35 to 59 must have a risk of developing breast cancer in the next five years equal to or greater than the 60-year-old. That risk is calculated by computer, based on such factors as number of first-degree relatives (mother, daughter, sister) with breast cancer, whether a woman has children, age at first delivery, age at first menstrual period, or if she has been diagnosed with noninvasive breast cancer, called lobular carcinoma in situ.

Women at increased risk for blood clots and pregnant women aren't eligible. Those taking hormone replacements for menopausal symptoms or women using oral contraceptives cannot take part unless they stop these medications.

Half the women receive a non-medicinal placebo, a look-alike pill containing no drugs. The others take tamoxifen twice daily — a total of 20 milligrams. The pills are dispensed randomly so that only the computer knows for sure which women are on a placebo or on the real thing, although given the nature of some side effects, many women can figure that out for themselves.

All participants are required to have blood tests, a pelvic exam, a mammogram and physical examination before being accepted. Women 55 and over need an electrocardiogram (ECG).

There is precious little science to support NCI's claim that tamoxifen may reduce breast cancer by "one-third or more," but coming from such a prestigious organization it makes the prospects of joining the trial attractive to women who believe that having the known risk factors almost guarantees that they'll get the disease. But if the NCI knew that tamoxifen was such an effective preventative drug, then surely it would be using it for that purpose, as opposed to testing it.

In addition to overstating the possible benefits of tamoxifen, the organizers have consistently understated the potential risks. A pamphlet produced by the NSABP promoting the trial has much to say about the risk of women developing breast cancer, but not a single reference to any side effects of the drug. Not a word. The brochure, given routinely to women in Canada and the United States who inquire about the trials, boasts not only that women who join the BCPT will contribute to medical knowledge "that may decrease the occurrence of this deadly disease," but also that tamoxifen may reduce deaths from heart disease in postmenopausal women and "can reduce" osteoporosis. There is scientific evidence to support the latter two claims, but one might expect a more balanced discussion of the pros and cons of a drug coming from such a major, publicly funded medical organization.

The NCI and Fisher's group aren't the only ones expressing some dramatic pre-trial predictions. In Australia, where the study has been going more than a year, Dr. John Forbes, professor of surgical oncology at the University of Newcastle, New South Wales, said tamoxifen may prevent up to 200,000 breast cancers a year.

Forbes advocates governments coordinating national policies on breast cancer to tackle such issues as improved treatment, early diagnosis, prevention, research priorities, education of women and doctors alike, and the development of centers of excellence. He says the tamoxifen study is key because, "it's the only one right now, it's likely to work and costs appear favorable." He says the study uses high-risk women "to maximize the gain and minimize the cost." This is because these women are "highly motivated" to prevent breast cancer, he says, and after talking to them for just a few minutes, you can see their high levels of "anxiety and concern." He says this concern is so overwhelming that all else is secondary, so the more detail you give these women about the risks, "the more determined the women are to take part."

Then again, if they're speaking to an "expert" who is sure that the trial will be a success, perhaps the risks don't sound all that daunting. Forbes, for example, dismissed reports on increased liver cancer risk of tamoxifen by saying it "appeared to be a total red herring. . . . Our current conclusion is . . . that it is likely tamoxifen protects against liver cancer."

Forbes concedes there are common side effects such as menstrual irregularities, early onset of menopause, vaginal spotting and hot flashes. As for the increased risk of uterine cancer, he says there is probably a two- to threefold increase, but that just makes it from "very uncommon" to "still uncommon" and remains smaller than the risk of women getting breast cancer in the trials. As for reports that tamoxifen may cause eye problems, including blindness, Forbes says there are isolated reports, but "it's rare and it's of doubtful significance." On blood clot risks, Forbes says it is "very difficult" to decipher medical reports, but even so, they exclude anyone with a history of the problem. Unlike the situation in England, the United States and Canada, Forbes says there has been only "patchy" interest in the Australian media about the trials. He says doctors are already being asked by women to prescribe tamoxifen as a preventative.

In Italy, Dr. Virgilio Sacchini, a surgeon with the National Cancer Institute of Milan and national coordinator of the Italian Chemoprevention Trial of Breast Cancer with Tamoxifen, says they are so concerned about the evidence of the drug causing endometrial cancer that their trial of 20,000 patients is restricted to women aged 35 to 70 who have had a hysterectomy. (In Italy, with extraordinarily high hysterectomy rates, that gives them 500,000 women to choose from.) The Italian trial, which began in September 1992, has signed up more than 2,000 women.

Sacchini said a recent experiment in Bologna showed a risk of liver cancer in rats taking tamoxifen, "but it's not a very high risk. It's the same as the risk of rats taking a contraceptive pill. . . . The major risk of tamoxifen is endometrial cancer. . . . There has been no controversy in Italy over the trial, because we do not have the same risks."

Funded by the Italian government and the Italian League Against Cancer, their equivalent of the American Cancer Society, women are being recruited in 40 centers throughout the country. The total budget is only US $100,000, but that's because Italy's state medical plan pays for the mammography, blood work and all the other regular tests associated with the trial. Some 79 percent of the women in the trial are between 45 and 65 years old, the age at which women are most at risk for developing breast cancer. About 10 percent of the women had a first-degree relative (mother, sister, aunt) diagnosed with breast cancer.

While the Italians seem to have avoided the controversy by changing the rules of the study, concern over side effects, while not widely publicized, may still account for the fact that instead of the 3,000 women enrolled in Australia and New Zealand, fewer than 300 have in what is supposed to be a $2.5 million-a-year trial once their target numbers are reached. (For the first three years, they're getting by on grants of $50,000 a year from Australia's National Health and Medical Research Council.) In the United States and Canada, where the target is 16,000, about 11,000 have joined, some 1,300 in Canada and the rest in the States. And the United Kingdom study, which hopes to attract 15,000 women — about the same number who die of breast cancer each year there — also remains well short of the target population.

Why such a poor response from women?

Dr. Richard Margolese, chief oncologist at Jewish General Hospital in Montreal, head of the Canadian section of the BCPT, and an enthusiastic and highly public booster for the trials, blames the media.

"It's not true that women are being experimented on," he said, without being asked, adding that "women aren't thronging to join," because of the bad press the study is getting. In fact, until the Poisson affair broke, the overwhelming bulk of media coverage was positive. The "bad press" came in as more scientific data emerged showing the possible downside of this experiment in human lives. And that was before Poisson's clinical fabrications cast even more doubt on the process.

Margolese, former president of the National Cancer Institute of Canada, said that when side effects such as liver cancer are mentioned, it's not put into perspective. "If you go on a picnic and get stung by a bee, is it likely? No, but you should know it can happen."

But giving pills to healthy women without knowing the outcome isn't exactly a picnic. And contracting liver or uterine cancer, or lethal blood clots, transcends your average bee sting.

For example, the February 18, 1994, edition of *Science* magazine reported that 4 of 23 women who took tamoxifen as part of an earlier clinical trial beginning in 1981 subsequently developed uterine cancer and died. That trial was conducted under the auspices of Dr. Fisher and his Pittsburgh team.

The significance of this information is that women like Bobbe Rigler, when they joined the current trial, were told that tamoxifen users who developed uterine cancer had been successfully treated and "no deaths from uterine cancer were reported."

Not any more. Yet both the NCI and Fisher refused to release specific details to *Science* magazine. Fisher said he sent a paper to NCI that was still in the peer-review process for potential publication in the NCI journal, no doubt a friendly publication for BCPT boosters, given its direct and massive commitment to the study.

Science writes that the "new data" on endometrial cancer mortality may rekindle the controversy over the risks of the BCPT.

After all, those deaths, and recent Swedish trials — one where two women on tamoxifen developed liver cancer and another suggesting a 50 percent increase in new cancers, including gastrointestinal, among breast-cancer patients treated with tamoxifen — have already caused the U.S. leaders to change their consent form, and not for the first time. The form must now include more prominent and updated information on the risks of the test — particularly data showing that it may cause other cancers, such as liver and uterine cancer, along with lethal blood clots.

Rather than claiming that there are no reported deaths from uterine cancer and that uterine cancers that have occurred in tamoxifen trials "have been caught at an early stage," Fisher and Jeffrey Abrams, the NCI's senior investigator at the Clinical Trials Evaluation Program, recommended changing the consent forms to say: "Uterine cancer is a potentially life-threatening illness" and "The level of increased risk of uterine cancer associated with tamoxifen is still uncertain."

University of Wisconsin cancer researcher Richard Love, an outspoken critic of the trials, told *Science* magazine that the risks of lethal blood clots and endometrial cancer are likely to exceed expected benefits such as improved cardiovascular health and reduced osteoporosis. Pointing out that younger women aren't normally at risk for these ailments anyway, Love said the BCPT is "absolutely premature for premenopausal women."

As for Fisher, his confidence in the trials remained unshaken. He argued that changes to the BCPT consent forms were just routine revisions. "This would be done if aspirin were being used for this trial and something unexpected were seen with aspirin."

Well, tamoxifen is not aspirin. And just how "unexpected" were these uterine cancer deaths anyway? The four deaths may have been "new" in Fisher's trials, but the warnings have been around for years in numerous other clinical tests.

As far back as 1975, signs of the problem became evident. That year, Los Angeles physicians Harry K. Ziel and William D. Finkle published a paper in the *New England Journal of Medicine*, which, while not directly on topic, showed a direct link between the growing use of conjugated estrogen therapy and a dramatic increase in uterine cancer over the previous decade. A 1989 Swedish trial, also published in the *New England Journal of Medicine*, reinforced the tamoxifen-endometrial cancer link. Lars E. Rutqvist of Sweden's Karolinska Institute reported in that trial that breast-cancer patients receiving doses of tamoxifen twice as large as those in the BCPT study had an increased risk of dying of endometrial cancer. In a June 1991 letter to *The Lancet*, the prestigious British medical journal, three University of Southern California doctors warned against the use of tamoxifen in premenopausal women because of the different hormonal effects shown in various tests of younger women with the drug. In what has proven to be a prescient paragraph, the doctors wrote: "That an increase in ovarian cancer patients treated with tamoxifen has not been reported so far is not necessarily reassuring. The drug has generally been used for only short periods, predominantly in postmenopausal women or in combination with chemotherapy known to inhibit ovarian function."

In addition, an overview of 133 clinical trials involving 75,000 women and published in the January 4, 1992, issue of *The Lancet* also refers to the "excess" numbers of nonfatal endometrial cancers associated with tamoxifen. The National Cancer Institute itself sponsored a 1991 study showing that 20 mg of tamoxifen a day, which is the BCPT dose, increases the risk of endometrial cancer about fivefold. And in April 1993, Dr. Bruno Cutuli of the Centre Paul Strauss in Strasbourg, France, told a conference on screening methodology that about 16 women out of 432 treated for breast cancer with adjuvant tamoxifen had subsequently developed endometrial cancer.

Dr. Jack Cuzick, chairman of the working group for the U.K. study, concedes "there will be a small increased risk of endometrial (uterine) cancer" for women in the study, but says this must be thoroughly explained to women before they commit themselves to the five-year regimen.

One Scandinavian study of 1,800 women with breast cancer showed that 13 of the 900 on tamoxifen developed uterine cancer, while only 2 of the 900 on a placebo did. Another study showed that 9 of 1,439 women taking tamoxifen developed uterine cancer, compared to 2 of 1,453 women on a placebo. The BCPT-revised consent form used in the United States uses a more favorable study than that, saying that clinical trials show "that 9 out of 3,097 women on tamoxifen developed uterine cancer (0.3%) versus 4 out of 3,091 women not treated with tamoxifen (0.1%)." That's still more than double the rate when tamoxifen is involved.

Supporters of the current trial have consistently downplayed the risks associated with prolonged intake of tamoxifen, including the risk of uterine cancer, arguing that because women in the trial will be constantly monitored, the presence of that cancer would be caught early enough to correct it in any event. Statistician Richard Peto, a leading British supporter of the trial, was quoted as saying the risk was "no big deal" because uterine cancer is curable by a hysterectomy. It may not be a "big deal" to him, but for a woman it's a major concern — particularly for the thousands of premenopausal women already involved in the trial who are not likely that keen on losing their uterus to a surgeon's scalpel.

Ottawa oncologist Dr. Shail Verma, founder of a group of health experts called Access to Effective Cancer Care in Ontario, which lobbies for a more sensible distribution of cancer research dollars in Ontario, supports the BCPT trial generally, but with considerable reservations. Verma told a Breast Cancer Action Ottawa meeting that the Scandinavian study showing 13 cases of uterine cancer in 1,800 women is "still low, but it's a sixfold increase from what we thought before."

And since uterine cancer can take up to ten years to develop, it's not exactly certain that links between the trials and this kind of cancer will be discovered. In addition, these tests were on women who already had breast cancer, unlike the women in the BCPT. And they were not on tamoxifen for as long as those women will be, a factor that increases the ultimate risks. Add to that recent studies showing tamoxifen-induced uterine cancer is a more deadly strain of the disease, and it doesn't inspire confidence.

What's more, all the current clinical trials on these "high-risk" women are testing premenopausal women. To the extent that solid scientific evidence exists — and there really are few direct comparisons that can be made for this group — even on the matter of tamoxifen reducing the odds of recurrence of breast cancer, turning 50 makes a dramatic difference. Indeed, for postmenopausal women aged between 50 and 59, tamoxifen has been shown to reduce the risk of recurrence by 28 percent, compared to 29 percent for chemotherapy. For women aged 60 to 69, tamoxifen reduces that risk by 29 percent, compared to 20 percent for chemotherapy. Compare that to women under 50, where for both premenopausal and postmenopausal women, tamoxifen's success rate drops to just 12 percent, compared to 36 or 37 percent for chemotherapy.

All the major scientific studies on tamoxifen have shown a consistent pattern indicating it is not effective for women under 50 and can even be harmful. Yet the BCPT researchers are welcoming younger women if they meet the so-called "high-risk" criteria for breast cancer.

Even the Physician's Desk Reference, a medical bible on pharmaceuticals published by Medical Economics Data of New Jersey "with the co-operation of the manufacturers whose products appear," which puts the most positive spin on various drugs, gives tamoxifen a dubious report in its 1992 edition. In the entry for Nolvadex, the trade name for tamoxifen, manufactured by ICI Pharma, under a subhead "Warnings," it was conceded that "visual disturbance including corneal changes, cataracts and retinopathy have been reported in patients receiving Nolvadex." It says endometrial cancer was "noted" in a large randomized trial in Sweden of 40 mg of adjuvant tamoxifen per day (twice that taken in the BCPT) for 2–5 years." And the reference adds that "Novaldex may cause fetal harm when administered to a pregnant woman. . . ."

Dr. Samuel Epstein, writing in 1993 in the *International Journal of Health Sciences*, even before news that Fisher's group had found a growing number of endometrial cancers (including four deaths) in his earlier studies, asserted that the tamoxifen trial "is a prospective experiment in human carcinogenesis whose scientific invalidity is compounded by a misleading patient consent form, trivializing risks and exaggerating benefits; participating oncologists and institutions clearly risk future malpractice claims."

"It should further be emphasized," he wrote, "that the median follow-up for all seven reported tamoxifen trials was only 80 months.

Very few healthy women have taken the drug for more than five years. Thus, tamoxifen may well be a much more potent human carcinogen than is currently recognized."

And on May 28, 1994, *The Lancet* published results of a U.K. study in the Pilot Breast Cancer Prevention Trial at the Royal Marsden Hospital showing that "women taking tamoxifen had a significantly larger uterus and a lower impedance to blood flow in the uterine arteries. Thirty-nine percent of women taking tamoxifen had histological evidence of an abnormal endometrium compared with 10 percent in the control group. Ten patients in the tamoxifen group (16 percent) had atypical hyperplasia and another five (8 percent) had a polyp. . . . These findings confirm that tamoxifen can cause potentially malignant changes in the endometrium of postmenopausal women."

Further evidence of the potential dangers of the BCPT came in July 1993 when the prestigious British Medical Research Council (MRC) formally announced its refusal to join two other major British cancer research charities — the Imperial Cancer Research Fund and Cancer Research Campaign — in the US $7.5 million study of 15,000 women who are healthy, but whose family has a history of breast cancer.

The MRC lists among its concerns the fact that tamoxifen has been shown to induce liver tumors in rats at exposures similar to those to be used in the trial on humans. And because there is "only limited information about tamoxifen's long-term effects in healthy people . . . the Council decided that it could only support a carefully controlled trial in women who had a particularly high — at least four times greater than normal — risk of developing breast cancer."

The Council said the dose of the drug given to animals was proportionately higher than that to be given the women. "However in the human the drug accumulates in the blood over a much longer period, so that eventually the same blood levels are reached."

Supporters of the trial have tended to dismiss the concerns about liver cancer on the odd grounds that it was only discovered in rats. In fact, that's not true. A Swedish test with tamoxifen resulted in two women getting liver cancer. But even if it were true, many diseases are first discovered in rats. The MRC takes it seriously enough that it is continuing its research and, to date, all its in-house testing has done is reinforce its concerns.

The Truth About Breast Cancer

In a prepared statement, MRC Second Secretary Dr. David Evered said that in women with proven breast cancer "the potential benefits of tamoxifen substantially outweigh the risks. But we are less certain about the benefits for women who do not have breast cancer. We hope that our new studies will provide firm evidence on which women and their doctors can make up their minds."

Writing in the February 1992, MRC *Bulletin*, lay member and well-known author Carolyn Faulder, whose books include *Breast Cancer* and *Whose Body Is It?*, published a lengthy review of the U.K. trial at the request of the MRC Secretariat, entitled "Better safe than sorry."

Faulder writes that "the ethical issues under consideration include the usual but nonetheless essential scientific and human dimensions; less usually, they extend beyond these areas into the domain of public health policy. Here the main ethical concern regards the degree and type of medical intervention we, as a society, should accept or want to accept in the cause of preventive health."

The MRC, Faulder goes on to say, had problems even with the term "high risk" (in reference to breast-cancer risk). It felt the term was "imprecise and . . . tended to raise anxiety levels. . . . Tamoxifen has become the victim of its success. The word has got around. Tamoxifen stops cancer, ergo all women at risk who don't mind taking a pill every day should be allowed access to it. Quite unscientific, of course, but the enthusiasm of many doctors for using the drug for treatment purposes fans the flames and makes it much more difficult to test it, as it should be tested, within the framework of a double blind randomised trial."

In addition, trial officials have suggested they may drop the placebo arm of the trial if they don't meet their target of 15,000 women from 15 centers within three years. Faulder writes that such a "major alteration" could "negate the value of the trial."

She also points out that 25 percent of the women eventually dropped out (compared to just 5 percent in the Italian trial) and half the women invited to participate in the pilot study have said no, in spite of tamoxifen's reputation. "It really will not do to describe the refuseniks as people unable to cope with their fear of cancer, except by denial, or the drop-outs as women with a low internal locus of control. Could it not be something much more simple, as, for instance, that some women do not relish the prospect of being on a drug for five years; or, conversely, that other women are not prepared to accept the one-in-two chance of taking a dummy for five years?

"As for the drop-outs, are they perhaps disillusioned to discover that the minor side effects they had been told might occur, turn out to be not so minor and not even the ones they had expected? . . . They could also be far less acceptable to healthy women than to women who are already being treated for cancer. . . ."

Faulder called the initial consent form "a travesty of what seeking informed consent should be about. It mentions only two side effects — mild nausea and headaches — and describes them as a short-term effect for between 1 and 5 percent of women receiving the drug. In fact, these are less commonly complained of than hot flashes, weight gain, vaginal discharge and menstrual changes.

"... To say 'there are no long-term effects which have been identified so far,' is simply not true, vis, the concern about endometrial cancer and the visual disorders which can occur." She added that the information leaflet for the major trial presented to the ethical review was an improvement on the initial attempt, "but it still left much to be desired."

Responding to the MRC attacks, Dr. Jack Cuzick of the Imperial Cancer Research Fund said the MRC's suggestion that the trial should be done only in women at fourfold risk and over 40 "amounts to refusing to support it, as there are not sufficient women in this group to get a reliable answer. I am still fully convinced that this trial is a very important and appropriate initiative and we are going ahead."

Cuzick added he was "very surprised and concerned" that the MRC has "overridden judgements of the cancer charities, the Committee on Safety of Medicines, the FDA in America, the manufacturers and government ministers, who have approved it."

Professor Gordon McVie of the Cancer Research Campaign said he, too, was concerned about the MRC's decision because the tamoxifen trial represents such a good opportunity to respond to growing pressure to shift the emphasis in cancer research from treatment to prevention.

But the MRC was not objecting to that shift. It too has felt the growing pressure from cancer activists to go beyond current treatments. Its objections are that this particular prevention technique may not only fail, but also cause other diseases as bad as, or even worse than, the breast cancer it may or may not prevent.

The Truth About Breast Cancer

On April 28, 1993, Trevor J. Powles of the Royal Marsden Hospital spoke in support of the trials at a meeting of the International Association for Breast Cancer Research in Banff, Alberta. "All information [from the British trial]," he said, "points to a fairly significant prevention" rate of between 20 and 50 percent. It would be at least a decade, however, before the trials could confirm whether tamoxifen was safe for widespread use. "The potential benefits are enormous, and appear to far outweigh the potential risks . . . but having convincing evidence will take at least ten more years," he said.

Not surprisingly, all the controversy in England has made it more difficult to recruit volunteers, but even so, officials at the Royal Marsden Hospital report that women are signing up for the tests.

One of those women, quoted in the December 2, 1993, London *Times*, is Suzy Tremaine, 45, of Cuckfield, West Sussex.

She said she readily volunteered to be a guinea pig six months earlier because her sister had undergone a mastectomy 12 years before.

"I don't know whether I'm on tamoxifen or the placebo — but whatever it is I feel great on it. Breast cancer is a very frightening disease and I'm happy to be part of something which could help prevent it," said Tremaine.

But not all women are willing to take the chance with a drug that, although successful for some things, was not designed for use in healthy women and has rarely been used regularly for prolonged periods.

Despite putting a brave face to the study, by late May 1994, the British had managed to recruit only 200 of the 15,000 women they wanted. But a statement from Dr. Cuzick reported in *The Times* made it sound as if the program was just being launched and everything was fine. The story cites the controversy over the MRC's withdrawal from the study over their concerns the drug might cause liver cancer, but adds that the organizers say, "These doubts . . . have now been dispelled and the trial has the support of the Medicines Control Agency." If anything, concerns over liver cancer have increased and the story doesn't mention all the other side effects, some of them deadly.

What's more, Cuzick seems to be confusing scientifically confirmed risk with fond hope when he claims that over ten years, 4 percent of the volunteers would likely have developed breast cancer, but, "We think we can halve that, possibly more, possibly less. Against that, the number getting endometrial cancer will increase from 0.3 percent to 0.6 or 0.9 percent," he said. "The simplest way of putting it is that for every endometrial cancer we cause, we will prevent four breast cancers."

Even the most highly regarded institutions can't always be trusted to deliver unvarnished science and/or medical information to the public. Many NCI publications, for example, still paint a one-sided picture of the BCPT, eschewing a balanced approach for a definite advocacy role in encouraging women to enter clinical tests. "Patients who take part in research make an important contribution to medical science and have the first chance to benefit from improved treatment methods," says one NCI brochure entitled "Adjuvant Therapy: Facts for Women with Breast Cancer." This brochure, last revised in July 1987, is still being distributed to women. On tamoxifen, it claims the drug is "tolerated well by most patients. However, it does cause short-term side effects related to lowered levels of estrogen such as hot flashes. Long-term side effects of tamoxifen are unknown at present but appear to be minimal." Hardly.

Even though the bulk of the medical/cancer establishment is convinced the tamoxifen trial is a good one, medical science has a spotty track record in the area of clinical trials. In his opening statement at an October 22, 1992, Congressional hearing into the flaws of the original consent form and other serious problems with the study, Donald M. Payne, the Democratic representative from New Jersey, said the Public Health Service has "a tarnished history regarding the ethical treatment of patients in federally-funded research," citing the "infamous" Tuskegee Study where more than 400 black American men with syphilis were "studied" for 40 years but not given treatment to cure their disease. At least 28 died and many more became seriously ill before the study was stopped in 1972.

A January 1994 essay by Dr. Douglas G. Altman, head of the Medical Statistics Laboratory, Imperial Cancer Research Fund, London — a British sponsor of the tamoxifen trial — argued in the *British Medical Journal* against the proliferation of medical testing. He wrote that "the effects of the pressure to publish may be seen most clearly in the increase in scientific fraud, much of which is relatively minor and is likely to escape detection. . . . The poor quality of much medical research is widely acknowledged, yet disturbingly the leaders of the medical profession seem only minimally concerned about the problem and make no apparent efforts to find a solution. . . . As the system encourages poor research it is the system that should be changed. We need less research, better research, and research done for the right reasons. Abandoning using the number of publications as a measure of ability would be a start."

The first detailed U.S. national survey of misconduct in science, published in *American Scientist* magazine in November 1993, showed that 43 percent of students and 50 percent of faculty members reported direct knowledge of more than one kind of misconduct in their labs, from faking results to withholding findings from competitors. From 6 to 9 percent of students and faculty in various disciplines said they had direct knowledge of faculty members who had plagiarized or falsified data. Asked about their students, one-third of faculty members said they had direct evidence of this misconduct.

Between June 1992 and March 1994, more than 300 allegations of fraud in scientific research were reported to the National Institutes of Health. The Office of Research Integrity studies about 75 cases each year. About 30 percent involve plagiarism, and most are in basic science, not clinical research. One problem is that people who report this misconduct often get victimized themselves. Dr. Richard Horton, North American editor of *The Lancet*, told *U.S.A. Today* that "the power structure works against whistle-blowers. . . . Junior people tend to get victimized if they make a claim against a colleague." And Representative John Dingell of Michigan, whose committee oversees federal scientific research, added: "The public should really be concerned that the scientists have an attitude of 'the public be damned, catch me if you can.'" Dingell said his committee has "received enormous abuse from the scientific community" for investigating misconduct cases.

The January/February 1994 issue of *Ms* magazine points out another example of scientific liberties taken by the medical establishment. The magazine cautions women using the NCI's CancerFax service to be wary because there are two different information lines updated monthly: one for doctors and one for patients. "A word to the wise," writes Maryann Napoli, associate director of the Center for Medical Consumers in New York City, "while doctors get state-of-the-art info, patients get a watered-down, sometimes misleading, version."

When the tamoxifen trials were set up, all the correct procedures were apparently followed. In October 1990, the NCI advisory board, which included Dr. Bernard Fisher, approved the study. In February 1991, Fisher was chosen from peer-reviewed applications to carry out the trial. The Oncologic Advisory Committee of the FDA held a public hearing on the study protocol in July 1991, and on April 29, 1992, they began to recruit women for the trial. National Institutes of Health (NIH) Director Dr. Bernadine Healy said at the time that "for NIH, the scientific evidence is clear. . . . We do not enter into trials lightly. We do not conduct trials without believing, based on scientific evidence, that those most in need of the answers will reap more benefits than undergo risks. I believe this trial of tamoxifen is well grounded in science."

But the National Women's Health Network opposed the trial "on the grounds that there is little evidence to support the protective effects claimed; that women eligible for enrolment are not truly at high risk for breast cancer; and that tamoxifen is too toxic for use in healthy women."

On December 11, 1991, in a letter from the National Women's Health Network program director Cindy Pearson to Dr. Ruth Merkatz, special assistant to the FDA commissioner, Pearson analyzed Fisher's original four-page consent form clause by clause. She argued that each woman in the BCPT "should know her own, individual risk [of developing breast cancer] rather than simply a general range of eligibility, so she can weigh the risks and benefits of her own participation in the trial. This is especially important given that the potential for risk is similar to the potential for benefit." Pearson said the liver cancer information on the consent form "is wrong," and cites scientific data to back that up. She added that the discussion on endometrial cancer on the form "should be expanded to make clear that when it occurs, it is treated by removal of the woman's uterus."

For all their protestations about the critics, however, Fisher and the NCI approved a revised consent form on January 13, 1992, expanding it to seven pages from the original four, including considerably more information on the known scientific risks of using tamoxifen. On the question of costs, moreover, the new form says that the placebo and tamoxifen will be provided by the ICI Pharmaceuticals Group through the NCI, but "other medications and all physicians' or hospital costs will be charged to me in the same fashion as if I were not part of this study. In the event that my insurance company will not cover the cost of the above procedures, these costs will be defrayed by other sources." It also rules out any "monetary compensation" for illness or injury from the trial.

Unfortunately, even if the model consent form approved by the NCI for the study hadn't been loaded in favor of the study — and if most doctors weren't encouraging women to enrol — the majority of U.S. centers conducting the BCPT trials throughout the country were editing out important chunks of the proposed form, so that the consent form being presented to women was even more flawed than the NCI-BCPT approved model consent form.

On October 22, 1992, Dr. Diana Zuckerman, a professional staff member of the Congressional Human Resources and Intergovernmental Relations Subcommittee, and staff consultant Naomi Schegloff reported to committee chairman Representative Donald Payne on their examination of 268 BCPT consent forms from medical centers around the country, comparing them to the NCI-approved model.

Incredibly, they discovered that 182 (68%) omitted or altered one or more of the key points; 131 (49%) did not mention that treatment for endometrial cancer is a hysterectomy, often coupled with radiation therapy; 140 (52%) minimized the risk of liver cancer (and 10 omitted any mention of liver cancer altogether); 69 (26%) failed to warn women that they could not use IUDs, oral contraceptives, or both while on tamoxifen; 40 (15%) minimized potential eye damage, including 3 forms that made no mention at all of eye damage in humans or in rats; and 29 (11%) did not warn women that they could not start or would have to discontinue estrogen replacement therapy to participate in the trial.

It got worse. A total of 166 (62%) of these consent forms provided "misleading information or no information about thrombo-embolic [blood clot] risks (3 predicted deaths for the present study and 2 deaths from Fisher's NSABP B-14 study)." Of those 166 forms, 61 changed the three predicted "deaths" to three predicted "cases," which Zuckerman and Schegloff called "a gross misrepresentation." Another 49 left out any mention of death related to thrombo-embolic events, past or present, and 29 did not mention the three deaths predicted in the current study. Another 15 cited incorrect numbers, 7 listed the predicted deaths but omitted the data on deaths from Fisher's previous study, and 5 mentioned the possibility of death "without including specific numbers."

The growing controversy prompted several Canadian hospitals to alter their consent forms, bringing them more into line with known tamoxifen risks. The Royal Victoria Hospital in Montreal, for example, approved a five-page addendum to the original nine-page form in February 1994. One significant change was that instead of simply saying that tamoxifen use "may" be related to endometrial cancers or blood clots in the lungs, it says, "Some human studies have shown that tamoxifen is related to endometrial cancers and to blood clots in the lungs." In a letter explaining the changes, Dr. Allan Sniderman, chairman of the hospital's Institutional Review Board, said that the changes were necessary to keep up to date because "knowledge accumulates continually and what has been learned must be incorporated at regular intervals." In an interview, Sniderman said he insisted on inserting the phrase, "I may or may not benefit from participating in this study," because he wanted this made explicit. If the benefit was a sure thing, there wouldn't be a trial. "As in any trial," he said, "it is conceivable that more harm is done than good. . . . Although it's a trial, people presume that there's a benefit to participation. They don't see the negatives."

Montreal's Jewish General Hospital, where Dr. Richard Margolese is the principal investigator for the trials, also changed its consent forms in 1994. Although it's still softer on the risks than the Royal Victoria Hospital, it does concede in the revised version that "some human studies have shown that tamoxifen use is related to endometrial cancers and blood clots in the lungs." The original version, approved in October 1992, dismissed the side effects as "usually mild," and said a "slightly increased risk" of uterine cancer had been reported but is thought to be about the same as seen in women taking routine postmenopausal therapy.

In Canada, about ten hospitals or universities are involved in the BCPT. Each has an ethics committee that must approve the study before the institution takes part in it. While the revised U.S. consent form is seven pages long, the Canadian form is just a little over two pages. It claims the side effects of tamoxifen are "usually mild" and downplays the risks of other cancers, devoting just 18 lines of print to cover the entire area of "risks and benefits." And for those women who may develop some "illness or injury" from the trial, it states that while "treatment will always be available to you," the hospital "has no special program for providing compensation for research related injuries." The U.S. consent form also states that "no monetary compensation" is available in the event of illness or injury, "but that any immediate emergency medical treatment that may be necessary will be made available to me without charge." It is silent on the question of long-term medical treatment, which could result from some of the more serious side effects, however.

U.S. law requires research sponsored by the NCI to use a model consent form, but there are also provisions for local input. Margolese says the Canadian study is using the NCI model form with "only a few changes" in things that are not appropriate to Canada, such as references to medical insurance. That's not true. The Canadian consent form is a pale imitation of the U.S. version, particularly in the area of warning participants about the dangers of tamoxifen.

After Fisher's fall as head of the NSABP over the Poisson affair, Margolese appeared on the Canadian Broadcasting Corporation's program *Medicine File*, insisting that Fisher got a raw deal over all the controversy. He brushed off concerns about the side effects of tamoxifen, saying that uterine cancer cases connected to tamoxifen had been "cured" by removing the uterus.

Granted, that was before news of the deaths from uterine cancer in Fisher's studies. On a 1993 Breast Cancer Action Montreal panel where Margolese debated Dr. Adriane Fugh-Berman (of the National Women's Health Network), however, he said that "one of the tragedies is only 1 percent of all the women with breast cancer in North America enter these trials." He conceded that "there are some uncertainties" associated with the drug.

"We take risks all the time," he said. "We take risks when we drive our car; you all know that. We take risks when we go skiing, or play tennis, you know that, people are injured. . . . So the question is, How serious is the risk? How worrisome is it, and against what should it be weighed?"

Then, in a bizarre exercise of medical doublespeak, Margolese said, "It's not fair to say that tamoxifen should not be given to healthy women. We're not giving it to healthy women. We are giving it to women who have a high risk of breast cancer, and although their health is good, it's sort of incorrect to suggest that they are healthy women altogether."

Fugh-Berman told the audience that the use of tamoxifen on healthy women for breast cancer prevention is "unconscionable" and a "dangerous precedent" in health research. She said tamoxifen, with its long list of side effects, "isn't disease prevention, it's disease substitution."

The August 1991 edition of *Health News*, published by the University of Toronto's prestigious Faculty of Medicine and still being handed out at public forums on cancer, also seriously understates the risk, claiming tamoxifen's short-term side effects "are negligible and well-tolerated." It says one "drawback" is that tamoxifen triggers or worsens menopausal symptoms such as hot flashes. Their October 1991 edition describes tamoxifen as "a well-tolerated, synthetic anti-estrogen with few side effects. . . ."

For all that, Fisher strongly criticized doctors in a 1991 article for enrolling fewer than 4 percent of breast-cancer patients in clinical trials, saying that the low figure "hardly indicates adequate use of a process that not only promotes superior patient care but also provides physicians with the opportunity to evaluate therapies potentially more effective than those being used." And Margolese complained in 1993 that the controversy had made it more difficult to enrol women, even though tamoxifen is "a safe drug. . . . The ethical thing is to do the trial and find the answer. The naysayers are going to keep us from finding out how to help women. This [trial] is something we can do here and now. I think not to do it would be a tragedy."

From the early days of the tamoxifen trial, many women, reassured by their physicians that the risks were small, displayed a high level of confidence in using the drug as an unproven preventative tool. A September 1992 news story by journalist Terry Gilbert in Calgary on the BCPT in that city, for example, features 65-year-old Ailsa Greenwood, a trial volunteer. "If this prevents it for my daughters or granddaughters, then it's worth it," she said, although Greenwood has no family history of breast cancer. She qualifies as "high risk" simply because she is over 60 years old. In the story, Anita Hades, coordinator of the study at Calgary's Tom Baker Cancer Centre, offers the remarkable prediction that the study will show that tamoxifen will cut the incidence of breast cancer in high-risk women by as much as 50 percent. "It's really the first thing of this magnitude looking at prevention. We have to look at things from a prevention focus. It's the only way to go," said Hades. Greenwood said she was not troubled by the possible side effects. "It makes you think. But at my age these things can happen anyway." True. But her statistical chances of suffering side effects on tamoxifen are much higher than her odds of getting breast cancer if she wasn't on tamoxifen.

A March 20, 1992, story in *Maclean's* magazine about the Canadian part of the BCPT quotes Dr. Michael Pollak, an associate professor of medicine at McGill University in Montreal, saying, "Every time we have checked out this drug [tamoxifen] so far, we have discovered good things about it. But it has never been used for prevention on a wide scale. This will be one of the largest clinical trials ever undertaken in the history of medicine."

All the more reason, say the critics, to be certain before getting in too deep.

One woman who didn't fall for the hype was Helen Apouchtine, a 39-year-old Ottawa civil servant. Even though study officials have said that women with previous endometrial problems would be wise to skip the test, Apouchtine says that none of the several doctors she consulted about the BCPT advised her to stay out of the trial despite the fact that she had a serious endometrial problem in May 1992, when her gynecologist discovered an "enormous fibroid the size of a five-month fetus," which was removed by major surgery. Indeed, despite her reading of the growing list of real and potential side effects from tamoxifen, she says all the doctors she consulted were pushing her to sign up.

A July 1993 mammogram discovered a pre-cancerous microcalcification, which was later removed by a needle aspiration, but Apouchtine said her surgeon "scared me half to death. He told me I could get a mastectomy and the chances were reduced by 97 percent of it ever recurring. That was a shock to me for him to tell me on the one hand I didn't even have breast cancer, then to speak of a mastectomy on the other hand."

As it happened, Apouchtine was referred to Margolese. "He only told me the positive things about tamoxifen," she says. "I asked about blood clots and eye problems, but he said, 'Oh, the dangers are really marginal. Not to worry.'"

Like most women in this position, she had only a few weeks to decide because she had to enter the trial before her radiation treatments began. "It's very stressful to put all that on you and not give you the information you need to make an intelligent choice," she said, adding that other doctors she consulted were also pushing her to join the trial. "All this stuff is going through your mind when you're already scared. I could hardly breathe when the biopsy results came back and showed something there. . . . You don't know what to expect. . . . And then you're being pressured to get into this trial."

In the end, Apouchtine decided not to join. "I really was going to do it. . . . I thought if I don't do this, I'll get breast cancer. What an idiot. But then I'd look at the articles and read about the problems. So I thought if I was going to worry about this for the next five years, I didn't want to go ahead. Even if I had known for sure it would help, I would have done it. But I don't know that. Nobody does. And in fact, it might hurt."

An Ottawa psychologist who did not want her name used was 48 in September 1991 when a mammography led to a biopsy which, in turn, discovered a pre-cancer in situ in her breast. An aunt in Montreal who had gone to Margolese with her breast cancer convinced her to follow suit. Like most women in this situation, she read everything she could. At first, Margolese told her she'd only confuse herself, "but I'm a health professional too, and when he [Margolese] saw how serious I was and how important it was to me, he directed me to some reading. It's true he has a manner that some people find difficult. He is not as warm as some people are. And he is certainly gung ho about tamoxifen."

A self-confessed health nut, she had a good diet, worked out regularly and generally avoided medication. "I don't even like aspirin. I take supplements to up my yin yang. But I guess I've compartmentalized this in my mind. I believe the benefits outweigh the risks. My way of handling that risk is to keep up to date on the latest literature, and if anything comes up, I get myself checked. . . . If the risk gets too high, or serious things begin to happen, then I'll get off it."

In the end, she went for the test for two reasons: first, she felt she'd be more closely monitored; second, "I was somewhat swayed by his

[Margolese's] emotional support for tamoxifen because I was feeling lost and scared. I was probably clutching at anything. Even though he told me my life was not in danger, I was very, very scared. That's where I'd say my consent was less informed than it would be now."

After the Poisson scandal broke, she said she was initially concerned, but felt better after reading a letter in the Montreal *Gazette* signed by Margolese and a group of other doctors assuring women that the overall test results were not affected by the medical mischief.

Many women, of course, feel it's better to "do something" than sit around and worry.

In London, England, part-time auxiliary nurse Frances Sladden from Grays, Essex, told *The Times* that she overcame her early doubts and volunteered for the trial. Sladden, whose sister had breast cancer, said, "The side-effects are minimal and if it stopped me and helped thousands or millions of other ladies not to get breast cancer it will be well worth it."

Mary Lou Urquhart, 52, of Hamilton, Ontario, certainly has a family history of the disease. Her sister in Vancouver got breast cancer at 40, had both breasts removed and takes tamoxifen. Her mother, who lives in California, also read about the trial and sent her a clipping, and she saw a show about it on her local television station, CHCH-TV. She also had an aunt who died of breast cancer. She said doctors told her she had a 19 percent chance of getting breast cancer within the next five years, so the trial is "an option you have to think about. You don't enter it lightly. You're committing yourself to five years of taking the pills."

"There are a lot of things you have to weigh," such as her own family history of heart disease and blood clots. "I did waffle. But it's a decision I made and I'm glad about it."

Despite all the controversy, however, in the United States, at least, there is no sign that fewer patients are interested in enrolling in scientific studies. A May 25 article in the *New York Times* says that in the wake of the scandal, researchers worried that the public would lose faith in these scientific studies, that fewer doctors would refer patients to them and that fewer of those patients would sign up. "But, so far, that has not happened," wrote Gina Kolata.

In Canada, however, there was one public rupture of medical solidarity when the Hamilton Regional Cancer Centre decided the risk of tamoxifen was too great and they would pull out of the trial. Of the 85 women already enrolled in the trial at that center, 10 decided to stay in and will be monitored by the Hamilton researchers for as long as it lasts. Dr. Andrew Arnold, head of medical oncology at the center, said, "We felt very uncomfortable going on participating in a trial in which some people might develop cancers as part of the trial. It's a very, very difficult issue."

Indeed. But surely Arnold knew long before the fraudulent data controversy that tamoxifen had been shown to cause uterine and other cancers.

Ottawa's Dr. Shail Verma says there are many good things about tamoxifen, but "today it is generating more questions than answers.

"Anybody who has breast cancer should ask their doctor, 'What is my risk?'

". . . tamoxifen is beginning to be applied as a primary prevention agency. We don't want it to be the thalidomide of the 21st century. I don't think it will be anything like that . . . but there shouldn't be a person who believes we [doctors] have all the answers to breast cancer. We don't."

And in Mill Valley, California, Bobbe Rigler says she's aware of the risks, but because of the rigorous and regular scrutiny of women in the trial — a checkup every six months, including a mammogram — she says any problems would be found early anyway. Although it can't hurt, it doesn't always help either. For some cancers, it doesn't matter when they're discovered. Once found, it's too late. For others, that's not true. And with the new information on tamoxifen-induced uterine cancers being more aggressive, earlier discovery may not compensate.

Even so, Rigler says her risks are "minute," far less than her chances of getting breast cancer.

"I felt that it was worth the risk. Quite frankly, I can't see any thinking woman not taking part if she's high risk."

3   Fatal Flaws

ON MAY 9, 1992, MICHIGAN DEMO-
cratic Congressman John Dingell, chair-
man of the Subcommittee on Oversight and Investigations of the U.S.
House of Representatives, delivered the 102nd Shattuck Lecture to the
annual meeting of the Massachusetts Medical Society in Boston.

Dingell, a no-nonsense, well-informed critic of the medical establishment, delivered a stinging speech on misconduct in medical research.

It is, he said, more common than we think.

Citing a 1992 survey sponsored by the American Association for the
Advancement of Science (AAAS), Dingell said that 27 percent of a group
of scientists surveyed acknowledged they had personally encountered
research they suspected was falsified, fabricated or plagiarized during
the previous ten years.

Worse, in private interviews with some 20 leading scientists,
Dingell's committee discovered that "almost all" cited examples of
misconduct they had witnessed, whistle-blowers they had seen harassed

or other matters engendering concern. "Yet none were willing to testify, write open letters or even have their names used publicly, for fear of retaliation."

Dingell went on to cite several examples of scientific misconduct, along with disturbing cases of principled scientists who were vilified by the scientific community for reporting the misconduct.

Just as people say you should not believe everything you read in the newspapers, you should also be skeptical of much of what you read in scientific research papers and scientific journals.

"Every time a researcher takes taxpayer money and publishes fabricated, falsified or plagiarized findings," Dingell said, "the taxpayer has in effect been swindled."

A dramatic example of this received worldwide attention in March 1994 when journalist John Crewdson of the *Chicago Tribune* reported that the NSABP, America's oldest and largest breast-cancer research group, had conducted no audit of patient treatment records for the previous year despite knowing since 1991 that some of the data supplied by Dr. Roger Poisson of Montreal's St. Luc Hospital had been falsified.

In addition, the key element of trust, so critical to successful patient-doctor-researcher relationships, was also seriously eroded, not just by Poisson's inexcusable actions, but by the studied inactions of Fisher, the National Cancer Institute, the National Institutes of Health and others inside the medical establishment.

Montreal's Dr. Richard Margolese, the leading Canadian advocate of the tamoxifen trials, admits that he and other doctors involved in the NSABP research work were told about the discrepancies in Poisson's work in the fall of 1993, although he said none of them had any idea of the extent of the fabrications. Nor, it seems, did they ask. Margolese, who co-published work with Fisher and other NSABP physicians, told the Montreal *Gazette* that when he personally met Poisson a few months after hearing about the problems, he did not pursue details. "I didn't pry. He [Poisson] told me he was going through certain travails. I didn't ask him for anything more."

Wasn't it his business to pry? After all, Margolese was actively signing up volunteers for the BCPT during this time. Wouldn't he want to be sure whether or not the falsified data had a direct bearing on the tamoxifen trials? Apparently not.

As for Fisher, who was regarded as the Wayne Gretzky of breast-cancer research until the scandal blackened his career, the *Tribune* revelations led him merely to ask the public to trust him. He said — and this turned out not to be true — that when the tests had been re-analyzed without Poisson's data, the results were the same. These landmark tests, of course, dramatically changed the way breast surgeons approached their patients — lumpectomies replaced mastectomies as the surgery of choice in most cases. And much of the NSABP data involved tamoxifen, leading directly to the current high level of faith in that drug, which, in turn, helped prompt the cancer establishment to test it as a preventative drug.

But how are we to trust Fisher when he sat on this information for several months without even telling the NCI about it and, some four years after the discrepancies were discovered, still balked at publishing the complete data so that all interested parties could satisfy themselves that the flawed data did not skew the overall results?

Fisher claimed that as soon as Poisson's misbehavior was discovered, the Montreal doctor was cut off from the program and his input, significant in some of the studies, was immediately excised.

If that were true, why, in a 1992 article in the *Journal of the National Cancer Institute* entitled "Lumpectomy for Breast Cancer: An Update of the NSABP Experience," written by Fisher, his assistant Carol Redmond and others, do they still cite Poisson in a footnoted NSABP study he co-authored with both Fisher and Redmond? And why — two years after Poisson's contributions were supposedly cancelled — does this same article list Poisson and St. Luc Hospital under an appendix detailing "Institutions contributing significant numbers of patients to these studies"?

Why didn't Fisher change his audit procedures after the NCI asked him to do that in January 1993 when they had expressed concern that the relatively small number of cases Fisher's team selected for re-audit contributed to the study group's "inability to detect problems"? Why didn't he follow the usual procedure and order an outside audit immediately, rather than keep it in-house and secret?

Why did Fisher virtually go into hiding for a time after the scandal broke, offering only a brief CBS interview in which he said, "Women can be assured that the treatments they have received, a lumpectomy or other treatment based upon our findings, have received highly appropriate therapy"?

How did the public know that? Even when the NCI finally ordered an outside audit and ultimately dumped Fisher and Redmond from the project's leadership, it remained uncertain about just how useful that audit would be. Will they be able to have access to all the raw data from past years, for example? Not likely. They can't replay the situations with thousands of patients. They, too, will have to accept on faith the data they find.

Even the NCI's assurances are hardly comforting in light of its initial reaction to the scandal. Less than a week after offering public assurances that the falsified data did not affect the overall studies, the NCI admitted it did not know whether this was true or not. In the wake of the *Chicago Tribune* stories, the NCI said it had "re-analyzed all of the studies" and had confirmed "the original results and conclusions of the trials." Not true. A few days later, the NCI admitted this when spokesman Paul van Nevel said the original statement was being rewritten and another NCI official, Dr. Michael A. Friedman, subsequently said, "We have never reviewed all the primary data in these studies. We reviewed the summary analysis that was provided to us."

Eventually, the NCI ordered the University of Pittsburgh to stop recruiting patients in the 14 NSABP cancer studies, including the tamoxifen study, until an investigation was completed. In the meantime, the tens of thousands of people already involved in these studies or treatments would continue as if nothing had happened. Fisher says he asked for administrative leave as principal investigator but would continue as a senior clinical researcher advising on the science of the project. But NCI officials say they fired him. Dr. Greg Curt even admitted to the *New York Times* that the NCI was partly to blame for the mess. "We let things slip as well. The audit process fell behind and we share that responsibility." True. But, unlike Poisson, Fisher or Redmond, nobody at the NCI or NIH was punished for their sins, even though the NCI knew about the falsified data three years before it was made public and the NIH had two years' notice. Neither health organization did much with this knowledge until forced to act when the *Chicago Tribune* told the world about it.

In the midst of all this, U.S. investigators found discrepancies in breast-cancer files at Montreal's St. Mary's Hospital, but they turned out to be minor. Poisson himself, in an open letter to the Montreal newspaper *La Presse* on March 30, claimed his only crime was caring more about the health of women than about "blindly obeying" rigid scientific rules. He accused U.S. officials of persecuting him publicly "when a single comment or warning would have sufficed." He claimed he bent the rules to allow some patients into the protocols even though they didn't qualify because that way they were assured of better treatment. Critics dismissed the claim as self-serving, saying all patients had access to the latest cancer treatment, whether they were enrolled in the studies or not.

In late March, both *Time* and *Newsweek* magazines published prominent stories on the controversy. *Time* quoted Poisson saying "the irregularities were very minor" and insisting that he did not order progress reports on a dead woman as had been claimed in the media. A staff member did it without his knowledge he said, and was fired as a result. Cynthia Pearson of the National Women's Health Network told *Newsweek*, "This might have been less sensational if it had come from Fisher or NCI and they said 'we're horrified, and we're going to make sure it never happens again.'" But because the fraud was reported in a newspaper, she said, "Women feel they weren't being told information that affects their lives and are upset because they think someone made a conscious decision to hide it."

In the April 6 *Journal of the National Cancer Institute*, the editors wrote that its "primary concern . . . is to provide the best possible information to patients and physicians who are dealing with life-threatening illness and complicated treatment decisions. This fraud is of such a scale as to cause some patients to question the validity of their therapeutic choices. The public trust and confidence is both precious and fragile. Hence, the full publication and complete re-analyses of all studies is necessary to restore full credibility in the clinical trials process and to permit the scientific community to properly evaluate the findings."

Such action might not have been necessary, of course, had the NCI acted earlier on its own knowledge of the fraud. But it didn't, opting instead to wait — along with everybody else involved — until the scandal was publicized before displaying any outward concerns.

That same issue of the NCI journal contained an essay by three NCI doctors entitled "Tamoxifen: Trials, Tribulations, and Trade-offs," reviewing the various studies and including — at long last — the fact that tamoxifen increases the relative risk of endometrial cancer by two to three times. Even so, they wrote that the matter of the risks versus the potential benefits of tamoxifen as a chemopreventative agent for breast cancer "can be properly answered only by a formal trial, such as the BCPT. . . ."

The journal also published the long-awaited data by Fisher and his colleagues showing that four tamoxifen-treated women had died of uterine cancer in an earlier study. Even so, it concluded that "benefit greatly outweighs risk."

Maybe so. But three days later the Food and Drug Administration upgraded warnings about tamoxifen, finally acknowledging what studies had long shown, that it increases a woman's chance by two to three times of getting cancer of the uterus. "Tamoxifen is a valuable treatment for breast cancer, but it is important for women to recognize that there are side effects," said FDA commissioner Dr. David Kessler. "If symptoms appear, do not ignore them." Zeneca Pharmaceuticals, the drug's U.S. manufacturer, sent letters to 380,000 doctors and other health-care professionals telling them about the FDA warnings. Zeneca, in addition to making tamoxifen, was also a major player in promoting pink ribbons for breast-cancer activism and designating April as cancer month.

In Canada, where the scandal had actually begun, the *Canadian Medical Association Journal* published a study in its April 1, 1994, edition concluding that "one randomized clinical trial can have an immediate and profound effect on medical practice." It referred, of course, to the original publication of the results of the NSABP trial in 1977, which dramatically altered the standard Halsted radical mastectomy to more breast-conserving surgery such as lumpectomy. The impact of the NSABP findings has been dramatic. In 1980 in Ontario, for example, radical surgery was used 77.5 percent of the time, while breast-conserving surgery was performed in just 12.5 percent of cases. By 1989, the two procedures were almost equal in popularity. The concern for women was that their decision to save their breasts by opting for lumpectomies instead of mastectomies was based primarily on studies showing that the breast-conserving approach was as safe as lopping off the entire breast. Unfortunately, the studies appeared to be based partially on falsehoods. Although subsequent studies "confirmed" the earlier results, a particular study can affect treatment techniques and it can also affect the outcome of further studies because much of science is cobbled together like building blocks piled one on top of the other, with scientists making certain assumptions based on the previous study, which in turn leads them to the next block.

Dr. Judith P. Swazey, president of The Acadia Institute in Bar Harbor, Maine, has been studying the question of scientific misconduct for 20 years. On the CBC radio science show, *Quirks and Quarks*, she said that often "insiders know that something wrong is going on and they are very reluctant to make that knowledge public outside of their professional group. They view it as an act of disloyalty to their colleagues. They think if they ignore it, it will simply go away and not be discovered."

Those who defend Poisson say he didn't twist his research for personal gain. Well, not exactly. His hospital did receive over $1 million in NCI research grants as a result of his work, money the NCI is now attempting to recover. And the entire system of academic progress and prestige is based on the number of publications you churn out, the prestige of those publications and the importance of the studies you are associated with. Despite Fisher's attempt to downgrade Poisson as a bit player in the NASBP affairs, Poisson, was, in fact, a major contributor over many years to several studies.

Dr. John Bailar, chairman of the Department of Epidemiology and Biostatistics at McGill University's Faculty of Medicine in Montreal, told a CBC audience that "the whole system of rewards for scientific work is related to publication and particularly to the publication of what you can call positive findings. Something new. People are not as much interested in experimental work or other kinds of science that may be carried out very carefully and comes to a conclusion that our prior beliefs were true." He said confirmatory work is "important, but it isn't exciting. And that isn't what people get Nobel prizes for. It isn't what they get their jobs for, or their promotions or their academic tenure. That isn't how they tend to get their next contract or grant for research support. All of the rewards are tied to publication, especially the positive findings, and so there is a lot of pressure on scientists to come up with what are considered positive findings that some scientific journal will want to publish."

In the mid-1980s, Dr. Arthur Schafer, director of the Centre for Professional and Applied Ethics at the University of Manitoba, was invited by Fisher to speak to over 1,000 physicians and surgeons participating in the NASBP trial at a meeting in San Antonio, Texas, on the subject of medical ethics. Schafer, reminiscing about the experience on the CBC radio show *Sunday Morning*, said the question at the time was that many of the doctors felt it was unethical to invite their patients to participate in the trials "since they had to pretend to their patients, or had to assert to their patients, that they didn't know which treatment was better [mastectomy or lumpectomy]. Some of them found it embarrassing to admit this." But Schafer said they all favored one or the other based on their own "pre-scientific feelings, because the test results weren't in and no one really knew, but they sort of knew. The problem was, of course, they knew different things . . . so the ethical problem really was on the other side. The question was, Was it ethical to enrol the patients, rather than was it ethical to exclude them."

At the time the Poisson scandal became public, another major medical public inquiry was underway in Canada, a judicial investigation into HIV-tainted blood that infected more than 1,000 Canadians, condemning them and some of their family members to death by AIDS because of transfusions they had received before the Red Cross began testing for the AIDS virus in 1985.

Schafer told a CBC reporter that both the tainted blood scandal and the fabricated breast-cancer study show that medical science has a serious problem on its hands. "We've been relying on an honor system and an audit system. Maybe there needs to be more audit, more actual on-site checks," he said. "Maybe we need more medical ethics . . . greater stress on research ethics in our medical schools and our research institutions. As well as stiffer legal punishment. I wonder whether people who violate their trust ought to be able to continue to practice medicine, for example?"

In the House of Commons, Reform Party MP Jan Brown said Canadian women were "outraged" by news of the Poisson affair. "The medical community has known about this for three years. The Canadian public has been misled by yet another health-related cover-up."

Brown demanded a federal investigation. Oddly, Health Minister Diane Marleau said that "no Canadian dollars were used to fund any of the research" under dispute. So what? Surely the issue is the potential impact upon Canadian women, not who paid for the studies? Anyway, Canadians funds were used to support the hospital Poisson worked for and the bills of his patients under Canada's universal health care system. And with some 1,500 Canadian women enrolled in the tamoxifen trials, you'd expect Marleau to show more interest. She did say, however, that she'd meet federal health officials about the matter. In a follow-up question from Brown a month later about the possible impact of this scandal on Canadian women, Marleau again stressed the odd notion that it was not really her problem because the study was funded by the United States. In late March, having said nothing for weeks about it, Marleau suddenly found herself "really overwhelmed" by the scandal and awarded Montreal's Hôtel Dieu Hospital and four other hospitals across the country $500,000 over five years to set up a breast-cancer information-exchange network.

Shortly after news of Poisson's misadventures became public, and about the same time the NCI commissioned three statisticians to conduct an independent analysis of the flawed Canadian data, Quebec's Corporation Professionelle des Médecins announced that it, too, was investigating the situation. Poisson had already been barred by the U.S. Office of Research Integrity from performing U.S.-funded research for eight years, the stiffest penalty it had ever imposed in a scientific misconduct case.

In Montreal, however, the medical establishment was busy doing damage control. Margolese and five other doctors, in a letter to the Montreal *Gazette*, said flatly that women in the studies or treated as a result of previous studies "can be assured of the appropriateness of their therapy." They claimed the trials had all been re-analyzed without Poisson's data by both the NSABP and the NCI. "The results in every protocol came out the same." At that point, of course, they had not been re-analyzed.

As for the Quebec investigation, the man in charge of the province's professional association for doctors, Dr. Augustin Roy, said the Poisson case was "very complex" and urged people to get all the facts before condemning the doctor. "We must be very careful before passing judgment," Roy said, typical of the approach he had taken in his 30 years of running the province-wide organization. At a 1993 function in his honor, for example, Roy said of the Corporation Professionelle des Médecins, "It's a little like it were my wife and you, you were my children. And one has a tendency to protect one's children. I shouldn't, but it's like a second nature." Apparently so. In the past, he had dismissed women who complained of sexual misconduct by doctors as being "crazy" or motivated by "vengeance." And in 1992, Roy refused to do anything about Hector Warnes, a psychiatrist who came to work in Quebec after losing his license next door in Ontario because he had had sex with a patient.

In 1993, the Quebec government's Office des Professions charged Roy with "meddling" in disciplinary proceedings against doctors, saying in a report that "the public does not receive the protection which it has the right to expect from the Corporation Professionelle des Médecins." That involved the case of Dr. Carlo Vernacchia, a general practitioner who'd already done time for raping and sodomizing a patient and indecently assaulting another, and was charged for the third time in his professional career with a sex crime against another female patient. Yet, after his bail hearing on the third charge, Vernacchia was back at work, still free to conduct gynecological examinations with no restrictions on his practice. Even before the third charge, government officials asked Roy why the physicians' corporation had not put in place restrictions such as insisting a nurse be present when he was with a female patient, for example. Roy replied that Vernacchia had paid his debt to society, and anyway, twice yearly visits to his office by Corporation executives was enough.

It wasn't surprising, then, that some breast-cancer activists were not too excited when the corporation announced it would investigate the Poisson affair.

Unlike the Canadian federal government, which saw no reason to get involved, U.S. political officials took a more active role. In Washington, Dingell's committee convened Congressional hearings into the fraudulent data scandal in April, but Fisher, citing health reasons, refused to testify. Dr. Thomas Detre, Fisher's boss in his capacity as senior vice-chancellor of the University of Pittsburgh, said he suspected Poisson's type of cheating "happens perhaps more frequently than we are aware of," adding that seemingly trivial actions, such as changing dates in a clinical trial, can lead to errors in determining the effectiveness of a therapy being studied.

NIH head Dr. Harold Varmus, and Dr. Samuel Broder, his NCI counterpart, both apologized to the committee over delays in sorting out the problems in federally financed breast-cancer studies, announcing they had imposed stricter rules and would now conduct surprise inspections yearly to monitor research at 20 percent of recipients of federal grants. Shifting the blame from their own organizations to Fisher, however, they publicly accused the veteran doctor of having an arrogant and cavalier attitude in dealing with federal officials and of failing to publish a timely correction of the falsified data.

Cindy Pearson, of the National Women's Health Network, said the tamoxifen preventative trial should be stopped. She testified along with Fran Visco of the National Breast Cancer Coalition and Jill Lea Sigal of Alexandria, Virginia, all of whom said they had lost faith in the NCI and that reports of the falsified data had left thousands of women terrified and anxious about whether they'd received proper therapy by choosing a lumpectomy over mastectomy. Sigal, 32, who chose lumpectomy with radiation for her treatment six months earlier, said, "There is a crisis of confidence and credibility as it pertains to NCI and other organizations associated with this study." Pearson added, "To let this trial proceed is to watch women die of trust."

Another twist flowing from the hearings was that in the late 1980s, officials of the University of Pittsburgh had solicited a $600,000 gift from the ICI Pharmaceuticals Group, the British tamoxifen manufacturer, for an endowed chair in Fisher's honor. Dingell called this "not quite cricket." Other gifts bumped the total endowment to $1.2 million, not enough to establish a chair. According to Detre, however, Fisher had expressed a personal dislike for such recognition anyway, although Dingell pointed out that at the time of the hearing, Fisher listed himself as the ICI Professor of Surgery in *American Men and Women of Science*. In *Who's Who in America*, Fisher was listed as ICI-Pharma professor of surgery. University of Pittsburgh officials claimed the listings were clerical errors — an unlikely explanation given the fact that such publications routinely send their subjects their own entry for editing and approval before actually publishing them.

To further allay the fears of women as a result of the Poisson scandal and its dramatic fall-out, in late April the *Journal of the American Medical Association* rushed a new study into print. It involved the records of more than 5,800 patients and was led by Anna Lee-Feldstein, an assistant professor of Biostatistics at the University of California, Irvine, College of Medicine. Among other things, it compared survival rates for different therapies among women with cancers that had not spread to the lymph nodes. For women over 50 who had had lumpectomies combined with radiation, 91 percent survived at least five years, compared to 79.7 percent of women who had had a mastectomy. For women under 50, there was no significant difference in survival rates.

Shortly after that, the NCI demonstrated it was cracking down when it suspended both Louisiana State University and Tulane University from NCI-sponsored clinical studies after an audit found "unacceptably high rates of unconfirmed data entries" and other "inadequacies" in their record keeping. Unlike the Poisson case, however, there was no suggestion of falsified or altered data.

In May, the NCI threatened to cut off its $16 million funding to the University of Pittsburgh to coordinate various studies unless the university dumped Fisher — whom they wanted to keep as scientific director instead of chairman — and his deputy, Dr. Carol Redmond, from leadership roles in the project. Four days later, the university announced the two physicians would remain involved in the project, but in lesser roles. A joint announcement "recognized Dr. Fisher and Dr. Redmond had valuable insight into the program and can certainly remain involved with the research."

At the same time, the NCI announced it had tightened its own grip on the process. Among other things, it would "now require immediate re-analysis and publication of all trials affected by scientific misconduct" and strengthen all phases of NSABP auditing activities, including on-site visits. It also created a new branch, the Clinical Trials Monitoring Branch. Its May 4 journal reported that the NCI had asked the University of Pittsburgh to replace NSABP's principal investigator (Fisher), to appoint an executive officer for its grants and to develop a plan for orderly succession of leadership responsibilities at NSABP. It said Fisher had "stepped aside" and the university had named Dr. Ronald Herberman, director of the Pittsburgh Cancer Center, as interim NSABP leader, with Dr. Donald Trump named to oversee the daily operations of the NSABP offices.

In a lengthy letter published in the May 19 *New England Journal of Medicine*, Fisher and Redmond defended their actions, arguing that there was no real need for the public to know, since Poisson's data did not change anything. They claimed that "we had repeatedly reanalyzed the data during the investigation, and the findings convinced us and others at the NIH that none of our original conclusions were affected by excluding Dr. Poisson's patients and there was therefore no issue of public health. Second, Dr. MacFarlane [Dorothy MacFarlane, NCI chief of Quality Assurance and Compliance] stated that her office would have released details publicly if it had appeared that the fraudulent data had caused a health catastrophe." Indeed, that same issue of the *New England Journal of Medicine* also contained letters on the topic from Poisson; MacFarlane; NCI's Dr. Samuel Broder; University of Pittsburgh's George M. Bernier, Jr.; St. Luc Hospital's Dr. P. Michel Huet; and University of Montreal's Dr. Gilles Richer, all defending their own actions — or inactions — in the affair.

Despite widespread public concern about the risks of tamoxifen, however (particularly its use in prevention — something for which it was never designed), an FDA advisory committee recommended on June 7 that recruiting for the BCPT, suspended in April in the wake of the scandal, could be resumed as soon as possible. Dr. Janet Osuch of the American Cancer Society told the FDA's advisory committee that killing the trial, which already had 11,000 U.S. women enrolled, would "set back any future prevention in breast cancer many years." Dr. Joseph Costantino of the University of Pittsburgh testified that over a three-year period, tamoxifen would prevent 133 cases of breast cancer in women in the trial, along with 45 cases of heart disease, but would cause 83 cases of uterine cancer, plus other health problems, such as liver cancer. NCI's Dr. Leslie Ford, who oversees the study, said the institute would now begin risk assessments on new patients interested in the study but would not officially enrol them until the consent form strengthened the warnings (once again) about uterine cancer and other health concerns.

On June 10, in a generally sympathetic interview on NBC's *20/20* with network medical specialist Dr. Timothy Johnson, Fisher, described as a "veritable giant in the field," was shown at a public speech to medical researchers — at which he received a standing ovation — saying, "Eight weeks ago my life, that of my associates, and that of the entire NSABP precipitously began to unravel."

NBC quoted Jill Sigal of Alexandria saying, "How many women, as I did, made their decision to have a lumpectomy on the basis of their study? How many women must now wonder, as I do every day, if they have made the wrong decision?" Immediately following that, however, Dr. Bruce Chabner of the NCI downplayed the extent of Poisson's fabrications. "I think it's important to understand what the fabrication was," he said. "It wasn't changing the outcome of the study." Johnson told viewers it took eight months for Fisher's staff to investigate the initial allegation before telling the NCI, then quoted Chabner saying, "Our rules were he was supposed to notify us immediately if there was any evidence of fabrications, fraud or scientific misconduct." Johnson did not, however, ask Chabner why the NCI didn't act on the problem for three years. Another clip, from NCI director Samuel Broder, also blamed Fisher for his "personal arrogance," but avoided any reference to the NCI's lack of swift action in the matter.

Fisher was asked how he felt about women being confused over whether a lumpectomy is as effective as a mastectomy or not. "To me that is very sad," he said. "That would have been the last thing I ever would have wanted to happen to women in my life . . . and I would be blamed for that."

On June 13 in Nashville, Fisher bade an emotional farewell to his colleagues at the NSABP. He apologized for the confusion caused by the scandal, but urged doctors and other researchers to continue their work despite the uproar from the tainted studies.

That same day, by a unanimous vote of its board of scientific counsellors, the NCI voted to hold open bidding for the 35-year-old cancer research project now located at the University of Pittsburgh, giving other institutions a chance to take over the $25 million annual budget. Broder said that was the only way to restore the NSABP "to its previous glory."

4

Ranking
the
Risks

IN NOVEMBER 1993, CBC'S FLAGSHIP
show, *Prime Time News*, broadcast "A Family Portrait," the moving story of the Anthony family of Newfoundland, where five of the six sisters developed breast cancer. Two of them died from it, one a 35-year-old mother of six children. Three had double mastectomies.

The other sister, Joan, wasn't diagnosed with the disease, but opted to have both breasts removed anyway. Just as well as it turned out. Post-operative studies on her breasts showed that within a year, she, too, would have had full-blown breast cancer.

"I'd get up every morning and go into the bathroom and look in the shower door, look in the glass. And I'd say, 'Why am I going to take two healthy breasts off? I mean, they look fine, right?' But then I'd think, 'Well, you don't know what's inside until they come off. Not every mammogram will pick up a lump and by the time I find them, it will be too late.'

"I'm telling you it was really hard," she said. "It was hard looking at yourself and all that. You'd get in the shower and it was dreadful. But the way I felt, my five sisters had that done and they could learn to live with it and cope with it, why can't I? I'm just as strong as they are."

Familial breast cancer, while not usually as dramatic as that experienced by the Anthony family, is perhaps the best known of the so-called risk factors, but represents only between 5 and 10 percent of all breast cancers. Scientists believe that the breast-cancer gene is so powerful that if mothers have it, there is a 50–50 chance the daughters will inherit it too.

Overall, women with all the known "risk" factors represent between 25 and 30 percent of all breast cancers. The rest are diagnosed in women who have no known risk factors, other than the fact that they are women.

The well-known "one-in-eight" — which used to be one-in-nine in the United States until the NCI changed it to reflect the lifetime risk to age 95 instead of 85 — is the most frequently quoted measure of the risk of breast cancer to individual women. It's also the most frightening. But despite the horrific numbers it represents, it does not mean that one of every eight women alive today is about to suddenly discover she has breast cancer. What it does represent is the lifetime probability for all women, assuming they live to be 95.

A more useful measure, and slightly more comforting, is the risk at any given age in five-year intervals. By age 30, for example, an American woman has 1 chance in 2,525 of getting breast cancer. By age 35, it's 1 in 622; age 40, 1 in 217; age 45, 1 in 93; age 50, 1 in 50; age 55, 1 in 33; age 60, 1 in 24; age 65, 1 in 17; age 70, 1 in 14; age 75, 1 in 11; age 80, 1 in 10; age 85, 1 in 9; and over, 1 in 8.

Another problem with that number is that it applies globally, to all women in those age groups. Since breast cancer isn't applicable to all women equally, however, it isn't all that useful. After all, those numbers include women who are at very high risk and women who have virtually no risk, so the one-in-eight cannot be applied equally among all women.

Dr. Susan Love, co-author of *Dr. Susan Love's Breast Book*, wrote: "This figure will be an overestimate for the woman with no risk factors and an underestimate for the one with risk factors, but no help at all to the forty-year-old woman who is sitting in your office."

Viewed in a more positive light, the one-in-eight means that the average woman has an 87.5 percent chance of not getting breast cancer in her lifetime. On the other hand, the lifetime risk in 1940 was 1 in 20, and incidence of the disease rose 25 percent between 1973 and 1988. Between 1980 and 1988, it increased by 15 percent in Canadian women and 21 percent in the United States. In Ontario, breast cancer has risen from 24 percent of all cancers in women in 1987 to almost 30 percent today. Even with major technological and pharmaceutical advances, the mortality rate is not improving. In the United States, a new breast cancer is diagnosed every 3 minutes, and a woman dies of the disease every 12 minutes. Despite the much higher risk for postmenopausal women, breast cancer accounts for 14 percent of all deaths in women between the ages of 25 and 49, and it remains the biggest killer of all women aged 35 to 54.

While the statistical risks of cancer are easy to calculate, there is still apparently widespread misunderstanding among the public. A 1991 survey of 1,350 women in Alberta, for example, found that 65 percent of the women aged 40 to 74 years knew that lifetime risk for breast cancer is 10 percent or more, but only 30 percent knew the incidence of the disease increases with age. In addition, women under 50 believed they were at much higher risk than older women.

While all women are obviously not born equal in terms of breast cancer, evaluating risk gets more muddied because the incidence of cancer varies considerably in various parts of the world for reasons that are not always obvious. Women in North America, for example, have about 30 times more breast cancer but only half as much uterine cervix cancer as women in Western Africa and Central America. Japanese women who emigrate to Hawaii have half the risk of contracting stomach cancer their grandmothers had at the same age, but double the risk of breast cancer.

According to the World Health Organization (WHO), about 1 in 11 women in industrialized countries will develop breast cancer. That's slightly less than the U.S. one-in-eight rate and about five times the rate in Japan. In Canada, it's roughly one in nine, based on a woman living until the age of 85. A 1986 comparison of 15 countries around the world found the lowest rates in Japan, at 11 breast cancers for every 100,000 women, while it was 50 per 100,000 in New Zealand and 46 in Germany, followed closely by the United States, Australia and Canada. Australia and New Zealand have the highest rates for premenopausal women, while the United States has the highest postmenopausal rates.

From region to region around the world, there is tremendous variation. In Geneva, for example, the incidence rate is double that for women living in Navarra, Spain. And white females living in the San Francisco Bay area have almost twice as much chance of being diagnosed with the disease as women in Newfoundland.

A 1992 *Atlas of Cancer Mortality in the European Economic Community*, produced by the WHO's International Agency for Research on Cancer, demonstrates the extraordinary range of breast-cancer mortality rates in Europe. While the rate of breast-cancer deaths per 100,000 women using 1989 figures was 84 in the United States, it was 87 in England and Wales, 95 in France and just 65 in Germany.

A few patterns can be discerned, however. The disease shows a clear north-south gradient: rates are much higher in eastern Ireland and southern and southeast England, above average in Denmark and well below average in southern Italy. The highest mortality rate as a percentage of fatal cancer in women was 29 percent in the East Midlands. The lowest was 9.6 in Basilicata in southern Italy.

Women living in urban areas are also at greater risk than their rural counterparts, but trends like these have not made scientists certain about the whys and wherefores of the disease. The following write-up from the *Atlas* about breast cancer graphically illustrates the diversity of possible causes.

Breast cancer incidence is about 30 percent higher in residents of urban areas compared to rural population groups and similarly elevated among black compared to white members of the same community. Although a large proportion of breast cancer seems to be related to environmental or lifestyle factors and, therefore, theoretically avoidable, the factors which influence breast cancer risk are not yet obvious.

The risk of breast cancer is increased by around 50 percent in nulliparous [childless] compared to parous women. Risk increases with increasing age at first birth until a first birth occurring after the age of [approximately] 35 years carries a higher risk than nulliparity, indicating that first childbirth after this age no longer confers protection against breast cancer. . . . [One study] estimated that a 3.5 percent increase in relative risk is associated with every year of increase in age at first birth.

Proposed protective effects of late age at menarche [first menstrual period], of parity [giving birth] and of breast-feeding remain controversial. Risk is increased by a late age at menopause . . . and an early menopause, whether natural or artificial . . . contributes to reducing risk.

Consistent evidence supports an increased risk in "young" women associated with prolonged use [over five years] of oral contraceptives; "young" implies less than 35 years and perhaps less than 45. . . . Fortunately, at these ages, breast cancer risk is very low and there appears to be no evidence to date that use of oral contraceptives influences the risk of breast cancer at the older ages at which the disease is commoner.

In relation to menopausal hormone replacement therapy, the risk for breast cancer is elevated 30–50 percent among long-term (i.e., 5–10 years) users. . . . The few data extant on combined estrogen-progestin treatment suggest that the risk may be greater than for estrogens alone . . .

Although an anti-estrogenic effect of cigarettes . . . could theoretically lead to some protection against breast cancer, the majority of published studies have given negative results. . . . Radiation to the breast in high doses has been shown to increase the risk of mammary cancer; exposure around the menarche is associated with particularly high risk . . .

The risk of breast cancer appears to rise with increasing body mass index among postmenopausal women. . . . Former college athletes have been found to have a reduced risk of breast cancer compared with non-athletes . . . as have ballet dancers. . . . This may be associated with physical activity or reduced body weight around menarche, early adolescence or throughout lifetime.

The association with diet, particularly fat intake, is the subject of much research and debate. . . . Although an association between risk of breast cancer and saturated fat intake in postmenopausal women is biologically plausible . . . the evidence from studies in human subjects with breast cancer is contradictory. Studies in Greece . . . and Italy . . . have suggested that green vegetable consumption is an indicator of a low-risk dietary pattern. This may simply reflect low intake of fat or calories, or suggest that some constituent of green vegetables is protective. . . . A modest increase in risk of breast cancer with increased alcohol intake has been observed consistently in a large number of studies . . .

Of the other factors for breast cancer studied, a positive family history has the effect of increasing the risk of breast cancer . . . with the maximum effect apparent in postmenopausal women who have a first-degree relative with breast cancer at premenopausal ages.

Although probably becoming more homogeneous, diets still vary considerably within the EEC-9 countries, as do national patterns of fertility, age-at-first-pregnancy, etc. The existence of a four-fold variation in risk of mortality within the EEC demands investigation. If the age of first full-term pregnancy is truly the major factor in Europe in the determination of risk for this cancer, then incidence of this form of malignancy is bound to increase, unless there are major advances in the success of early diagnosis or treatment.

And so the question remains: Why do women (and some men) get breast cancer?

Unfortunately, science can't answer that question with any degree of certainty, although it has determined a list of risk factors.

Dr. Andrea Manni, professor of medicine, University Hospital at Penn State, says, "Although certain risk factors have clearly been established, there is very little, in general, a woman can do to significantly decrease her risk to develop breast cancer. This is because very little is still known on the etiology [combined causes] of the disease."

The issue of risk is all the more baffling because not all breast cancers are the same. Some are fast, some slow. Some spread, some don't. Nor do scientists agree on all the risk factors. There's widespread agreement on the impact of family history, for example, but great controversy over environmental risks. Even where researchers do agree, however, there is no real understanding of the connection between these factors and the disease itself. Most women with breast cancer have none of the established risks, while one woman can have numerous risk factors and never get the disease.

Adding to the confusion, and the fear, is the fact that the cancer research community itself is schizophrenic about risk factors. When they want to promote clinical trials like the tamoxifen trial on "high-risk" women who do not have breast cancer, there is considerable emphasis on the risk. Indeed, in Canada and the United States, all women over age 60 are considered eligible because they are in the "high-risk" category — an obvious absurdity. (It's true that breast-cancer incidence increases dramatically with age, but the majority of older women still do not get the disease.) But when the cancer establishment wants to present a happy face to the world, arguing that they are winning the war against breast cancer — although they aren't — the risk factors are downplayed.

So what are the established risk factors?

Age, for one. A woman over 50, for example, has a much higher risk than a woman in her 30s. Then there's the country of birth, with North American and Northern European women being in the high-risk group, while those in Asia and Africa are at low risk for breast cancer. Urban women have a higher risk than rural women on average, and women in the northern United States a higher risk than their sisters in the southern part of the country. Childless women have a higher risk than women who have borne children. And women who have their first full-term pregnancy over the age of 30 are at greater risk than those who have their first child before the age of 20. Women who don't breast-feed see their risk increase, just as women with early menarche and/or late menopause and women who have already had cancer in one breast or have a history of breast problems do. Body shape and weight are also factors, along with breast radiation. And then there's the family history connection, and, it is believed, long-term use of oral contraceptives.

Other factors often mentioned are high-fat and low-fibre diets, alcohol and caffeine consumption, environmental toxins and long-term hormone replacement therapy.

Although the science is lacking to support it, more and more women are becoming convinced that stress is a major factor in causing the disease. A 1994 survey of breast-cancer survivors for Canada's National Forum on Breast Cancer, for example, found that 38.4 percent of the respondents named stress as the cause, prompting Pat Kelly, founder of the Burlington Breast Cancer Support Services in Ontario, to tell a journalist, "Sadly, it appears that due to the lack of true knowledge about the causes of breast cancer, women often look inward for the reason."

While women are beginning to talk more freely about stress, even though there is little scientific evidence to support it as a cancer cause, one risk factor few are talking about is abortion. Several serious scientific studies suggest that abortion, whether induced or natural, does increase the risk of breast cancer. These findings, however, are generally ignored by the media and the cancer establishment, no doubt because of the evocative political realities associated with the abortion issue.

Although widespread public attention to breast cancer is relatively new, thanks largely to the political activism of breast-cancer survivors, women have worried about the disease for a long time. In the book *Cancer of the Breast* by Drs. William L. Donegan and John S. Spratt, Donegan writes that "breast tumors were described by the Egyptians 3000 years before Christ. Subsequently, Greek and Roman physicians wrote about it, and the record continued through the Middle Ages and into modern times."

Writing in *The Times* of London, on February 11, 1993, Dr. Thomas Stuttaford cites the 1751 *Chambers Encyclopaedia* describing breast cancer as "a most dread disease, particularly of the celibate and barren." That was the same week the NCI in the United States reported that lesbians were two to three times more likely to develop breast cancer than heterosexual women, adding that "there is no immediately obvious single explanation for the difference."

Knowledge of the disease has grown over the centuries, but not that much, at least not in ways that make much difference to women. Doctors and scientists still don't know what causes this cancer or, for the most part, what cures it.

Scientific studies *have* managed to do two things, however: they have increased the lifespan of some breast-cancer victims, and they have isolated the aforementioned risk factors.

But the cancer establishment alternates between downplaying the risks of cancer and overplaying the risks, depending upon the situation.

The Truth About Breast Cancer

A February 1993 article by *New York Times* writer Gina Kolata cites both the American Cancer Society and the National Cancer Institute arguing that "there is not now nor was there ever an epidemic of breast cancer in this country. The increase was more a statistical illusion, they say, resulting from an increased use of X-ray screening that caught cancers early."

This is not true. Numerous scientific studies show that while some of the increase is due to earlier detection through X-ray screening, much of it isn't. For example, a study by five doctors published in the April 1991 *American Journal of Public Health* found that by using detailed records from Atlanta between 1979 and 1986, the average annual age-adjusted incidence of invasive breast cancer rose 29 percent among white women and 41 percent among blacks. Incidence increased in all age groups. They acknowledged the trend toward earlier detection, but concluded specifically that "increased detection accounts for some but not all of the rising incidence of breast cancer in the United States." Also, regardless of when and how cancer is found, it's still breast cancer. Sometimes it helps to find it early, but not always.

The fact is, the statistics speak for themselves. Between 1980 and 1987, the reported age-adjusted incidence rates of breast cancer in the United States alone rose from 85 per 100,000 women to 112 per 100,000, a 31.7 percent increase. Between 1973 and 1988, the estimated number of new cases of breast cancer in the United States almost doubled, from 73,000 to 135,000, an annual increase of 1.8 percent. For women aged 50 and over, the average rate increased 32.1 percent between 1973/74 and 1987/88. While the disease is far more common in postmenopausal women, the incidence rate in younger, premenopausal women increased by 8 percent between 1973/74 and 1987/88 — and between 1980 and 1988 it slid upwards from 27.5 cases per 100,000 women to 32.8.

Granted, the death rate has remained relatively constant, as the cancer establishment claims — 26.8 deaths per 100,000 women in 1973/74 and 27.3 per cent in 1987/88 — but that's still a slight percentage increase, and a huge increase in the actual numbers of women dying of the disease. Despite the much-ballyhooed and extraordinarily expensive technological and pharmaceutical breakthroughs, that situation is not improving either. Regardless of what the cancer authorities like to claim, breast-cancer incidence and deaths are increasing around the world. And the cancer organizations often do little to advance under-standing of the disease. Instead, they collect money, sustain their own bureaucracies and walk lockstep with the pharmaceutical companies in drug-based research. They don't want to let the public know that they are really losing the war against cancer.

This is what they call success: the fact that there is no per-capita increase in breast cancer among young women in their 20s and 30s. More are getting the disease — and dying from it — but they explain that away by saying that's only because there are more of them in the population. Wonderful. No doubt this "statistical illusion" will come as consider-able comfort to the families of all those women who are dying, knowing that the problem isn't getting worse, just that more women are getting the disease and dying from it. What's more, by putting a positive spin on increased incidence and deaths, the cancer experts can avoid explain-ing why, after 20 years of all-out warfare, and billions of dollars spent in research and treatment, the numbers are not improving, no matter how these people wish to color them.

The *Times* article quotes Dr. Larry Kessler, chief of the Applied Research Branch at the NCI, saying, "It's inappropriate to say there's an epidemic."

It also cites Frances Visco, president of the National Breast Cancer Coalition, saying, "If you already have 1 in 8 women getting breast cancer in their lifetime and you already have 2.5 million who have the disease and 50 percent of those diagnosed are dead in 10 years, those are pretty horrible statistics. I certainly believe they rise to epidemic proportions."

Exactly.

Another way of measuring breast cancer, and a chilling indicator of the dramatic connection between aging and increased risk of breast cancer, is something called age-specific incidence rates. That simply means the total number of cases of breast cancer diagnosed in each specified age group divided by the total number of women in that group during a specified time period. In the United States, for the five-year period from 1984 to 1988, for example, the rate for women aged 20 to 24 was 0.9 per 100,000. That goes up to 66.2 in the 30–34 range, 187.4 for women aged 45 to 49, 220 in the 50–54 category, 390.7 aged 65 to 69, to a high of 461.4 for women aged 75 to 79. After that it drops slightly to 451.3 per 100,000 for women aged 80 to 84, and down to 411.9 for women aged 85 and over.

It is true that some of the increased incidence results from two statistical realities — lead-time bias and length bias. Lead-time bias applies to cancers picked up by screening that would normally have been found later, but are reported as new cases. This increases the reported incidence without changing the actual incidence of the disease. Length bias stems from the fact that breast-cancer tumors develop at different rates, which means that tumors with long preclinical phases are more likely to be picked up by screening than cancers that grow faster. Thus, changes in detection practice can result in different types of breast cancer being grouped into the same incidence rate.

For all that, however, a December 1991 report from the U.S. General Accounting Office concluded that both forms of bias "account for some of the dramatic increase" and "exactly how much of the increase is 'real' (indicative of higher levels of breast cancer) is not known. Further, explanations for any real increase in incidence are largely unsatisfactory in that the majority of women diagnosed with breast cancer continue to have no known risk factors for the disease. As a result of these uncertainties, we conclude that, as NCI states in its most recent statistical review, the increased incidence in breast cancer remains 'a major concern' that is unexplained."

But the increase in cancer rates demands an explanation.

A July 30, 1992, article in the *New England Journal of Medicine* concluded that "[l]arge variations in the rates of breast cancer among countries and over time within countries and large increases in the rates of breast cancer among populations migrating from nations with a low incidence to those with a high incidence indicate the existence of major nongenetic determinants of breast cancer and the potential for prevention."

The review article, written by Drs. Jay R. Harris, Marc E. Lippman, Umberto Veronesi and Walter Willett, was the first of a three-part series on the disease. It points out that many of the risk factors "are generally associated with only weak or moderate elevations of risk," but this changes in certain subgroups of these variables — for example, a family history of breast cancer at a young age or a family history of bilateral disease (cancer in both breasts).

"A family history of breast cancer, particularly when the diagnosis was made in the mother or a sister at a young age, can be an important risk factor for breast cancer. As compared with the risk among women having no first-degree relatives with breast cancer, overall the relative risk is on the order of 1.5 to 2 for women who have one first-degree relative with breast cancer and may be as high as 4 to 6 for those with two affected first-degree relatives. The risks are heightened if the cancer was bilateral."

Until late 1993, most research suggested that a woman's risk was up to three times higher if her mother or sister had had the disease before menopause. But a Harvard Medical School survey of 117,988 women argued that the role of heredity was much smaller, a risk 2.1 times higher if her mother had had breast cancer before age 50, and 2.3 times higher if her sister had had it. While 82 percent of breast-cancer patients have no family history of the disease, studies on the subject have often relied on women's recollection of family history. Researchers believe that some women may have overestimated the prevalence of the disease in their family.

The Harris article calls early menarche "a well-established but weak risk factor." The relative risk is about 1.2 for women in whom menarche occurred before age 12 compared to women in whom it occurred at the age of at least 14. "However, this variable may account for a substantial part of the international differences, because the contrasts are more substantial; in China the average age at menarche is 17 years, as compared with 12.8 years in the United States."

In March 1993, the *Journal of the American Medical Association* published results of a five-year study analyzing deaths among nearly 42,000 Iowa women aged 55 to 69 which showed mortality linked to waist-hip ratios. A six-inch increase in the waist of a woman with 40-inch hips was associated with a 60 percent increase in mortality risk — but the links between central obesity and breast cancer were shown to be strongest in women with a family history of the disease. Women with the highest waist-hip ratio were at three times the risk of dying from breast cancer as women with the lowest ratios.

In 1990, another U.S. study linked body shape — pear- or apple-shaped bodies — with the risk of breast cancer, concluding that women who were apple-shaped and carried their weight around their waist had more chance of breast cancer than pear-shaped women, whose weight is concentrated more on the hips and thighs. But, as often happens when studying the uncertain, researchers from the Memorial Sloan-Kettering Cancer Center reported in the March 1, 1993, *Annals of Internal Medicine* that their study of 313 white American women undergoing breast biopsy found no link to the waist-to-hip ratio, although obesity was seen as a risk factor, particularly for postmenopausal women. (In the article by Dr. Jay R. Harris et al., however, obesity in premenopausal women was associated with *reduced* incidence.)

Dr. Elin Sigurdson of the Fox Chase Cancer Center was quoted on the new study saying it "proves pretty conclusively that [body shape] isn't a real risk," adding that judging a woman's risk by body shape is "highly simplistic and far too crude to put any reliance on it." But the University of Florida's Dr. David Schapira, an author of the earlier report, argued the number of patients in the new report was too small to draw any conclusions. "One has to be extremely careful about how to interpret," he said. "I hardly think it refutes" the connection.

Yet another study, released in late March 1993 by the NCI in Washington, concluded that taller women have a 50 to 80 percent higher risk of getting breast cancer than women who are closer to five feet tall. The five-year study involved more than 1,500 women with breast cancer and almost 2,000 who did not have the disease. Some researchers believe the differences are connected to socioeconomic status, breast size or how breast tissue cells divide. The study also showed that extra weight in women under 50 decreases their risk of getting breast cancer, while added pounds on older women *increases* the risk.

The largest unresolved risk factor in connection with breast cancer, and a major focus of ongoing studies since the early 1970s, is the impact of oral contraceptives. During the more than 30 years since the Pill was introduced, some 3 billion women have used it, and right now, over 60 million women worldwide are on the Pill. Both estrogen and progesterone are contained in every pill taken during a cycle of use. Until the last few years, scientific studies found no connection between the Pill and breast cancer, but more recent studies suggest a possible link in some groups of users.

Seattle doctor David B. Thomas of the Fred Hutchinson Cancer Center, writing in the March 3, 1993, edition of the *Journal of the*

National Cancer Institute, said it is "reasonable to suspect that use of oral contraceptives at different ages could have different effects on breast cancer development, although we cannot predict a priori which circumstances of use would most likely enhance or reduce risk." He says that because of the widespread use of this drug, "even a small increment in risk attributable" to it "might therefore result in large numbers of additional breast cancers. It is, thus, of major public health importance either to rule out with reasonable certainty the existence of an unfavorable effect of oral contraceptives on risk of breast cancer or, if such an effect exists, to accurately quantitate it and determine the circumstances under which it occurs."

After reviewing much of the previous data on the subject, Thomas concludes: it is "likely that prolonged use of oral contraceptives has led to a true increase in risk of breast cancer in young women," particularly those who began taking contraceptives in their teenage years. Overall, Thomas argues for more study, saying there is reason for concern but "at the present time, it would not be sound public health policy to warn women against using these highly effective means of contraception on the basis of their possible adverse effect on breast cancer risk."

On May 17, 1994, Nigel Hawkes wrote in *The Times* about a BBC current affairs program, *Dispatches,* which highlighted work published in the April 1994 *Journal of the National Cancer Institute.* He suggested that young women have "a significantly increased risk of breast cancer" if they began taking the Pill as teenagers. And an American study by Dr. Emily White shows that women under 35 who used the Pill for more than ten years had a 70 percent increased risk, compared with women who had never taken the Pill or had done so for only a year.

But less than 2 percent of all new cases come from that age group, so the 70 percent increase is still a small number. "It means that instead of one in 500 women developing the disease before the age of 35, it is one in 300," writes Hawkes. True enough. But given the millions of women who fit this increased-risk category, that change in status from the Pill, while statistically small, still becomes something more significant than a mathematical dispute to hundreds of women around the world whose breast cancer may be tied to contraceptive use.

Dr. Valerie Beral of the Imperial Cancer Research Fund acknowledges the increased risk for younger women but believes this risk disappears as the women get older. She bases her argument on the fact that eight out of ten women now in their late 40s and six out of ten in their early 50s had taken the Pill when they were younger than 35 with no evidence of increased risk. "If the Pill was going to have a serious, long-term risk of breast cancer, we should have started to see the effect by now," she told a conference organized by *The Lancet* in April 1994 in Bruges, Belgium. The use of oral contraceptives increases the risk 50 percent while being used, but the risk drops rapidly after the drug is stopped.

But Hawkes also cites epidemiologist Kim McPherson of the London School of Hygiene and Tropical Medicine, who has used computer simulations to calculate how the increased risk would affect the overall incidence if it were assumed it is not merely a transient effect. And although McPherson points out it is only a projection based on assumptions that may not prove to be true, the result of that would be a catastrophic increase in the number of cases, by 30 to 40 percent by the end of the century.

"In some birth control programs in America," writes Hawkes, "girls as young as 12 or even, astonishingly, ten, are being given the Pill. Girls who menstruate early are known to be at greater risk, in any case, but those who give the Pill to such young girls justify it by comparing its risks with those of pregnancy."

Which brings us to the impact of abortion on breast cancer, the risk factor that dares not speak its name.

You won't find it listed in the standard risk material dispatched by the breast-cancer societies or appearing in most newspaper, magazine or television lists of breast-cancer risks. But despite that, a host of scientific studies show that abortion, either spontaneous (miscarriages) or induced, increases the risk of the disease. The first significant study to draw the causal relationship between a first-trimester abortion and breast cancer came from University of Southern California's School of Medicine, Department of Family and Preventive Practice, by M.C. Pike et al. and published in the 1981 *British Journal of Cancer*. It was a case-control study of 163 breast-cancer patients who were younger than 33 at diagnosis, which found that abortion "was associated with a 2.4-fold increase in breast cancer risk," dropping to a relative risk of 1.8 among women who subsequently bore at least one child. Pike et al. also concluded that prolonged oral contraceptive use increases the risk.

This study prompted a flurry of medical criticism and a rash of studies disputing the findings. The politics of the debate were odd. One 1983 NCI study claimed in its summary that abortion "was not associated with an elevated risk," yet the numbers contained in its own charts clearly showed the opposite.

A 1985 study by six Japanese physicians looking at occurrence of breast cancer in relation to diet and reproductive history also concluded that "a past history of both natural abortion and of benign breast disease were significantly associated with the disease." Part of a series of studies aimed at finding factors to explain dramatic differences in breast-cancer rates between Japanese women in Japan, Japanese women in Hawaii and Caucasian women in Hawaii, it involved only 212 women from each group, but did show a significant risk elevation (1.91) for spontaneous abortion and also a higher risk (1.51) for induced abortions.

This was followed by a 1986 cohort study by Connecticut Cancer Epidemiology Unit physician O.C. Hadjimichael and two other doctors of 3,315 women who delivered livebirth children between 1946 and 1965 in a group of private gynecology practices in Connecticut. They were checked through to 1980 for incidence of cancer, and women who got breast cancer were compared to women in the cohort who didn't. Although it precludes adjustment for certain known risk factors, such as family history of the disease, the study concluded that "a spontaneous abortion before this livebirth was associated with a 3.5-fold increase in the risk of breast cancer. The elevation in risk was independent of some of the major risk factors of breast cancer and became more pronounced as the number of years since the abortion increased." The study did not analyze nulliparous women and, since induced abortions were illegal in Connecticut at the time, all abortions were presumed to be spontaneous.

On the other hand, a large, 1987 case-control study published in the *International Journal of Epidemiology* concerning 2,389 women in northern Italy found "little relation of breast cancer risk with abortions or miscarriages" — roughly the same conclusions drawn by a Danish study published in the 1988 *British Journal of Cancer*.

In 1988 a large case-control study of more than 8,000 women on the impact of both induced and spontaneous abortions was published in the *American Journal of Epidemiology* by Boston University School of Medicine epidemiologist Lynn Rosenberg and five colleagues.

Rosenberg et al. downplayed the risks of abortion, even though some of their own tables showed a statistically significant risk elevation (relative risk of 2.1) in women who had had induced vs. spontaneous abortions. Also worth noting was that of the more than 8,000 women in the study (patients and controls) only nine had their first induced abortion after age 30 and then went on to have more children. All nine of them got breast cancer. Even so, the study authors concluded that "the risk of breast cancer is not materially affected by abortion." Anti-abortion critics argued that the study was guilty of political-economic bias. It was sponsored not only by the NCI and FDA, both of which tend to underplay the abortion issue, but also by drug companies, including birth control pill giant Organon and abortion pill manufacturer Hoechst AG, parent company of Roussel-UCLAF.

In the early 1990s, a series of studies was undertaken on the subject, and although many found a relationship between abortion and breast cancer — though some didn't — the cancer establishment and the media studiously avoided the findings. To cite one important example, the major 1992 update of breast-cancer risk factors by Jay R. Harris and colleagues mentioned earlier in this chapter does not even mention abortion as a risk factor for breast cancer. (It was published in the *New England Journal of Medicine*, which itself has a pro-choice editorial bias.) Also, during subcommittee hearings held by members of the Health and Welfare Committee on the status of women in Canada in 1992, Ottawa doctor Libuse Gilka presented a paper called "The Women's Right to Know," regarding the risk of abortion and breast cancer — but the committee's final report does not mention it as a factor.

In November 1993, when Alliance for Life President Bernadette Mysko of Saskatoon, Saskatchewan, sent a lengthy fax to provincial medical officials concerning the connection between breast cancer and abortion, she received an angry call from a senior physician accusing her of trying to "scare" women. "He said he'd never heard of such a thing and that there is no basis in fact for it," said Mysko. "He said if I could provide him with legitimate references, he'd go over to the university library and check them out. So I sent him the references, and guess what, we haven't heard a thing from him. . . . I guess we have to have a few more women die before people will begin to pay attention to this. Why can't women simply be told the truth? It doesn't matter where you stand on abortion. Why can't you be told the truth and then make your own decision accordingly?"

Typical, too, of the media bias on the issue was the March 1994 visit to Ottawa by Cincinnati doctor John C. Wilke, long-time president of the International Right to Life Federation. Wilke, whose daily radio program is carried on almost 300 stations, spoke to Action Life (Ottawa) Inc. on the link between abortion and breast cancer.

He argues that a first pregnancy permanently changes the structure of the breast, prompting the flow of estrogen and other hormones in a woman's system and resulting in rapid growth in size and dramatic change to the internal structure. "Cells, previously dormant, rapidly grow into a system of branching ducts and gland cells capable of producing milk. Once this growth, change and maturing is complete, there is no further significant change the rest of her life. Once mature, the chance of the breast developing cancer is much less. When these cells are changing and transitional, they are less stable and have much greater potential of becoming cancerous. If she completes her first pregnancy, this unstable period passes and her gland cells mature and stabilize.

"But if she interrupts her pregnancy, in its early phase — 90 percent of abortions are done in the first trimester — she in effect stops the development of the cells at this unstable transitional phase. It seems apparent that cancerous changes can and do occur more frequently among these transitional cells of a woman who has terminated her pregnancy. If she aborts more than once before completing a pregnancy, her chance for cancer increases even more. A subsequent full term pregnancy helps, but sadly never removes the sharply increased threat of cancer."

Wilke says women who carry their first baby to term cut their odds for breast cancer almost in half. Since over 800,000 women abort their first pregnancy each year, he argues that, of this group, 10 percent, or 80,000 women, would have developed breast cancer. Because of the abortion, however, "the number of cancer cases will increase to 120,000. Of these extra 40,000 cases, 25 percent, or 10,000 additional women, will die of breast cancer every year."

Whether one agrees with Wilke or not, he produces a host of respectable scientific studies to support his case. But the media simply isn't interested. The day after his formal speech, Wilke met with a group of federal politicians and political aides, setting aside time for interviews with members of the Parliamentary Press Gallery, the so-called elite of the national media corps. Only two reporters showed up — in stark contrast to the numbers attending a news conference held two days earlier by a Canadian company seeking more federal funds to help develop an AIDS drug. That session drew a large crowd of journalists and resulted in prominent news stories in most major Canadian newspapers and across television networks. Wilke's comments, on the other hand, were virtually ignored.

Another measure of the relative importance governments place on abortion access and breast cancer is that despite widespread access to publicly funded abortions in 17 Toronto hospitals, the Ontario government alone spends $7 million a year subsidizing just four privately operated abortion clinics in that city's downtown core — more than the annual total spent on breast-cancer research by the federal government and all the provincial governments combined.

Doctors have long believed that breast-feeding at younger ages and for longer periods lowers the risk, but only until a woman enters menopause. A large study directed by Dr. Polly A. Newcomb of the University of Wisconsin and published in the *New England Journal of Medicine* in January 1994 found that women who began nursing in their teens and continue for at least six months cut the cancer risk almost in half. Even women who begin breast-feeding in their 20s could enjoy a 22 percent risk reduction. The study was based on a review of 5,878 breast-cancer patients in Wisconsin, Massachusetts, Maine and New Hampshire, comparing their nursing habits with 8,216 women who did not have breast cancer. Even so, the researchers are not certain why breast-feeding would affect cancer, speculating it may change hormone secretions, interrupt ovulation or cause a physical change in the breast. In any event, Dr. Newcomb told the *New York Times* there are a number of reasons to breast-feed. "First and foremost is to provide the child with complete nutrition and psychological benefits. But a woman might also consider the possibility that this could reduce her risk of breast cancer."

Two controversial risk factors blamed for breast cancer and a host of other serious health problems are alcohol and cigarettes. In June 1994, an American Cancer Society survey of 604,412 women who were initially cancer-free found that smokers were 25 percent more likely than nonsmokers or ex-smokers to die of breast cancer. The study, directed by epidemiologist Eugenia Calle, does not suggest that smoking causes breast cancer, only that women who don't smoke have a better chance of avoiding the disease. "For example," she told Associated Press, "smokers may have impaired immune systems, they may not obtain routine (mammograms), or smoking may cause a direct deleterious effect on survival." The risk, up to 75 percent greater for women who smoked two packs a day or more, grew with the number of cigarettes smoked. Previous studies had argued smoking could actually reduce breast cancer by decreasing a woman's estrogen.

In May 1993, a study conducted by Marsha E. Reichman for the National Institutes of Health found that two alcoholic drinks a day could raise hormone levels enough in women to increase breast-cancer risk by 40 to 100 percent over women who do not drink at all. Reichman said it was the first study "to suggest that the mechanism by which alcohol affects breast cancer risk may be the increase in hormones caused by alcohol." The 34 women in the study were tested for effects of alcohol through six menstrual cycles. Blood tests showed increases in estrogen of up to 31.9 percent during the middle phase of the menstrual cycle for women who were drinking. Urine tests also found a similar hike in estrogen excreted during the final phase of the cycle.

Estrogen, of course, has long been believed to be a major player in breast cancer, which is one reason why the growing use of hormone replacement therapy as a treatment for menopause has become so controversial. However, a June 1994 document called the *Canadian Menopause Consensus Conference by the Society of Obstetricians and Gynaecologists of Canada* stated that "the benefits of hormone replacement therapy greatly outweigh the risks." About 4 million Canadian women, average age 51, were either going through menopause or on the verge of it. The therapy, using estrogen and progesterone, helps control menopausal symptoms, but has also been shown to reduce the risk of heart disease, the main cause of postmenopausal deaths in women, by 50 percent. It's also been shown to reduce bone loss. It treats such menopausal symptoms as hot flashes, vaginal dryness, insomnia, frequent urination, migraines, fluctuations in sexual desire, crying jags and panic attacks.

So what's the controversy? Why have only about 11 percent of Canadian women aged 50 and older filled prescriptions for estrogen replacement therapy?

Well, studies have suggested that women on estrogen have three times the risk of developing endometrial cancer, and one study showed that seven out of ten women gave fear of developing breast cancer as their reason for avoiding the therapy. The study officials argued that progesterone is added to the therapy to protect a woman from developing endometrial cancer, but so far, at least, it has not been shown to have any major impact on breast cancer.

Dr. Lynn Rosenberg of the epidemiology unit at Boston University School of Medicine told *The Toronto Star* in June 1994 that "[t]he benefits of hormone replacement have been overstated and the risks have been understated." When the Canadian Cancer Society says replacement therapy "doesn't appear to significantly increase the risk of breast cancer," it is hardly the same as saying there is no risk and it is not reassuring to women who worry more about this disease than any other.

Although the risks of hormone replacement therapy are not clear, hormones are being investigated as a means of decreasing breast cancer. In March 1994, Dr. Darcy Spicer, an assistant professor of medicine at the University of Southern California and principal author of a study published in the NCI journal, reported that efforts to find a hormonal contraceptive that also lowers a woman's risk of breast cancer look promising. The ongoing study involves giving women a monthly injection of a hormone called gonadotropin hormone-releasing agonist (GnRHA), which suppresses ovarian function. Doctors then give the women small doses of estrogen and progesterone. Mammograms have shown a reduction in breast-tissue density after one year on the hormones. Spicer says the treatment may also lower the lifetime breast-cancer risk by almost one-third if used for five years and by more than 50 percent if used for ten years. The study continues.

Some 50 million women in the United States and millions more elsewhere are possibly putting themselves at risk by using petrochemical hair dyes. Several studies suggest strong links between these dyes and various forms of cancer, including non-Hodgkin's lymphoma deaths in women, multiple myeloma, leukemia, ovarian cancer and, to a lesser extent, breast cancer. But a joint study by the American Cancer Society and the Food and Drug Administration published in February 1994 found "almost no connection between hair dyes and fatal cancers." The study, published in the *Journal of the National Cancer Institute* did, however, recommend "removal of carcinogens from hair dyes and appropriate labelling of hair coloring products."

However, well-known cancer industry critic Dr. Samuel Epstein, chairman of the Cancer Prevention Coalition and a professor of medicine at the University of Illinois, attacked the study in a February 16 letter in the *New York Times* as being "seriously flawed in design and interpretation." On the question of breast cancer, Epstein wrote the study's "negative findings . . . are further invalidated by . . . [its] failure to analyze for other critical risk factors besides hair dyes, particularly duration of oral contraceptive use and age at onset; duration and dosage of estrogen replacement therapy; and history of mammography. The last is particularly important, as repeated mammography in healthy premenopausal women has been consistently associated with excess breast cancer mortality in some eight randomized controlled trials over the last decade."

Epstein calls "recklessly misleading" an editorial accompanying the study that dismissed any cancer risk from hair dyes and recommended against further studies on the subject. "There is substantial evidence on the carcinogenic hazards of petrochemical hair dyes. Their use represents a major class of avoidable cancer risks. . . . Legislative and regulatory action is now decades overdue. While waiting, women should switch to noncarcinogenic organic hair dyes."

Finally, it wouldn't be America if growing concerns about breast-cancer risk didn't ignite the entrepreneurial spirit and spawn a whole new industry to cash in on that anxiety.

This latest growth industry is called breast-cancer risk analysis. For $350 or so — rarely covered by insurance — you, too, can have your specific risk of breast cancer analyzed by experts. An October 1992 feature in *Vogue* by writer Joan Walsh, whose mother died of breast cancer at age 45, lionizes Patricia Kelly, a nationally known geneticist and pioneer in cancer-risk analysis. Since the late 1970s, Kelly has counselled more than a thousand families and individuals in her role as director of medical genetics and cancer-risk counselling at the Los Angeles-based

Salick Health Care, Inc. Walsh writes that the three-session process begins with a detailed family history-taking, "moving on to general background about cancer and heredity, and concluding with . . . [Kelly's] assessment of an individual's risk over time," which, in Walsh's case, was estimated to be about 15 percent to age 70 — slightly more than double the average woman's risk.

Kelly argues that risk counselling sometimes has implications for a woman's medical care that don't always please the physician. She told of seeing two women in one week with benign breast disease and a family history of breast cancer, whose physicians had recommended preventative mastectomy, even though, as she advised the women, only one variety of the condition, called atypia, actually increases a woman's risk in these circumstances. Atypia adds about a 10 percent risk of developing breast cancer over 15 years. UCLA's Dr. Susan Love, while praising Kelly's work, says that it is also "something breast surgeons can do, and ideally should do — the risk information is out there. But many don't, and so there's a need for her service."

A feature story in the January-February issue of *Health* written by Lisa Davis also explores the work of Kelly and other risk-analysis counsellors. It cites Barbara Blumberg, director of education at the Baylor-Susan G. Komen Breast Centers in Dallas, saying, "Most women grossly overestimate their risk. It's not unusual for me to hear someone say, 'I think my risk is 70 to 80 percent.' And that's because they know the average woman's risk is one in nine, and their mother had breast cancer, and so they triple it. Or quadruple it."

The story mentions 35-year-old Janet Argo of Dallas, one of Blumberg's patients, whose mother died of breast cancer in August 1992 after nine years of "a horrible, slow, painful suffering process. When I lost her I started thinking, 'Oh my gosh, this is going to happen to me.' I just thought I'm doomed. But then I had a series of one on one consultations with a risk counsellor, and I started to understand that I was only at slightly higher risk.

"Women ignore breast cancer because they are scared of the unknown. In reality, if you do find something, if you catch it early, there's a 95 percent chance that you'll be fine. Those are good odds. Ten years have passed since my mother was diagnosed, and they're doing a lot more aggressive treatment now. Her lump was big enough that she found it in the shower by accident. She wasn't doing monthly exams.

"Two months before she died my mother looked up at me and asked, 'Have you had a mammogram?' And I said, 'Yeah, I have.' She said, 'You have to keep up on them.' And I promised her I would."

Ironically, at Argo's age, some major studies show that regular mammograms can do more harm than good. In fact, according to the Canadian National Breast Screening Study, which followed nearly 909,000 women for seven years, the chance for survival was not increased when a tumor was found in a premenopausal woman through mammography, rather than through breast palpitations or breast self-examination.

While the Canadian study was controversial, it has nonetheless changed the way most physicians and the NCI approach mammography: now regular mammograms are not recommended until age 50, whereas in the past they were recommended beginning at age 40. Despite that, Lisa Davis writes in her article that "most radiologists set aside the Canadian data and insist that women in their forties ought to be getting tested. In fact, since tumors sometimes grow faster in younger women, many think that 40-to-50-year-olds should get mammograms every year instead of biannually."

What's more, in a section of the article dealing with "women at higher risk," Davis again recommends yearly mammograms beginning at 40 and describes uncritically the tamoxifen trial on healthy women. She does not mention the demonstrable health risks of tamoxifen itself — risks many authorities believe outweigh the possible benefits of using the drug as a so-called preventative.

No wonder women are so confused about risk.

Measured against the raw statistics, however, is the reality that most women know somebody — either a family member, a friend or a colleague — who died of breast cancer, or at least was diagnosed with it.

In scientific terms, of course, that is simply anecdotal evidence. But in human terms, it's more powerful than any study or statistic (or statement of reassurance).

5 Implants

FOR LINDA WILSON, BREAST CANCER was bad enough.

But her real battles began when she had reconstructive breast surgery in March 1985.

Wilson, a British Columbia bookkeeper and breast-cancer survivor and activist — one of the founders of the group I Know/Je Sais — later fought a losing legal battle against her doctors.

She testified in Ottawa in November 1991, before a federal subcommittee on the status of women studying breast cancer.

Here's part of her story:

From my own experiences with Meme implants, I can say there was and still is nothing beneficial. These implants, in less than three weeks, eroded through my skin, causing infection, tissue death and leaving big holes. The infection continued to run rampant even after I had them removed . . .

I lived almost a month in and out of one type of intravenous or antibiotic, even after they had been removed. . . . I had the most incredible [body] rash. . . . This again required further medication. Also, for some reason still unknown to me, one of my nipples began to bleed almost constantly, causing a lot of pain and resulting in the loss of part of it. It basically got what appeared to be eaten away.

I endured nine operations and five lengthy hospitalizations for chronic infections, resulting in approximately 180 days spent in one hospital or the other, and on top of that often required home-care nursing visits for weeks at a time . . .

All of this happened to me because of Meme implants. When the problem started and they had to be removed, the polyurethane covering, because of its break-down abilities, was completely left behind, hence it continued its destructive course.

I had never been informed that part of this implant's materials have the ability to disintegrate . . . and could lead in the long term to the possibility of cancer. I was never told that the company manufacturing this product was doing so in violation of many good manufacturing standards, the main one being sterility, and that because of this I would go on to suffer the invasion of my body by a fungus that was present on these implants before they left the factory.

I was also never told that the silicone gel used in implants had the ability to bleed through the shell containing it and also finds its way into my system, and possibly contribute to other serious and debilitating diseases involving one's immune system.

My initial surgery was in March 1985 and the doctor did not even tell me that he was going to use Meme implants. I never questioned him because, first, I trusted him and believed that no doctor would use anything before it had been proven safe by the appropriate authorities. Also, like most people, I believed that we had departments within the structure of Health and Welfare controlling and protecting us from possible health hazards brought about by medical products and devices, and that strict requirements from both manufacturers and distributors had to be met before devices, any devices, were allowed for sale.

. . . I am a woman who, under advisement and with trust, believed in the medical profession. My trust was abused.

She wasn't alone.

The sordid saga of silicone breast surgery, which became a mammoth industry by capitalizing on commercial greed, shoddy research, bureaucratic bungling and women's insecurities, actually began for the oldest of all reasons — sex.

American GIs prowling the streets of postwar Japan lusting for some civilian action complained that the breasts of Japanese prostitutes were too small.

Anxious to please their free-spending conquerors, and completely unaware of any physical dangers, thousands of Japanese women subjected themselves to injections of liquid silicone. The stuff was actually industrial-strength transformer coolant stolen from military supplies loaded on the local docks.

It didn't work. The silicone soon oozed out of the women's breasts and spread throughout their bodies.

But the notion of enhancing women's breasts didn't go away, and manufacturing companies began experimenting with different methods. Soon, various chemicals were added to the solution so the resulting scar tissue would keep the silicone from spreading, and within a decade, an estimated 50,000 American women, and untold thousands in Canada, Europe and elsewhere, had received silicone injections directly into their breasts.

While most women were buying the injections for cosmetic reasons — including some 10,000 showgirls and star-wannabees in Nevada alone — it wasn't long before the direct injections were replaced by silicone-filled breast implants. Breast-cancer victims were among the millions of women who underwent surgery to receive the implants. Many of these women, who had already suffered through a mastectomy, were hit again by the traumatic physical fall-out of some implants.

The idea of breast implants had been around for a long time before silicone was used. At the turn of the century, women were injected with paraffin, vegetable oil, lanolin or beeswax. Glass balls were even inserted into women's breasts in the 1930s, and in the 1950s plastics began to be used.

The vast majority of breast implants, of course, have nothing to do with breast cancer or other breast diseases. Rather, they are tied in with fashion and self-esteem. In *The Beauty Myth*, feminist writer Naomi Wolf writes, "Breast surgery in its mangling of erotic feeling, is a form of sexual mutilation."

Or, as British journalist Kate Muir pointed out in "The Implant Scandal," an article that appeared in *The Times Magazine* on May 7, 1994, "It is ironic that an operation designed, in cosmetic surgery cases, to increase sexiness does, in fact, reduce a woman's ability to feel sensation in her breasts. In most women, breasts grow and shrink again every month, and vary in sensitivity to touch. Growth and tinglings in the breasts signal the onset of pregnancy or a period. Yet the pressure and desire to be buxom is so strong that women will willingly insert foreign matter into their breasts which can render them stiff and insensitive."

In the early 1960s, Dow Corning Corporation, the world's largest silicone supplier, set up a center to aid medical research specifically to explore the medical uses of silicone. They obtained permission from the U.S. Food and Drug Administration in 1963 to pursue liquid silicone studies in animals and humans, and by 1965, Dow had developed the silicone-gel implant.

A 1967 article in the *Journal of Plastic and Reconstructive Surgery* by the late Dr. Franklin Ashley and other doctors, who at the time were working with the Dow center, says that the injection of liquid silicone into the breasts of Japanese apes and rhesus monkeys caused "marked fibrous response" and "destruction of local anatomy."

It also says that "a selected group of women" were repeatedly injected with 5 to 10 millilitres of liquid silicone in their breasts. The results of the experiment were never published, nor were they reported to the FDA. Studies on another 149 women reported to the FDA were also never published, and in 1967, faced with widespread reports of serious complaints about lumps, rock-hard breasts and silicone cysts, the FDA decided to put an end to these studies by revoking its permission to Dow.

Unfortunately, that did not end the affair. If anything, it provided even more impetus for Dow and other manufacturers to develop a more acceptable way of delivering the silicone to the breast.

In 1969, just two years after revoking Dow's permission to test liquid silicone, the FDA told Dow it could test the stuff after all, but could not inject it into women's breasts. Thanks largely to the activism of Dr. Edward Kopf, an assistant professor of plastic surgery at the University of Nevada School of Medicine, the State of Nevada outlawed injectable silicone in 1975. Both Colorado and California quickly followed suit, and it wasn't long before the practice became outlawed in all Western industrialized countries — although it's still practiced today in many Asian countries.

The next year, the U.S. Congress authorized the FDA to regulate medical devices, but because breast implants had already been on the market for about five years they were temporarily exempted from regulatory review. In Canada, medical devices were put under the Food and Drugs Act of 1954 under the category of "therapeutics." That law, a godsend to manufacturers, decreed that it was up to the government to prove a therapeutic was harmful to health before the product could be banned. But the government had no enforcement inspectors and didn't even require such devices to be registered with the federal government, which left manufacturers to do pretty well what they wanted. In fact, Canada didn't set up its Bureau of Medical Devices until 1974, and that was only in response to political pressure flowing from U.S. Congressional hearings into the disastrous Dalkon Shield — a celebrated "breakthrough" in birth control that ended up causing miscarriages, permanent sterility, pelvic infection and even several deaths.

While few North Americans took note, a 1986 report in the *British Journal of Plastic Surgery* did warn that the Meme implant was unsuitable for breast reconstruction because the plastic covering, developed for industrial purposes, tended to disintegrate in the body.

By 1988, six years after the U.S. FDA had announced that implants were potentially risky (and after Canada had approved a regulation requiring manufacturers to submit safety and efficacy data on any new devices to be implanted in the body for 30 days or more), serious health concerns over the Meme implant were growing. The FDA sharply criticized the manufacturer — Surgitek Inc. of Racine, Wisconsin, a subsidiary of Bristol-Myers Squibb Co. of New York City — for several violations in its plant in Paso Robles, California. Surgitek had acquired the Meme from Cooper Surgical in December 1988. Cooper, in turn, had bought it from Natural-Y Surgical Specialties of Los Angeles in 1987.

But Cooper sold it after learning that laboratory studies prepared for a lawsuit in Florida showed the polyurethane cover could release cancer-causing 2-4 toluene diamine, a compound the U.S. Environmental Protection Agency classifies as hazardous waste. The compound is considered so dangerous that the United States banned its use in hair dye in 1971. Cooper contacted the polyurethane manufacturer, Scotfoam Corporation of Eddystone, Pennsylvania, and was told the cover could indeed release the deadly chemical.

In his 1994 book *Safety Last*, science journalist Nicholas Regush of the Montreal *Gazette*, who played a major role in alerting both the American and Canadian public about the dangers of the Meme, quotes Scotfoam official Ed Griffiths as saying that he was surprised to learn polyurethane — which was used in oil filters, furniture and carburetors — was being used in a breast implant. Griffiths said the manufacturers "had been using our foam for many years and [when Regush informed him] it was the first time that I or anyone else at the company had heard about it."

In any event, FDA inspectors visited the Surgitek plant in Paso Robles for 16 days in July 1988, discovering, among other things, inadequate safeguards ensuring sterility, no record keeping of the raw materials used in the implants and poorly trained employees. Even so, the FDA did not order Surgitek to clean up its plant until eight months later.

While most women used implants for cosmetic reasons — as late as 1981 the American Society of Plastic and Reconstructive Surgeons Inc. diagnosed small breasts as a "disease" in a memo to the FDA — mastectomy survivors created special challenges. During the 1950s, Alberta-born Dr. William J. Pangman moved to Beverly Hills where he began to experiment on ways to rebuild the breast after cancer and other diseases and eventually created an implant named the Natural-Y, the grandfather of the Meme. Pangman, described by his colleagues as an extremely aggressive and ethical plastic surgeon, used a host of products, including fabric, plastics, foams and even glass, but only when patients insisted and only after he'd clearly warned them of possible dangers. Over a 20-year period, Pangman left a host of patents, one of which was leaked by a colleague in the late 1960s to a group of salesmen who, putting their own interpretation on it, promoted it as a prosthesis to repair breasts of patients who'd suffered catastrophic cancer.

This prosthesis was sold from 1969 until December 1990, but according to Canadian Dr. Pierre Blais, a recognized expert on implants and the man the Canadian government later fired for speaking out about the Meme, this prosthesis "left a trail of morbidity and mortality amongst patients who would have survived normally. But as far as many of the cancer patients were concerned, they didn't make it. Therefore, there were no data. . . . Now, amongst the patients who received this implant were mainly what is called poor prognosis cancer patients, who lasted an average of two, three, five years. Most of them had additional surgery and the data generated from this experiment were in effect lost. They were lost because they could not possibly have had any value. There was no control.

"The implant over the years mutated into other kinds of implants built according to the same structure, and as the years went by the promoters of the implant took shortcuts. They made the implant cheaper, more easily fabricated, more universal in appeal, easier to implant, more profitable to use.

"Eventually, in 1982, they renamed one version of it the Meme. The Meme originally was a joke. It was laughed at by the medical community. It was reviled in medical textbooks. It had an atrocious reputation and nobody trusted it, for many reasons. Through promotion and through use, perhaps by repetition, it developed a small following, which eventually grew to the point at which the original company, with the salesmen, sold itself to a much larger firm, which in turn audited the operation and became so appalled that they decided to jettison the company a year later. In turn they sold this company to a company that was associated with Bristol-Myers, and we now have the rest of the story . . ."

We certainly do. And it's not pretty.

Blais calls that story "an exercise in medical fraud . . . recognized as such from its inception . . . [with] a long trail of victims, women who have used it as well as surgeons who were convinced to implant it."

The silicone-gel-filled Meme was particularly popular because of its soft, foam covering. Unfortunately, it was that covering that so often broke down inside the woman's body.

In February 1985, Bryant Medical Products Inc. of Mississauga, Ontario, a distributor of medical devices, including competing breast implants, filed a formal complaint noting that the Department of Health and Welfare had never reviewed the Meme or the Replicon, another polyurethane-covered implant. In response, a federal inspector visited the Canadian distributor, Silimed Inc. (later Réal Laperriere Inc.) and was told the implants had been sold for about ten years in Canada. Two weeks later, federal health inspector Sylvain Boucher wrote the company asking them to register its product and asking for sales information to determine if a safety review was legally required. Four months after that, Boucher wrote to Réal Laperriere saying that Natural-Y implants had been sold by Weck, a division of Squibb Canada, since March 1976, so the implants did not require a safety review. He asked Laperriere to register the product and that would close the matter. Laperriere didn't bother to register it for another 44 months, and health department concerns that the Meme was not the same implant as the Natural-Y, and therefore shouldn't be exempt from formal safety review, were swept aside by senior officials.

In January 1989, Chris Batish, an organic chemist who headed a research team at the University of Florida, identified the highly toxic chemical, 2-4 toluene diamine, inside the Meme's coating. The chemical causes liver cancer in rats and mice and was suspected of also causing cancer in humans. Batish said he couldn't understand why Surgitek Inc. would use foam containing this chemical.

In March 1989, journalist Regush reported in the Montreal *Gazette* that because of serious health concerns, at least five Canadian federal scientists from the Department of Health and Welfare had urged that the Meme be withdrawn from the Canadian market, but senior officials had rejected the recommendation. Instead, the department had decided to wait for the implant's Canadian distributor, Réal Laperriere Inc. of Montreal, to voluntarily supply data proving the product's safety and efficacy. Laperriere, incidentally, had sold about 7,500 pairs of the Meme since 1984, but had taken four years before bothering to comply with federal law and register it with the Health Protection Branch of the Department of Health and Welfare.

Responding to the story, Dr. David Johnson, chief of the Research and Standards Division of the branch's Bureau of Radiation and Medical Devices, denied that federal scientists had recommended taking the Meme off the market, but Regush had minutes of the meeting written by Johnson that clearly stated that's exactly what the scientists had recommended. Three years earlier, federal scientist Pierre Blais, who would become the major combatant in the Meme story, had written an article raising questions about the implant's tendency to break apart and the lack of serious research on the long-term effects on the body of this action.

In typical fashion, the federal bureaucracies in both Canada and the United States circled the wagons against the growing criticism being levelled at the Meme. So, too, did the medical establishment — particularly plastic surgeons who were using the Meme and profiting handsomely from the $2,500 implantation operation. Despite the serious weight of evidence against the Meme, it took two more years to finally get it off the market, although even then, thousands of women were left with it inside their bodies. Many of these women, victimized once by breast cancer, were hurt again by shoddy technology and the shameful response by various authorities.

In March 1989, Surgitek officials dismissed the criticisms out of hand. Company spokesman Jim Kaufmann said the 20-year U.S. experience with the Meme proved they were safe. "We know the polyurethane foam is chemically safe," he said, dispensing with the laboratory tests that showed it wasn't by saying, "They heated the product in lye and heated it to 350 degrees Fahrenheit, clearly conditions that do not exist in the human body." In Montreal, Réal Laperriere echoed these assurances, saying he was glad Ottawa had asked for scientific information about the Meme. "When you sell something good, you are not afraid," he said.

Once again, Regush published a *Gazette* story showing that Canadian officials had ordered the destruction of a February 20, 1989, memo from senior health scientist Dr. Pierre Blais to his boss, Dr. Irwin Hinberg, in which Blais said the Meme and its analogs were "unfit for human implantation and . . . potentially hazardous to users." Hinberg returned the edited memo two weeks later with a handwritten note to "Please make the corrections suggested" by Dr. Johnson of Canada's Health Protection Branch. Among the "corrections" was the removal of Blais's references to the Meme being "unfit," the deletion of a line saying this was "discussed extensively at our Consensus Development Meeting of January 6, 1989," which Johnson had chaired, and the removal of a reference to a recommendation at that meeting that the Meme be reviewed under Section 28 of the Medical Devices Regulations. At that time, federal officials claimed the Meme didn't have to undergo scrutiny because it had been sold in Canada since 1981, predating 1983 regulatory changes concerning safety and efficacy. That wasn't true either, but again, federal officials took the manufacturer's word for it.

In April 1989, Minister of Health and Welfare Perrin Beatty appointed Montreal plastic surgeon Carolyn Kerrigan to investigate the safety of the Meme and report back by May 23. Kerrigan, head of plastic surgery at Royal Victoria Hospital, used the Meme in her own practice, and essentially relied on studies done by the U.S. manufacturers and conversations with other plastic surgeons who were also using the Meme, to report that there was no evidence the Meme was unsafe. Because of inadequate scientific data, however, she couldn't say it was safe either. Still, this report was enough for the health minister, senior health officials, and the plastic surgeons themselves to declare the Meme was safe. Dr. Roland Charbonneau, president of the Quebec Association of Plastic Surgeons, where the bulk of Meme implants were being used, praised Kerrigan's study as "superb" and called "unfounded" the allegations that because she was a plastic surgeon herself she was "trying to find something positive on the implant." Charbonneau went on to say, "We're not pushing to sell that implant. Our main concern is to reassure the population that the implant is safe."

Charbonneau's reassurances were cast in doubt by a 1989 Mayo Clinic research paper concerning polyurethane implants. The study noted that complications with the implants ". . . led us to abandoning the use of this implant some 15 years ago. It is our opinion that it not be used routinely until more extensive favorable trials are reported."

Still, nobody listened.

During that same period, officials in the Department of Health and Welfare tried to stop Dr. Pierre Blais from communicating with British Columbia lawyer Ulf Ottho, who had subpoenaed him to testify on behalf of Linda Wilson who was suing her doctor for malpractice. So anxious were federal officials to shut Blais up that Justice Department lawyer Debra Prupas even challenged the B.C. subpoena, arguing that it didn't apply under Ontario law. Instead, the health department "volunteered" Blais's boss Johnson as a witness, even though Johnson's expertise was on implanted heart pacemakers and radiation issues, while Blais was the recognized expert on implants. By this time, the implant business had grown to some $400 million a year in Canada and the United States, with more than 2 million women having acquired various kinds of breast implants, up to 20 percent of those victims of breast cancer or other breast diseases.

On July 17, 1989, Assistant Deputy Health Minister Albert Liston fired Blais, saying that Kerrigan's report showed the 49-year-old scientist was wrong about the dangers of the Meme. Blais, an internationally recognized expert on implant technology, with more than 150 published articles in professional journals, had spent 21 years with the government, but Liston's three-page letter said he was being fired for his "unsuitability for employment in the Public Service." Blais subsequently appealed his dismissal and won his case, but cut a deal and left the federal service.

With some plastic surgeons reporting that the Meme resulted in infection rates as high as 20 percent, the Wisconsin-based Surgitek organized a joint news conference in Montreal in October 1989, to counter these concerns. Dr. Roderick Hester of Atlanta, Georgia, cited the Kerrigan study and said, "The higher infection rate is a myth." Hester, chief of surgery at Colquitte County Memorial Hospital and a teacher at Atlanta's Emory University, claimed that several studies, including his own, show the breast implants have the same rate of infection as other implants, from 1 to 3 percent. Dr. Pierre Langlois of Quebec, in a statement endorsed by both the Quebec Association of Plastic Surgeons and the Canadian Society of Plastic Surgeons, went even further, claiming the Meme produced better results than conventional prostheses and that "the complication rate is lower."

In June 1990, a seven-member team of scientists at Laval University in Quebec City found that the Meme decomposes within two weeks of implantation and produces cancer-causing 2-4 toluene diamine. Even worse, the team, which included Pierre Blais, discovered that women who undergo surgery to have the implants removed are at greater risk of receiving high doses of carcinogens and toxins because of the extreme temperatures used by surgeons to stop bleeding from their use of electrosurgical tools to cut and seal the tissue. "It's obvious to anyone who knows about toxicology that this material should never have been used in a medical device," said Blais. As a result of this work, Dr. Robert

Guidoin, head of the team and chief of the university's laboratory of experimental surgery, called for a moratorium on the Meme. "Our studies," he said, "show the foam degrades very easily and rapidly and the formation of the [2-4 toluene diamine] is obvious."

A month later, a U.S. FDA official privately told journalist Nicholas Regush that "[t]here is no way we can keep an implant with a carcinogen on the market." But Surgitek official Jim Kaufmann said the company "has already completed much of the testing proposed by the FDA and we have seen no negative data that would suggest the product would not be approved."

In November 1990, officials of Canada's Department of Health and Welfare admitted that their laboratory tests had found traces of the cancer-causing chemical in the foam covering of the Meme, but they dismissed it as "insignificant and not worrisome" because of the small amounts. Douglas Shanklin, a pathologist at the University of Tennessee at Memphis, was quoted as saying, "The Meme represents an enormous uncontrolled experiment." And Nir Kossovsky, a pathologist at the University of California School of Medicine, said, "The choice of materials for this foam is so off base it's out of touch with the reality of today's efforts to develop durable implants."

In March 1991, a federal jury of five women and three men in New York City awarded a 46-year-old single woman $4.45 million in the first damage suit linking the Meme to breast cancer. The unnamed woman had had the Meme implanted in 1983 because her breasts sagged. She suffered inflammation for several weeks and had the Meme removed, but some of the foam had become entangled with her breast tissue when the implant had ruptured, causing silicone to travel as far as her uterus. The $4.45 million award was for loss of a breast and fear of future cancer. "We want this verdict to serve as a warning to women," said Denise Dunleavy, the woman's lawyer. Nearly 50 damage suits had been launched in Canada and the United States against the Meme.

On April 14, the *Sunday New York Times* published a devastating story on the Meme, citing FDA sources saying that on the basis of preliminary calculations, the implant might cause cancer at the annual rate of 200 to 400 cases for every million users.

The FDA could no longer ignore the problem. It convened a meeting in Washington on the Meme after its researchers found that significant levels of 2-4 toluene diamine were released by the foam covering when it decomposed under mild laboratory conditions. Canada announced it was sending an official to Washington to study the FDA results. The government's choice was Irwin Hinberg, still arguing that Canadian studies showed the Meme was safe. Meanwhile, Minister of Health and Welfare Perrin Beatty also continued to defend the Meme, saying he could not make a decision to ban the product based "on accusations or on newspaper headlines." Indeed, so convincing was Beatty's continual defence of the Meme that Hansards of his comments from the House of Commons were introduced as evidence at later U.S. Congressional hearings into the implant. The FDA, which had also been dragging its heels in the face of growing safety concerns, finally moved, if only slightly, giving manufacturers 90 days to file "premarket approval applications" containing evidence of the safety and effectiveness of implants.

At the same time, Blais and Guidoin announced in Quebec City that a study using about two dozen sets of mammograms sent to them from across the United States and Canada showed the Meme leaking badly, with fluid building between the implant and women's breast tissue. The women had suffered such problems as inflammation, infection, swollen underarms, joint pain and excessive weight loss. One set of mammograms showed a woman from Washington whose implant had burst, deflated and become stuck to her chest wall. There was leakage on both sides of her implant and her ribs were being eroded, Blais said.

On April 16, in a study later published in the U.S. journal *Clinical Chemistry*, Calgary researchers announced that they had found biological products of 2-4 toluene diamine in the urine of a 41-year-old woman relating to the breakdown of the foam covering of her Meme implant. They said more research was needed, but Ottawa replied that it would await the results of research being done by the implant manufacturers.

A day later, Bristol-Myers Squibb Company (owners of Surgitek of Racine, Wisconsin) suspended shipments of the Meme to the ten countries around the world where it was being used. They insisted it was safe and blamed "unsubstantiated but widespread media reports" for necessitating the action. The company also suspended distribution of the sister implant, Replicon, and asked doctors to stop using it pending completion of FDA studies. Canadian officials, who had been defending the product all the way, quickly followed suit and warned doctors to stop using the product. Even so, they played down the risks. Dr. Ernest Letourneau, director of the Department of Health and Welfare's Bureau of Radiation and Medical Devices, said, "Our overall advice is that the risk which is involved is very low and we are not recommending that the prosthesis be removed specifically for the fear of this chemical compound." In fact, as Blais had shown in his studies, the risk of removal could be more dangerous than the risks associated with leaving them in. Health department officials said the FDA findings suggested that the additional cancer risk to women with the Meme was equal to smoking one and a half cigarettes in a lifetime. This was not true, but it sounded reassuring.

Dr. Carolyn Kerrigan, who had assured the federal government two years earlier that the Meme posed no health hazard, admitted that soon after submitting her study she proposed another one into whether the implant's foam casing could cause cancer. She also confirmed part of the funding of the continuing study came from Surgitek, but she insisted there was no conflict between her tests and her continued use of the implant.

And Toronto plastic surgeon Dr. John Taylor, a spokesman for the Canadian Society for Aesthetic [Cosmetic] Surgery and member of the Canadian Society of Plastic Surgeons, said patients should "wait a few weeks until the dust has settled . . . until we know more about what's going on."

In a letter to FDA commissioner Dr. David Kessler, however, U.S. Congressman Ted Weiss, chairman of a subcommittee studying the controversy, said FDA scientists estimated the cancer risk could be more than 100 times the levels publicly reported by FDA officials. He said internal documents received by the subcommittee clearly show that FDA statements did "not accurately reflect the conclusions of FDA's own scientists." Weiss said the documents estimated the cancer risk at between 0.5 and 110 per million women exposed to the chemical in the implant and indicated that the scientists believed the higher risk numbers were more realistic. In the meantime, about 200,000 American women had been implanted with a Meme.

Still, Canadian health officials weren't prepared to give up on the Meme. In an extraordinary column published in the May 1, 1991, edition of *The Ottawa Citizen*, Assistant Deputy Health Minister Albert J. Liston wrote to "reassure your readers" and to scold the Meme critics for causing "unnecessary concern to the 17,000 Meme users in Canada to suggest that they will be affected either by a greatly increased cancer risk, or by the type of post-operative difficulty widely publicized in the past week."

A month later, researchers at the Aegis Analytical Laboratories Inc. in Nashville, Tennessee, found signs of 2-4 toluene diamine in the breast milk of a woman in her late 20s who had a Meme implant. Other tests by the firm had found the biological products of the cancer-causing compound in the urine of some women with the Meme as well. Mark Faulkner, executive vice-president of Aegis, told the *Gazette*'s Nicholas Regush that researchers "were surprised and concerned to find signs of the chemical in breast milk but are leaving any medical conclusions about the results to doctors" and the FDA. Some of the studies at Aegis were performed under contract for Surgitek and were sent to the company on May 10, which, in turn, passed it on to the FDA.

It got worse. Dr. Tom Sinclair, a researcher at the Royal Victoria Hospital in Montreal, told the annual conference of the Canadian Society of Plastic Surgeons that tiny particles of the polyurethane foam covering some breast implants, including the Meme, were found in surrounding tissues of women who were subjects of their study. "We analyzed 62 implants from 40 patients," he said. "Intact foam was recovered from 29 implants. In 33 implants we could not recover intact foam. All of the 33 specimens examined by standard light microscopy, except one — removed 17 years after implantation — had microscopic evidence of foam still present in [the tissue], even though we could not recover or physically detect it."

The problem is, pieces of foam get tangled with breast tissue, making their removal extremely difficult without removing some muscular and glandular tissue. Sinclair said the longer an implant was in place, the more difficult it was to recover intact foam. Ironically, the study was supervised by Dr. Carolyn Kerrigan, whose earlier study on behalf of the federal government concluded that Meme implants were not unsafe.

About that same time, Regush discovered that a 1987/88 study conducted on rats by pathologist Stephen Woodward at the Veterans Administration Medical Center in Nashville for Cooper Surgical, then the Meme's manufacturer, found that the foam in miniature implants in the animals disappeared up to 50 percent in two to eight months. Documents show that Cooper Surgical initiated studies at Vanderbilt University in Nashville in 1988 with researcher David Black to examine the chemistry of the foam. In February 1989, Surgitek, which now owned the product, showed continued interest in the project by sending details of Black's study proposals to Scotfoam Corporation, the foam's manufacturer. After that, however, the company decided not to fund the studies. In July 1991, officials for Bristol-Myers Squibb Company said the research on rats was not convincing enough to warrant funding more studies proposed by Black.

Despite everything, the newly minted Canada-wide support group for women with breast implants, called I Know/Je Sais, was shocked when Canada's new Health Minister Benoit Bouchard announced in July 1991 that the government would not compensate women who had had or had wanted to have their Meme implants removed. Why not? Because there was no scientific evidence to demonstrate how they are harmful to women, he said. The group's president, Marcella Tardiff of Montreal, had had bleeding cancerous tumors and had undergone seven biopsies and five operations, leading finally to a mastectomy. She had had her implants inserted in April 1990 and was hit by "immediate side effects. Numbness of the arms, absolutely no feeling around your breasts. You feel like you are walking around and there is a big empty hole there."

Testifying in February 1992, before a Commons subcommittee on breast cancer, Tardiff said her plastic surgeon had not told her anything about the implant. "He showed me no documents, no product, nothing. They put me to sleep. They did my mastectomy. I woke up, I had breasts. It was important. Use it any way you want to, the word is aesthetic. It is cosmetic because whether you're having a mastectomy . . . you want breasts. It's still cosmetic because you want to look physically feminine.

"My dream was totally shattered. Not more than four days after I had the implants the secretions, the swelling, the deforming of my face, the deforming of my breast, what I looked like — I couldn't believe that this was me. I went to see the doctor repeatedly. It's medical abuse. He told me in his office in front of my husband that I was a crazy person, that it was between my ears, that it was not true, that he'd never had any rejections, that this does not happen."

A month after Bouchard rejected compensation, Health Canada (formerly Department of Health and Welfare) officials finally admitted they'd goofed in permitting the Meme to be marketed without tests to ensure its safety. In an October 1990 letter to *Gazette* reporter Regush, Assistant Deputy Minister Albert J. Liston claimed his staff had "verified that the Meme in its present form has been sold in Canada since 1982," one year before regulatory changes would have required a pre-market safety review. But in August 1991, Marcel Chartrand, chief of media relations for Health Canada, told Regush in a telephone interview that "we are not able to produce conclusive evidence the Meme was sold in Canada before April 1983. I have nothing definitive. We haven't found any document that says the Meme was sold in 1982 or 1983." When political critics jumped on the statement, Chartrand said his comments did not constitute owning up to any wrongdoing. "It was no admission [of guilt]," he said. Perhaps not, unless you believe public officials have a responsibility to tell the truth and enforce their own regulations.

In any event, Chartrand's non-admission prompted the reluctant Bouchard to finally ask for a thorough review of the entire Meme controversy. It was an internal review, however. Bouchard refused a public inquiry on the matter.

While Bristol-Myers Squibb of New York City closed the plastic surgery unit that manufactured its Meme in Racine, and U.S. officials asked makers of breast implants to provide readily understandable information for patients on the risks of implantations, Canadian officials said a similar move wasn't necessary. And Canadian suporters of the Meme continued to do battle. A group of five Montreal plastic surgeons accused both Blais and Guidoin of deliberately trying to scare the public away from the Meme to create a market for a new prosthesis of their own. This was not true.

In November 1991, an expert review panel of the Canadian Medical Association (CMA) formed by Bouchard conveniently discovered that the Meme implants were safe after all. They said the risk of cancer was infinitesimal, and women didn't need to have them removed. Chairman Dr. David A. Boyes said the controversy was overblown by emotional accusations and very little scientific data. "We are satisfied at this time the implants are safe." They didn't even mention the other health risks of the Meme, such as autoimmune diseases like arthritis and lupus, serious infections, prolonged pain, hardening of the breasts, fatigue, blurred vision, memory loss, insomnia, hypertension, heart irregularities and rashes. Even Blais, the implant's most persistent critic, had put the cancer risk ninth or tenth.

Just when the stench couldn't possibly get any stronger, it did. Calgary scientist Dr. Hans Berkel, director of the Division of Epidemiology with the Alberta Cancer Board, announced a study of every woman in the province who had had an implant between 1974 and 1986. The women were traced until 1990. Using Alberta Health Care records, Berkel and his team found that 11,991 women between the ages of 20 and 65 underwent breast implant operations. That was four times the size of most major U.S. studies. The researchers collaborated with Dr. Dale Birdsell of the Foothills Hospital in Calgary, comparing the list of women who had a breast implant with one that showed how many Alberta women got breast cancer. There were 345 matches, but 307 of those had the surgery for reconstructive purposes, which meant they got the implant after breast-cancer surgery. That left only 38 women who contracted breast cancer following cosmetic surgery, actually lower than the number of cancers that might be expected in the normal female population of that size. So the study concluded that there was no scientific link between implants and breast cancer. (Berkel said the study did not differentiate between implants using silicone polymers and the newer Meme implant that used a polyurethane sponge as a surface coating.)

Berkel's study made headlines across North America when it was published June 18, 1992, in the prestigious *New England Journal of Medicine*. Co-authored by Birdsell and Dr. Heather Jenkins, the article concluded that "women who undergo breast augmentation with silicone implants have a lower risk of breast cancer than the general population. This finding suggests that these women are drawn from a population already at low risk and that the implants do not substantially increase the risk." The article was quickly embraced by several U.S. implant manufacturers named as defendants in U.S. lawsuits by women who had undergone the procedure and later suffered health problems. It also prompted breast implant giant Dow Corning to offer Berkel a $250,000 U.S. research grant, through the Medical Research Council, to continue his research. Berkel also published an editorial defending his position in the October 1992 edition of the *Canadian Medical Association Journal.*

In the same issue of the *New England Journal of Medicine,* Dr. Jack Fisher of the University of California Medical Center in San Diego wrote a stinging editorial attacking the FDA for displaying "insensitivity to the demonstrated needs of more than one million women who since 1963 have sought breast implantation for cosmetic or reconstructive purposes." Fisher said their actions against silicone implants "depended largely on the exaggerated claims of consumer-advocacy groups and on poorly documented assertions," ignoring what he called the "carefully considered position statements" of the American Medical Association, the American College of Surgeons, the American College of Radiology, the American College of Rheumatology, the Society of Surgical Oncologists and the American Society of Plastic and Reconstructive Surgeons Inc.

A year after Berkel's celebrated paper was published, he was fired without notice from his $140,000-a-year job by the Alberta Cancer Board, which accused him of serious flaws in his research. (Berkel, in turn, launched a $500,000 suit against the board for wrongful dismissal.) Despite the enormous favorable publicity garnered by Berkel's paper, the cancer board later launched an investigation into his work, using scientists from the United States, Ottawa and from inside the board itself. Dr. Heather Bryant, director of the cancer board's mammography screening program in Calgary, headed the investigation.

According to a November 9, 1993, *Calgary Herald* report citing Dr. Birdsell, who was not involved in the statistical calculations that were criticized, the main point of contention was that Berkel could not say accurately how many women with cosmetic breast implants, whose health care records were used in the study, left the province or changed their names through marriage. Also, in comparing records of women with cancer with those with implants, he was again unable to account for all those whose health care numbers had changed through marriage or for other reasons. Birdsell, whose own reputation was on the line in this study, said the accusations against Berkel were "nitpicky. There was never any suggestion of scientific misconduct."

On January 7, 1992, FDA commissioner Dr. David Kessler imposed a temporary, 45-day moratorium stopping doctors from putting silicone breast implants in patients because troubling questions remained about their safety. Kessler said it was not known how often the silicone implant leaked or broke, where the gel went in the body or what it did when it got there, or whether the devices increased a woman's risk of cancer. "Thirty years of use and we still don't know the answers to these questions," said Kessler. "There remain troubling questions about the safety of these implants. As physicians, our first obligation is to do no harm. We owe it to the American public to see to it that these questions are thoroughly investigated." Kessler said the FDA had received new "information [which] provides additional evidence that implants could possibly cause auto-immune or connective tissue disorders." At the time, an estimated 2.3 million American women had silicone-gel breast implants, and another 10,000 a month were getting them. Between 400,000 and 500,000 of those women had the implants following breast-cancer surgery. With the operation costing $2,500 or more, the industry gained some $25 million a month in the United States alone. In Canada, an estimated 150,000 women had breast implants — roughly 30,000 of them after breast-cancer surgery.

The day after Kessler's surprise announcement, Dow Corning Canada Inc., the country's major manufacturer of silicone implants, announced it was pulling them off the market until the FDA completed its safety review. Mentor Corp. of Santa Barbara, California, followed suit. Toronto plastic surgeon Michael Bederman, who had performed 4,000 breast augmentation operations over 16 years, said he would continue to do breast implants despite the controversy. Bederman told *The Globe and Mail*, "I believe it is an operation that is extremely safe and relatively risk-free. Two million women in the United States have had breast implants and, to date, there is still no hard evidence that the implants cause anything wrong. They make people happy, they give them more self-esteem and enhance their femininity."

They also make plastic surgeons rich.

Despite the temporary moratorium in the United States, Canadian officials refused to follow suit. Canadian medical experts, including Hans Berkel, were accusing the FDA of acting for political motives more than out of concern for scientific accuracy. British Columbia cancer specialist Dr. David Boyes, who headed a CMA review on the Meme a year earlier, said Canada "should not follow that [FDA] knee-jerk reaction and do what they did."

A day later, Health Minister Benoit Bouchard did just that, announcing a temporary moratorium on the sale of silicone-gel implants in Canada. "We have no new scientific information about the safety of these implants," Bouchard said. "The action we have taken is a temporary measure while we await and review information from the FDA." He added he was "disappointed" that the FDA had not complied to Canada's repeated request to provide the information it used in making its decision. "We don't understand. We would like to know if there is a problem for Canadian women." Bouchard said other countries such as Britain and Australia were equally upset. Spain and Australia also banned the implants, but most countries were waiting to see scientific proof of danger. "We are used to the hysteria that follows health warnings in the United States," said David Sharpe of the British Association of Aesthetic Plastic Surgeons.

The new information included additional reports from rheumatologists who reported seeing a growing number of autoimmune and connective-tissue disorders among implant recipients. In addition, the FDA obtained documents still under seal in several implant lawsuits suggesting that the manufacturers had concerns about the devices' safety way back in the 1970s.

On January 15, 1992, Dow Corning Corporation, a joint venture of Dow Chemical Co. and Corning Glass Works, and the leading maker of silicone breast implants, announced in Midland, Michigan, that it was halting production at Hemlock, Michigan, and Arlington, Tennessee — the two factories that produced the devices. The announcement came after widespread news stories in the United States that the company had ignored the advice of its own scientists to test the product more thoroughly. According to published memos, the company had allowed silicone-gel devices to be implanted in women before it had received the results of studies in animals. Even in the studies that were conducted, the implants had not been placed below the animals' breast tissue, as they always were in humans. The memos also indicated that Dow Corning had instructed its sales force to mislead plastic surgeons about the risk that silicone would leak into patients' bodies. Dow said its half-share in the company represented only about 1 percent of its total sales of $1.7 billion in the first nine months of 1991. But the threat of potential damage awards had driven Dow's share price down nearly $3 that week to around $52.

Robert Rylee, chairman of Dow Corning's health-care business, insisted that "the cumulative body of credible scientific evidence" showed the implants were "safe and effective. . . . At some point any company begins to wonder why it would spend any more time and money selling a product that's causing it so many difficulties." Rylee essentially argued that the company was forced out of business by bad publicity. Part of that publicity flowed from a liability case against the company in December, in which a Dow Corning marketing executive, asked by a group of plastic surgeons about the safety of the implants, wrote that "I assured them, with crossed fingers, that Dow Corning too had an active study underway."

More deception was unveiled in late January 1992, when corporate lawyers in New York said they had documents at least eight years earlier showing that breast-implant manufacturers knew the devices could be dangerous, but court-approved agreements kept the papers secret. Lawyers and consumer advocates argued that without the secrecy orders, the government probably would have stopped the sale of implants years earlier. Dr. Sidney Wolfe, director of the Washington-based Public Citizens' Health Research Group founded by Ralph Nader, told Reuters News Agency that "[m]ost of the documents that are being used belatedly by the federal government to properly regulate silicone breast implants have been locked up for eight years." If the FDA had access to them then, Wolfe said, "silicone breast implants would have been a dead product and hundreds of thousands of women implanted with these would have been spared."

Dow Corning lead counsel Dr. Frank Woodside, a Cincinnati lawyer, maintained that the devices were safe and said the FDA did have the relevant documents for years. "My personal belief is that there is no new evidence," he said. When it had announced the moratorium earlier that month, however, the FDA claimed it had new evidence and needed time to study it.

On February 10, 1992, Dow Corning released hundreds of internal memos, letters and other documents showing decades of complaints that its silicone-gel implants had caused medical problems and announcing that its chairman, John Ludington, was stepping down to become chairman emeritus as a result of the controversy.

In spite of this, the company continually insisted the implants were safe, but a 1985 memo from Bill Boley, a Dow Corning scientist, warned that more testing was needed to determine whether a particular formula of the silicone gel caused cancer. "Without this testing, I think we have excessive personal and corporate liability exposure," Boley wrote. Chairman Robert Rylee conceded that the documents represented a public relations disaster for his company but said the focus of attention should be on scientific data, not a collection of inflammatory company memos.

The memos, however, were hard to ignore. One dated March 9, 1971 — 21 years before the company released it — told of a New Orleans patient whose breast had become irritated about four months after she received an implant following a mastectomy. The doctor treating her twice thought it was an infection and gave her penicillin. The irritation returned, and after the third occurrence, the doctor discovered "the irritation had lacerated and the fluid was oozing from the wound." The doctor removed the implant and found it "was partially empty of gel and what gel was there was extremely fluid and oozed out of the prosthesis and the surrounding tissue."

On April 29, 1980, salesman Bob Schnabel wrote a memo to head-quarters relaying a doctor's complaint about a batch of implants that appeared to be leaking. "To put a questionable lot of mammaries on the market is inexcusable," Schnabel wrote. Rylee said the memo "looks bad," but added it "was written by a salesman who had an unhappy customer. While we're not happy about the memos, we have nothing to hide."

Not anymore perhaps. But they had been hiding them for 20 years.

In Canada, Health Minister Benoit Bouchard was hanging tough, steadfastly refusing to ban the silicone implants. "I'm still looking for scientific evidence that tells me, without any doubt, that those implants have had a negative effect on women," he said, apparently unaware of the evidence that had been piling up for years. Instead, Bouchard set up an independent committee of experts headed by Dr. Cornelia Baines of the University of Toronto to investigate whether silicone-gel breast implants are harmful. Shortly after that, Drs. Pierre Blais and Robert Guidoin at Quebec City's Laval University announced studies showing that the implants cause arthritis-like symptoms and nerve damage to some women over the long term.

On February 19, four silicone implant manufacturers told a U.S. federal advisory panel that any connection between the implants and users' health problems was a coincidence, but Dow Corning promised to pay for removing implants from women who could not afford to pay for removals ordered by their doctor. Representative Marilyn Lloyd, who had had a mastectomy because of breast cancer, said she would like to have an implant but said that because of the "unjustified" FDA moratorium "my quality of life has been put on hold." That sparked applause from women who had been sitting quietly in the hotel ballroom in Bethesda, Maryland, where the panel was meeting. Barbara Quinn of Atlanta, representing Bosom Buddies, a support group for women who have undergone mastectomies because of breast cancer, said reconstructive surgery meant "my self-esteem was restored. Why is the FDA denying cancer-maimed women the use of this device to make their bodies whole again? . . . If the government cannot or will not regulate tobacco products, they should not regulate women's breasts," she said.

A day later, the panel unanimously recommended that the U.S. government restrict silicone-gel breast implants to experiments and to women needing breast reconstruction. Nancy Dubler, a lawyer and one of nine voting members of the 24-member FDA panel, said the recommendation responded "to science on the one hand and compassion on the other." Perhaps. But it seemed an odd compromise. If the panel believed the implants were not safe, then why did they allow them in women who had already suffered the trauma of breast cancer? Another panel member, Dr. Julie Harris, said the evidence did not "provide the basis to conclude that silicone-gel breast implants are safe and effective. I do not find this evidence convincing, but it is disturbing." Medical school professor Dr. Elizabeth Connell, the panel's chairman, said the evidence was not conclusive that implant leaks are linked to cancer and autoimmune disease. "We have a possible association, and we need more research," she said.

In Quebec, however, plastic surgeons called reporters to a briefing to "counter the nonsense in newspapers and on TV." According to Dr. Jacques Charbonneau, president of the Quebec Association of Plastic

Surgeons, criticism of the implants was "medical terrorism." He insisted, "There are no scientific data to justify this." Then he made a curious assertion: Women with implants "are scared," he said. "They're having nightmares. If there's nothing scientific to justify this, it must stop." To support their case, the plastic surgeons cited Dr. Hans Berkel's sensational Alberta study, which was later discredited by the Alberta Cancer Board.

On March 19, 1992, Dow Corning made a joint announcement in Washington and Toronto that it was getting out of the breast-implant business completely. In the first salvo of a series of compensation packages designed by the manufacturers to stem the tide of court actions, Dow Corning announced that it was setting up a $10 million fund to monitor breast implants in women in the United States and Canada, and would provide up to $1,200 in financial assistance to American women who, on the advice of their doctors, wanted to have their implants removed but lacked the necessary insurance coverage. (It did not cover non-American women. The reason given is that in Canada, provincial health plans cover the removal when it is deemed a medical necessity.) The company held about 25 to 30 percent of the breast-implant market. Its decision to withdraw left two other U.S. manufacturers — McGhan NuSil Corporation and Mentor Corp., both based in Santa Barbara, California — with the market to themselves. With $250 million in liability insurance, Dow Corning was reportedly facing a potential liability of more than $1 billion in lawsuits from American women who were claiming serious health problems related to the implants.

In Canada, Benoit Bouchard was still procrastinating. The committee he had appointed two months earlier had concluded there wasn't enough evidence to decide whether the silicone implants were safe or unsafe. "More research will be required before we understand the biological behavior of the components of [silicone] implants," the report said. The committee suggested an odd compromise that would have allowed the silicone implants to be used by older women and cancer victims needing reconstructive surgery, but Bouchard said this would "discriminate among women" and could be a violation of the Charter of Rights and Freedoms. Instead, he announced a six-month extension of his moratorium on the use of implants and said another $1 million would be spent by the Laboratory Centre for Disease Control on an epidemiological study of the health risks of the implants.

He also commissioned a pollster, the Angus Reid Group, to survey women who had implants and to find out their experiences with them. As it turned out, 3,000 women, twice as many as expected, responded to the survey. The results, released in December 1992, showed 56 percent of the women were very satisfied with their implants, 22 percent were somewhat satisfied, 9 percent somewhat dissatisfied, and 12 percent very dissatisfied.

Some 77 percent said their original expectations had been met regarding such things as physical appearance (20 percent), no problems (18 percent), increased self-esteem (14 percent), no surprises (12 percent), and happy/no regrets (10 percent). On the other hand despite claims from manufacturers that there were few problems, 21 percent were disappointed, complaining of these things: "nothing but problems" (22 percent), breast hardened (13 percent), not enough or misleading information (13 percent) and unnatural appearance (10 percent). Asked whether given the chance they would have implant surgery again, 58 percent said they would, while 33 percent said no. A total of 23 percent said they had had complications within the first two weeks of surgery, and 53 percent had had problems at some point since their surgery. Of the respondents, 57 percent had silicone-gel implants, while 22 percent had saline implants, and 4 percent, a silicone-saline combination, both of which are less likely to cause problems. Twenty percent of the women had implants following a mastectomy for breast cancer.

Following an interview with Canadian Broadcasting Corporation radio journalist Judy Morrison on the implant controversy, Bouchard told Morrison he didn't understand "what all the fuss is about." He said maybe it was because he was a man, but added that he'd even asked his wife about it and she didn't understand either. Bouchard said he was going to hire a female assistant to advise him on such women's issues. "I was just stunned that he couldn't understand what women were worried about," says Morrison. "Unfortunately, the interview was over and we weren't taping. Maybe I should have pursued it more at the time, but I was so shocked I was at a loss for words. No wonder he took so long to act. He didn't know what the problem was."

In the meantime, the American Society of Plastic and Reconstructive Surgeons, which has many Canadian members as well, was raising $4 million from its membership for an advertising campaign to counter the negative publicity about implants. Jane Sprague Zones, a medical sociologist at the University of California in San Francisco and a member of the FDA advisory panel on implants, accused the doctors of being "more motivated by profit than medical concerns. . . . They view themselves as embattled, wronged, portrayed wrongly by the press," she said.

Dr. David Leitner, an assistant professor at the University of Vermont College of Medicine, removed nine silicone-gel implants shortly after the FDA moratorium was announced. "Seven have been broken and been leaking very badly — it looks like hot bubblegum coming out of the wound," Leitner told an *Ottawa Citizen* journalist. "Two or three years ago, I would not have been concerned about this, but looking at it now, I'm getting worried."

Women were also getting worried. So much so that Laura Thorpe of New Mexico, fearing her silicone-gel implants were making her ill, used a razor blade to remove them herself after her insurance company refused to pay for the operation.

Canadian government officials were embarrassed again in June 1992 with the release of documents indicating that they had given a clean bill of health to the Meme implant in 1989, while departmental bureaucrats wanted it taken off the market until safety research could be completed. Dr. Haim Ben-Simhon, a clinical adviser, wrote in a memo on January 10, 1989: "I believe the risk of severity of the complication outweighs the apparent possible advantage of such an implant." Two days later, Hripsime Shahbazian, a research scientist with the Department of Health and Welfare, wrote, "This is an urgent matter and needs immediate attention." At the time, the department had responded publicly by dismissing the critics and claiming the Meme was perfectly safe.

In November 1992, Dr. Pierre Blais and his Quebec City colleagues struck again, announcing that by using high-powered microscopes, they had found "huge amounts of infectious materials in both saline-filled and silicone-gel breast implants that have been removed mostly from Canadian and American women who are experiencing infection, respiratory and immune-system problems, swelling and fever. A couple of implants were so contaminated with fungi and other germs that they had turned coal black." Norman Anderson, an implant expert at Johns Hopkins University in Baltimore, a member of the FDA Advisory Committee on Breast Implants, told the Montreal *Gazette* that he had studied the findings of implant contamination with Blais, and that the electron-microscope pictures "show absolutely unacceptable levels of contamination." Anderson said Blais's work raised "root questions about the lack of (government) regulation of something as basic as proper sterilization of implants."

In January 1993, Bouchard finally moved, although he continued to insist, "There's no new evidence of problems or risk for women in terms of disease." Still, he announced a freeze on the sale and distribution of silicone breast implants in Canada. If manufacturers wanted to sell the devices, they would have to undertake and pay for clinical studies that would be strictly reviewed by Health Canada.

But Bouchard picked up on the American idea to allow implants in "exceptional circumstances," such as radical mastectomies or severe deformities, announcing that he'd changed health regulations to "allow access on compassionate grounds, to medical devices that have not yet met all regulatory requirements and have not been approved for sale in Canada."

That same month, a House Government Operations subcommittee report in Washington accused the FDA of not following up on its announced plans to investigate the safety of silicone implants. Recipients of all implants were supposed to have become part of a data base and a large-scale study. Women with previous implants were also encouraged to register with a national data base, whether they were satisfied with the implant or not. But the subcommittee said data collection was lagging badly and documentation on doctors' current practice — a major enforcement mechanism — was being sent to the manufacturers, not the FDA, a return to the old self-policing style that had caused so many problems to go unreported for so long. FDA Commissioner Dr. David Kessler replied that it was "ludicrous" to suggest that the public hearings had not affected medical practice. He noted that the number of implantations in 1992 had collapsed to a mere 3,500 — down from an average of 130,000 a year.

In March, researchers at the University of California-Davis reported that 16 of the 46 women studied showed an immune-system reaction to the breast implants in the form of very high levels of antibodies to collagen, a basic body protein. This figure was compared to a group of 45 women without implants but of similar age, where only one woman showed the same high level of antibodies.

But the champions of silicone implants weren't finished yet. In April 1993, a group of Toronto researchers headed by Wellesley Hospital plastic surgeon Dr. Walter Peters concluded that the implants do not cause arthritis or diseases of the immune system. Of the 500 women with silicone-gel implants that they studied, about 20 who had had implants inserted between 2 and 25 years before showed symptoms of immune-system illnesses — about the same percentage scientists could expect in women without an implant. Réal Laperriere, who owned exclusive rights to distribute the Meme in Canada until it was pulled from the market two years earlier, said the new study shows "what we've always known. . . . We knew the product was efficient."

Several class actions had been launched in both countries against the manufacturers. One in Ontario was undertaken on behalf of 8,500 women who had received implants manufactured by both Dow Corning Canada Inc. and McGhan NuSil Corporation of California. In Denver, a jury was not convinced that implants were the cause of problems of 30-year-old Tammy Turner McCartney. On June 11, 1993, the jury deliberated for less than two hours before siding with Dow Corning in a $7 million suit brought by McCartney, a former topless dancer, who said she suffered crippling fatigue and pain in her joints from her silicone-gel implant. Some jurors said they were offended by McCartney's lifestyle and the jury foreman said the jury did not believe the implants caused her health problems. Although about 5,400 cases were pending against the company and they were no longer marketing the implants, Dow Corning lawyers concentrated on McCartney's past. They told the jury she had had an abortion, had given a child up for adoption and was considering reconstructive surgery on her nose. Some jurors admitted the tactic influenced their decision.

David Bernick, a lawyer for the company, said he hoped the verdict would discourage women from filing similar lawsuits and assuage fears that the implants were not safe. McCartney's lawyer, Jo Stone, said the company's case was tried on "character assassination, not facts." She said Dow chose McCartney's case as part of a corporate strategy to dissuade other women from coming forward and to reduce damage awards.

By September 1993, looking for ways to mitigate future court judgments against the company, Dow Corning dramatically increased its proposal for a $10 million fund to help uninsured American women have implants removed by announcing a proposed $4.75 billion fund to serve as an insurance policy for American women with breast implants. The fund would be paid for over 30 years by implant manufacturers, physicians, insurance companies and others involved in implant surgery. That would give American women between $200,000 and $2 million each if approved at a fairness hearing. The manufacturers have insisted throughout that the implants were safe, but that a compensation package would be cheaper in the long run than fighting each individual case or class-action suit through the court system.

In November 1993, three studies — by the Mayo Clinic, University of Toronto and University of Maryland — were presented at a meeting of the American College of Rheumatology in San Antonio, Texas, claiming to show there was no link between silicone-gel breast implants and connective tissue disease, even though thousands of lawsuits contended otherwise. Dr. Ralph Cook, Dow's director of epidemiology, said initial concerns about the implants leaking or rupturing were based on anecdotal case reports. "Sound scientific research has shown no increased risk of breast cancer among women with breast implants and a similar picture is now emerging for connective tissue disease," he said.

At the time, things were taking a turn for the worse in the courts for the manufacturers. In December 1993, a jury awarded Mariann Hopkins, 48, $7.34 million in her suit in San Francisco Federal Court. Hopkins had had breast implants in 1977, which ruptured and were replaced in the mid-1980s. While Dow Corning said it would appeal the decision, evidence at the trial indicated that the company had a secret program designed to trick women into signing away their rights to launch legal claims if problems arose with their breast implants. A company salesman testified about the company's Product Replacement Expense Program (PREP). (A U.S. Congressional committee had learned about it and was pressing the company for details.) The program, offered in both the United States and Canada, apparently began in 1984 after the company paid $1.5 million to a woman who sued because her implant was leaking.

Dow Corning sent notices to plastic surgeons saying the company would pay them to obtain legal releases "in favor of both the surgeon and Dow Corning" from women who had leaking or ruptured silicone implants replaced. The company salesman told the jury that he was aware that once women signed the company's legal release in the warranty program, they waived "all their future rights from any problems they would have, forever."

In a 1986 four-page overview of the warranty program sent to plastic surgeons, the company announced that PREP was a five-year limited product warranty that would pay for "uninsured out-of-pocket costs," to a maximum of $600, to a patient for repair or replacement of ruptured gel implants. It also covered "removal of implants due to rejection, sensitization, allergenic or adverse immunological response." When ruptures occurred, doctors were asked to send the company a copy of the woman's medical file from the initial surgery, a copy of the corrective surgery plan, copies of bills for corrective surgery, information on the patient's insurance coverage and "the removed sterilized . . . implant." Then Dow Corning would send the doctor "a full general release for signature by the patient." Once that was returned, the company sent the surgeon a replacement implant or a product credit and a cheque "for up to $600" payable to the surgeon and patient.

In December 1993, the FDA and the American Medical Association (AMA) exchanged sharp words in the *Journal of the American Medical Association* when FDA Commissioner Dr. David Kessler attacked the AMA for advocating the continued availability of silicone breast implants for cosmetic purposes. The AMA's Council of Scientific Affairs opposed the FDA's moratorium on implant use, saying, "Women have the right to choose silicone-gel-filled or saline-filled breast implants for both augmentation and reconstruction." Kessler's essay, which followed the AMA report, accused the doctors of "abrogation of responsibility" to patients and of disregarding the FDA's statutory obligation to require that drugs and devices be shown to be safe and effective. The FDA received more than 23,000 reports of problems with implants in 1992 and more than 19,000 in 1993, but the AMA still insists the evidence is "anecdotal."

By the end of 1993, about 9,000 individual lawsuits and 41 class actions had been filed against Dow Corning Corporation and other manufacturers. Responding to this and growing public pressure, including formation of the National Breast Implant Plaintiffs' Coalition, on February 14, 1994, three U.S. health-care manufacturers announced yet another compensation package. The tentative agreement would provide more than $3 billion among them for a worldwide compensation fund for women who suffered ill health as a result of silicone breast implants. Dow Corning Corporation, Bristol-Myers Squibb Company and Baxter Healthcare Corporation said they had reached an agreement among themselves and with representatives of claimants that would lead to the three companies paying 80 percent of the estimated $4 billion settlement costs over the next 30 years. Dow Corning would pay the most, about $2 billion; Bristol-Myers Squibb would put in $1.154 billion; and Baxter Healthcare would pay $556 million. Even so, the bulk of all payments to the women would be recovered from insurance. Each breast-implant recipient would have the chance to accept or reject the settlement and pursue her insurance claim if she decided to opt out. Two other companies, the Minnesota Mining and Manufacturing Company (3M) and the General Electric Company, had not yet agreed to contribute to the fund. Nearly all the money would go to American women, leaving women in Canada, Europe and elsewhere scrambling over a small pot. Judge Sam C. Pointer, Jr., of Federal District Court in Birmingham, Alabama, announced he would review it after the pact was signed, before women could be notified and then join the settlement.

In the meantime, court losses continued to mount. On March 4, 1994, a Houston jury awarded three women a total of $27.9 million damages in a lawsuit charging the 3M Company and two small companies — McGhan NuSil Corporation and Inamed Corporation — with manufacturing silicone breast implants that leaked, causing severe illnesses. Darla Lawson, Susan Doss and Judy McMurry argued that the leaked silicone caused various nervous-system and immune-system disorders before the implants were removed in 1992. The companies argued that scientific evidence did not support the verdict. The 3M Company, based in St. Paul, Minnesota, was assessed $14 million of the punitive damages. Together, the payments from all three companies were considerably less than the $100 million sought by the women.

A week later, the Supreme Court of Canada agreed to hear an appeal by Dow Corning Corporation of a ruling that awarded $95,000 to Susan

Hollis, a British Columbia woman who had received the implants in 1983 when she was 23 to correct abnormalities in her breasts. She eventually noticed a lump in her right breast and experienced pain. By the time she had the implants removed in 1985, the one in her right breast had ruptured. The surgeon removed most of the silicone but couldn't find the silicone envelope surrounding the gel. Her physical condition deteriorated and the pain continued. In 1987, she had a double mastectomy. In 1990, a lower court ruled that Dow had been negligent for failing to warn the medical profession of the risk of rupture.

On March 23, in the largest settlement ever negotiated in a class-action lawsuit, the three implant manufacturers — Dow Corning, Bristol-Myers Squibb and Baxter Healthcare — gave final approval to their $3.7 billion compensation fund, releasing details of how the compensation would be paid. The complex deal involved a series of payments depending on the woman's age and severity of her medical problems. For example, a woman younger than 35 who was suffering from severe lupus would get $20 million over the 30-year life of the deal, while a woman suffering the same problem who was 56 or older would get only $1.5 million. A woman under 35 with serious neurological or muscular syndromes would receive $1 million, compared to $800,000 for a woman aged 41 to 45, and $500,000 for a woman 56 or more.

During that time, other smaller manufacturers joined the negotiations and by April 2, when Judge Sam C. Pointer, Jr., accepted the terms of the settlement in Birmingham, Alabama, there were nearly 60 companies involved and a total compensation package of $4.25 billion. The judge set a September 16 deadline for women filing a claim for damages under the deal's Current Disease Compensation Program. Women who had no symptoms but wanted to preserve their right to seek damages under the program had until December 1, 1994, to register. The arrangement applied to U.S. and foreign women who had received their implants before June 1, 1993. These figures are not as generous as they appear, however, for some of the money would never get into the hands of the women seeking compensation. About $1 billion of the pot was set aside for administrative and legal fees. Another $500 million was slotted into a special fund to pay for removal of implants or compensation for ruptured implants, none of it for women outside the United States. Of the remaining $2.7 billion, covering ten conditions, just $1.2

billion, less than half, was to be paid out immediately. The rest would be paid over the next three decades.

Non-American women were at a disadvantage if they signed on for the package. For one thing, Canadian women had until only June 7, 1994, to object to the terms of the settlement or to notify the court that they did not wish to participate. Non-American women who did accept the deal also lost the right to sue the manufacturer; only $32 million, or 3 percent, of the $4.25 billion package was available to women from outside the United States, even though about half the implants sold went to foreign women. (The manufacturers claimed foreign compensation was so low because these women have access to publicly funded health benefits U.S. women don't enjoy.) To make matters worse, timelines were short. Quebec lawyer Yves Lauzon, heading one of two provincial class-action lawsuits against the implant manufacturers, advised women to be wary about agreeing to the deal, warning they could jeopardize their chances of winning better awards by accepting the package.

One of 600 Ontario women involved in a class-action suit against U.S. manufacturers of silicone-gel implants was Jane Bloomfield, a 31-year-old London, Ontario, nurse, co-founder of the 400-member London-based Implant Support Group. She says her health problems started in 1981 when she received a saline-filled implant to correct her malformed left breast. A healthy person before that, she told a Montreal news conference that she soon began suffering migraine headaches and chronic fatigue after she had a silicone-gel prosthesis implanted following a 1989 mastectomy. Her original implant had hardened and was replaced the next year with a silicone model. During the next two years, she had each implant removed and replaced again. "I begged my surgeon to remove them," she said. The final one was removed in April 1993, but only after 14 operations and a total of 80 days in hospital. "My immune system is still out of whack," she said. "No breast implant is safe." The class-action suit continues.

While Canada and Australia have removed silicone-gel implants from the market, and at least 30,000 American women have had breast implants removed since silicone was banned (25,000 are suing manufacturers), thousands of British women, incredibly, are still having them implanted in their breasts. The British medical establishment defiantly dismisses the health risk — in return for handsome profits.

The May 7, 1994, edition of *The Times Magazine* quotes Peter Davis, a plastic surgeon at Harley Street and at St. Thomas's Hospital. Recommended as an expert on breast augmentation by the British Medical Association, Davis said: "The state of play here is that we feel this is a lot of balls. They're [Americans] making up some 'Hertzweiner Chicken Sandwich Syndrome,' some spurious disease that doesn't exist. There is no problem; it's just an American lawyer's dream." Davis has been doing 300 or 400 implants a year for the past 30 years. He does warn women of the risks, but says many are willing to go ahead anyway. "Things have improved a great deal. I used to get 70 percent of patients with hard boobs, but I now get 10 percent. Of course some breasts also get infected, 15 percent lose sensation in the nipple, and some get asymmetric and distorted later on. About 10 percent of implants burst over 10 years. Silicone of any sort bleeds into the body."

Jean Perrin, an antiques dealer in Devon, who now operates an informal telephone hotline for British women experiencing problems with implants, testifies to that. She had hers inserted in 1972, at age 43, after breast-feeding three children. When she got severe arthritis about ten years later, her doctor discovered one silicone implant had ruptured and was slowly leaking into her body. "Later, her second implant burst. The arthritis worsened, she had trouble climbing stairs, and then an undiagnosed virus landed her in hospital," wrote journalist Kate Muir. Perrin had her silicone implants replaced by saline ones, but her discussions with other women told her a number of doctors were ignoring warning signals. "Many women tell me that the surgeons who removed their implants are often totally uncooperative," says Perrin. "I suppose doctors feel that admitting anything is wrong would be impugning their reputations. But they must hear about what's going on abroad. They're turning a deaf ear to what is obvious to everyone else."

Muir points out that since silicone is also used in hundreds of penile and testicular implants every year, men too should be listening for the results of investigations underway at dozens of universities and hospitals into the safety of silicone. "Until full studies are available," she writes, "it would seem sensible for the Department of Health to take precautions, or at least warn women more fully of the risks. Are we dealing with a mass of 'spurious evidence' or a medical establishment in denial? If British experts take on an attitude of jolly reassurance, is it surprising that British women continue to queue up for the operation?"

As a final, bitter postscript to the implant controversy, the *New York Times* published a story on April 7, 1994, showing that Dow Corning had concerns about the silicone implants back in 1975 when its own internal study showed that D4, an agent in the silicone gel, harmed the immune system of mice. Lawyers representing breast-implant patients uncovered the study after sifting through 2 million pages of scientific documents provided by the company as part of a class-action suit against it. Had the study been made public in 1975, it may have prevented the marketing of silicone-gel implants in the first place, and saved millions of women the grief, agony and trauma of this whole sordid episode.

A month later, the newspaper published another story showing that 20 years earlier, Dow Corning had employed two scientific teams who had worked side by side for a decade on the nature of silicones. One group found that some silicones, including the type used in breast implants, were biologically active and that they altered the immune system. The other group concluded silicones were inert and safe for implants. The company accepted the findings of the second group, and pursued a commercial breast-implant business. According to former and present employees, they decided to halt research into the immunological activity of silicone in 1975.

Despite everything, Dr. Richard Mast, director of toxicology and bioscience research at Dow Corning, continues to proclaim the company's innocence.

"We've had 30 years of good results with implants," he said. "We've done a tremendous amount of epidemiology. No definite connection between our products and disease" has been proved.

There are thousands of women who would differ with that opinion.

Back in Canada, by June 1994, women faced such a confusing array of choices they practically had to be lawyers themselves to figure them out. The 30,000 Quebec women who had implants, for example, had until June 17 to opt out of the $4.25 billion global plan (of which only $32 million was set aside for foreign recipients, even though almost half of all implants went to non-American women). If they didn't opt out, they could not seek other legal remedies in the United States or Canada against the companies. They had another choice of joining two class-action suits in Quebec — there are also two in Ontario and one in Manitoba — which may, or may not, ultimately be a better deal. To add to the confusion, there was a stipulation that women now had until December 1, 1994, to opt into the settlement but that they could opt out after that if, because of a large number of claimants, they felt the amount they received was too low. And the manufacturers could also opt out if, in their view, too many women were pursuing independent legal actions against them.

Canadian critics said the corporate deal could mean Canadian women might get as little as $400 in compensation if they accepted the terms, compared to anywhere from $105,000 to $1.4 million for American women. The settlement offer was so blatantly biased against non-American women that in a rare legal move in late July 1994, Canada formally intervened in the case when the federal Department of Justice asked the U.S. District Court in Alabama to increase the share set aside for Canadians. Canada argues that between 4 and 15 percent of the implants were used by Canadian women, so Canada's share should reflect that.

Montreal lawyer Yves Lauzon, heading one of the two Quebec class-action lawsuits — the other was sponsored by the non-profit consumer group, L' Association Coopérative d'Économie Familiale du Centre de Montréal — told the Montreal *Gazette* in June 1994 that Quebec implant recipients "who don't want to sue in the U.S.A. have no advantage in excluding themselves" from the settlement. Lauzon said all Quebec women who received implants made by Dow Corning and Bristol-Myers Squibb were automatically included in the class actions. "Whether they exclude themselves from the U.S. settlement or not, all women maintain their recourses in Quebec," said Lauzon.

And Winnipeg lawyer Bob McRoberts said about 2,000 of the 150,000 Canadian recipients of silicone-filled implants had signed up with his Manitoba class action, registered with a U.S. affiliate of his in Washington. In Calgary, Lori Dobson, a member of I Know/Je Sais, the support-group network for women with faulty implants, told *The Globe and Mail* newspaper that "we are fumbling here in Canada. We are told we can opt in, opt out, join a class-action suit, settle or sue." Faced with the costs of paying for much of the reconstructive surgery and health care of victims of the implants, the governments of Ontario, British Columbia, Manitoba and New Brunswick all retained a U.S. law firm to discover whether there were legal means to get a better deal. The government of Alberta decided to join McRoberts' class-action suit in Manitoba for the same reason.

The situation got even more confusing on June 16, the day before the deadline for women in the United States, when six doctors published a study conducted by the Mayo Clinic in Rochester, New York, in the *New England Journal of Medicine*, which they claimed "found no association between breast implants and the connective-tissue diseases and other disorders that were studied."

Saying case reports "provide the weakest evidence of a cause-and-effect relation," they conducted a population-based, retrospective cohort study among 749 women in Olmsted County, Minnesota, who received implants between January 1, 1964, and December 31, 1991, along with 1,498 community controls. Only five implant recipients and ten of the non-recipients developed any of the connective-tissue diseases or other disorders that the researchers studied. The women were followed for an average of about eight years.

The timing of the publication — one day before the deadline — and the sponsorship of the research raised more than a few eyebrows. The research was supported by a small grant from the National Institutes of Health and by research grants from the American Society of Plastic and Reconstructive Surgery, hardly a dispassionate body when it comes to the field of breast implants. Dr. Sherine Gabriel, leader of the study, said the $175,000 grant from the plastic surgeons paid for most of the research, but insisted it did not in any way affect the study's outcome or how and when the results were made public. She said the manuscript was sent to the journal the previous fall and did not know why they waited until the day before the deadline to publish it.

Nevertheless, the journal ran an exceptionally strongly worded editorial by Dr. Marcia Angell rushing to the defense of the medical establishment and attacking the fact that so many courts have accepted the notion that implants cause these diseases "with so little evidence" to support it. "Despite the lack of published epidemiologic studies," she wrote, "the accumulated weight of anecdotes was taken by judges and juries as tantamount to proof of causation. Multimillion-dollar settlements

117

followed, along with poignant stories in the media and appearances by plaintiffs on talk shows. All this added to the weight of the anecdotes, which in a circular way became accepted by the courts and the public as nearly incontrovertible evidence. Three manufacturers of breast implants finally decided that a lump settlement would be less expensive than to go on losing cases one by one. . . ."

On June 18, the *New York Times* waded in with its editorial view. The paper disagreed with Angell's assertion that the FDA was "overly paternalistic and unnecessarily alarming" in taking the implants off the market two years earlier. Concluding that more research was needed, the *Times* said, "Even in hindsight it is hard to see how the FDA could have ignored the mounting anecdotal evidence that silicone implants were causing harm. The FDA banned the implants not on the grounds that they were unsafe, but that the manufacturers, despite decades of selling the devices, had failed to conduct the studies needed to show the safety and effectiveness of implants. The fact that scientists are still scurrying today to measure those effects is proof that the agency's judgment was right."

And on June 20, Dr. Sidney M. Wolfe, director of the Washington-based Public Citizens' Health Research Group, along with the group's staff attorney Joann C. Mott, wrote a letter to the *Times* saying the study sample in the Mayo Clinic article was too small to be the final word. "If there really was no link between silicone breast implants and disease, tens of thousands of women with silicone-related diseases would have to start believing their medical problems were caused by something else. Unfortunately, thousands of women have well-documented problems, unequivocally caused by silicone implants. There have been more than 10,000 women with reported cases of implant rupture, causing many to experience serious local or regional complications, such as scar tissue formation, severe pain and migration of silicone to adjacent lymph nodes and organs. There is also evidence of delayed diagnosis of breast cancer in women because the implants decrease the ability of mammograms to detect small breast cancers," they wrote.

Wolfe and Mott complained that the researchers, whose report was "greatly oversold" by the *New England Journal of Medicine* and the press, did not even look for such problems since they concentrated only on connective tissue diseases. And because they did not look, they "could not have found them."

The size of the study was also a problem, as Wolfe and Mott pointed out. "Given its sample size, the probability that the Mayo Clinic study would have detected a statistically significant doubling of the risk of connective tissue diseases among women with breast implants was only 31 percent."

After months of study, Birmingham Federal District Court Judge Sam C. Pointer, Jr., granted final approval for the $4.25 billion compensation agreement, the largest product liability settlement in U.S. history. The decision cleared the way for court-appointed administrators to begin deciding where there was enough money to pay the claims. Under the order, the manufacturers had to make their initial payments of more than $900 million in mid-October if no appeals were filed. More than 90,500 women had made claims, including 500 non-Americans, mainly Canadians and Australians. About 15,000 women, including about half those living outside the United States, had already rejected the pact.

Responding to complaints from Canada, Pointer increased the amount available to non-American women from $81 million to $96.6 million, but it still meant that Canadian women could get as little as $400 each and a maximum of $3,000 if they accepted the deal, compared to up to $1.4 million for American women. The judge also specifically excluded women from Australia, Ontario and Quebec from the deal because of their involvement in class actions, giving them six weeks to register if they wanted to sign up for the deal.

Joyce Attis, a Toronto breast-implant recipient and activist, said, "I think it stinks. It's deplorable. It's disgusting. I don't know why the judge thinks Canadian women are expendable." Attis said her implants, which she had removed in 1992, caused her to suffer rheumatoid arthritis, symptoms of lupus and rashes, and led to a hysterectomy.

In October 1994, two new studies — one at the University of Maryland Medical Center, the other at Harvard Medical School — found no evidence linking silicone-gel implants and connective tissue disease.

While scientists, doctors, lawyers, manufacturers and judges can argue forever about statistical probabilities and absolute scientific proof, and experts may dismiss the problems as merely "anecdotal" evidence, those anecdotes have real names and faces and lives, many of which were seriously harmed after the implantation of silicone-gel breast implants.

One of those women is Johanne Morrissette, 30, of Pierrefonds, Quebec. In June 1994, she launched a $207,000 lawsuit against her Montreal plastic surgeon, Dr. Hugo Ciaburro.

She had first received implants in 1986, but in 1991 decided to have an enlargement. Her lawsuit claims that one of the old implants ruptured during the operation and caused liquid to spill into the open wound. The new implants did not fit and Dr. Ciaburro implanted smaller ones, causing her chest cavities to become deformed, she says. Because of that, her two breasts were not symmetrical. The right one was pointed up, while the left slumped down. She also experienced excruciating pain.

"I was afraid of cancer, obviously," Morrissette told a Montreal *Gazette* reporter. "I underwent the mammograms for a while, but they found nothing."

The suit claims Morrissette was embarrassed by her physical appearance at a time in her life when she was single and looks were important to her. When she went to the emergency room at Notre Dame Hospital in July 1991, doctors found inflammation of the right breast. For months afterwards, she says, it was subject to leaks from her wounds.

"Contrary to all expectations, [Morrissette] was left with serious scars extremely visible and painful," the suit states.

While her experiences may not be real enough to convince a peer-review group at the Mayo Clinic or the *New England Journal of Medicine*, they are a reality for her, and similar painful ordeals have disrupted the lives of tens of thousands of women around the world who have had problems with silicone-gel breast implants and are simply demanding justice.

6 Candid Cameras

WHEN DR. ANTHONY MILLER'S SEVEN-year, $20 million National Breast Screening Study (NBSS) of 90,000 women was released in October 1992, the medical establishment went ballistic.

The battle continues.

Why? The answer, alas, has more to do with big bucks than good science.

Mammography, you see, is big business.

Although it is only one form of breast-cancer screening, it is one of the most prevalent. Other forms of screening include breast self-examination (BSE), breast palpitation by a physician, thermography, ultrasound and magnetic resonance imaging (MRI). The last three haven't caught on because thermography is seen as unreliable, ultrasound is insensitive and MRI is prohibitively expensive. In the medical community, and in the minds of most politicians, mammography is supreme.

So by concluding that regular mammograms for women under 50 were not only unnecessary, but could actually be harmful — and even casting doubt on the medical shibboleth that mammograms by themselves save lives of women over 50 — Miller's study threatened to undercut a multi-billion-dollar industry directly and loosen the planks of political platforms that use support for widespread mammography to demonstrate that politicians are fighting the scourge of breast cancer.

Even before the study was released, some preliminary findings made their way into the media purporting to show that mammograms even increased mortality by 50 percent in younger women, prompting this headline in *The Sunday Times* of London: "Women Who Have Breast Scanning Are More Likely to Die of Cancer." Miller and the study's deputy director, Dr. Cornelia Baines, have since put that charge to rest, but not before critics pounced on it to malign the entire study. Steven Feig of Jefferson Medical College in Philadelphia told *Science* magazine in May 1992, for example: "It would be a tragedy if younger women were dissuaded from having mammograms because of mistaken results from a flawed study." And Dr. Peter Scholefield, special adviser to the chief executive officer of the National Cancer Institute of Canada and secretary to the policy advisory group appointed by the NCI and the Department of Health and Welfare to assist the survey, said Miller was "unethical" in discussing the findings before they were officially released. "It is most unfortunate," he told *The Toronto Star*. One reason he gave for his concern was curious, however. "This country is about to embark on an $80 million a year screening program. There are tremendous stakes involved here."

Baines responded that "those of us who believe that there is still no compelling evidence to support breast screening programs for women under 50 years of age sometimes feel that we are sailing in the eye of a hurricane."

The debate over mammography has polarized large segments of the medical community as well as breast-cancer activists and politicians. Much of the disagreement is based on conflicting scientific evidence, but it goes well beyond science into politics and profit. Not all defenders of mammography are motivated by profit, of course, but many seem to be, just as politicians pushing these machines often appear to be pandering to the gods of the instant fix, the magical, high-tech answer to a disease we can't understand and often can't defeat.

Mammography has its legitimate place, but universal, frequent mammography programs may prove to be more damaging than helpful, particularly when young women are routinely tested, even those in their 40s. For women over 50, the evidence for annual testing is stronger, but for premenopausal women, who tend to be more likely to have regular mammograms than older women, the bulk of scientific evidence is against them.

One of the major issues in mammography is cost. Is it worth the cost, or could some of the money being poured into machines be better spent researching prevention? Considerable evidence shows that often breast self-examination or, better still, breast palpitation by a doctor, is just as effective and considerably cheaper. If mammography did reduce the death rate, as its supporters claim, the critics would be muted. But there is considerable science supporting a viewpoint contrary to the claims of mammography advocates on just how effective it really is in helping women survive.

Still, for politicians trying to decide where to invest scarce public resources, and being buffeted on all sides by breast-cancer activists demanding action, mammography offers an easy response. Just as old-time politicians constantly built new roads to demonstrate their commitment to the electorate, today's politicians are buying new machines to visibly provide evidence of their fight against breast cancer.

The virulence of the criticism of Miller's report is a stark reminder of just how divisive the issue has become. Asked about this criticism, Miller said some of it was "intemperate, but only by those people with preconceived notions that were challenged by this research. When you challenge someone's cherished beliefs, there is a tendency to shoot the messenger — and there were some pretty strong interest groups that were challenged by this study. The American Cancer Society had based an entire program and philosophy on the recommendation of mammograms for women under the age of 50. And then there were the radiologists, and General Electric.

"Whenever you are in a highly-politicized field like breast cancer research, you are bound to find this. . . . When people make their living at a certain practice, and research shows many patients do not need a certain common treatment, you will be attacked."

Sound a bit too cynical? Well, witness two *unsigned* articles in the March 9, 1994, edition of the *Journal of the American Medical Association*. The first trumpets the glorious news that they may have found a way to entice even more younger women to attend mammography clinics. "Tailored letters and telephone calls may emerge as effective new weapons in the stepped-up fight against breast cancer. The tactics can't come quickly enough," writes the author, adding that according to the National Center for Health Statistics in Hyattsville, Maryland, the number of women over 40 receiving a mammogram in the past year nearly doubled, from 17 to 33 percent between 1987 and 1990. That, according to Dr. Nancy Breen, an economist at the National Cancer Institute's Applied Research Branch in Bethesda, Maryland, and co-author of an analysis on mammography statistics, is "the good news." As she puts it, "the figures suggest something out there is working."

The "bad news," however, is that two-thirds of women over 40 did not have a mammogram the previous year, and 38 percent had never had one. "The women we really need to target now are those with lower levels of education and those who are poor," said Breen.

The second article in the same edition of the journal reports that all 10,000 mammography facilities in the United States were given until October 1 to meet new federal quality standards and be certified by the U.S. Food and Drug Administration in order to stay in business. This touches on the fact that many of these facilities have not been meeting high professional standards. In many instances, machines designed for other things are being used for mammography, untrained clerical helpers are doing the tests and unskilled people reading them.

The article cites FDA Commissioner Dr. David Kessler making the scientifically debatable claim that "good screening mammograms, taken in time, interpreted by an experienced physician, and, if necessary, followed by appropriate treatment, can reduce breast cancer mortality in older women by 30 percent providing that the mammogram is of high quality, produced by a competent technologist operating specially designed, well-maintained equipment, and read by a trained physician." Several earlier scientific studies did attribute such impressive life-saving numbers to mammography, but more current studies, including

Miller's, have cast enough serious doubt upon those rosy predictions that you might expect the FDA chief to be more circumspect.

In the interests of improving mammography in the United States, the FDA began last January to hire and train the first of the 250 to 300 inspectors it says will be responsible for policing those facilities when inspections begin in October. While nobody can quarrel with tougher standards — though after being used on millions of women for two decades, it's about time — experience in the enforcement of medical standards is not reassuring.

In October 1994, Kessler, calling it "a major step up in quality," announced 9,700 U.S. mammography clinics met the new standards. The remaining 1,300 did not, however, and had been warned by letter. Critics complained that the *standards* were too low and still meant improperly trained doctors, inadequate quality controls and wild fluctuations in the amount of radiation used, from too low to be useful to too high to be safe.

A graphic example of how regulations and practice often fail to mesh is contained in a May 2, 1994, article in the *Wall Street Journal* showing that despite the toughly worded regulations of the Safe Medical Devices Act requiring hospitals and doctors to disclose malfunctions of medical equipment, the law is often ignored. Since 1985, manufacturers of such devices have been required to report problems, but scores of them haven't bothered. And it's not just the small, fly-by-night operations either. FDA inspectors discovered that even industry leaders such as C.R. Bard Inc. didn't report 229 incidents involving its cardiac angioplasty catheters, and Eli Lilly & Co Cardiac Pacemakers Inc. unit didn't disclose more than 600 patient problems related to its insulin infusion pump. Realizing they couldn't count on the manufacturers to rat on their own shortcomings — why would they ever have thought they could? — the U.S. government passed a law in 1990 requiring hospitals and doctors to report problems, but in a February 1994 letter to Representative John Dingell, the General Accounting Office, Congress's investigative arm, said hospitals and other health providers were largely disregarding the law. The Colorado Department of Health, for example, visited 175 health-care facilities and found only 36 percent of them fully complying and only 26 percent of personnel understood their legal reporting requirements under the law.

Fact is, there are 14,000 mammography machines installed in the United States alone and thousands more in Canada, Europe and elsewhere. According to an analysis by the National Cancer Institute in the United States, that's two to three times more than are needed. About 24 million mammograms are performed each year in the United States, 90 percent of them routine screenings on asymptomatic women. General Electric sells more than $100 million a year in mammography machines, and Du Pont is a leader in sales of mammography film. Both companies actively market mammography to younger women, despite the apparent scientific risks involved. One Du Pont television ad, for example, claims the company's new film "makes it safer to start mammography early." Both companies also contribute to the American Cancer Society, which, incredibly, continues to advise women in their 40s to have regular mammograms, despite significant scientific evidence to the contrary, and despite the recent decision by the National Cancer Institute to stop advising mammograms for women under 50.

It is, in fact, the practice of entrepreneurship not just by corporations but by doctors themselves that contributes substantially to the problems associated with the excessive use of mammography. Toronto's Dr. Miller cautions, "Entrepreneurship is not always backed up by good, solid science. . . . In the United States, the women are really organized politically to put pressure for breast cancer control programs. And so, everybody is desperate to come forward with something that works. But the panic or political pressure puts people at risk of coming on a bandwagon prematurely.

"Entrepreneurship in medicine creates false expectations. And when the expectations are not delivered, it really is a form of fraud. The pressure to find cures for everything I think contributes to some of the entrepreneurship. And, also, some of it is just desperation. And some of it — even among the professions — represents hope that is not always justified by the science," said Miller.

He adds that most physicians are conscientiously trying to follow national guidelines, "But if the guidelines that come down from on high are flawed — which is the case in using mammograms under age 50 — then, those guys down in the trenches are going to do a hell of a lot of unjustified medicine. And that is precisely what has been going on."

In a 1993 paper accepted by the Surgical Oncology Clinics of North America on public expectations of breast-cancer control and the law, Dr. John Spratt of the University of Louisville School of Medicine argued, "When overpromotion of the idea that the probability of dying from cancer can be reduced by screening and earlier diagnosis, but the desired objectives are not attainable, then the ground is laid for malpractice suits. In the case of breast cancer, the malpractice claims problem has become significant, while in parallel, screening has become more widespread." Spratt said a recent review of Blue Cross/Blue Shield payments for mammograms in Kentucky "revealed that three-fifths of all mammograms were being performed on the wrong age group, including patients as young as age 8."

Miller called it "criminal" to begin mammography on girls that young. "The younger you start exposing the breast to radiation, the higher the probability you are going to produce a breast cancer over the course of a life span. . . . The thing about radiation is, the effects are cumulative over time. And if you start doing low-dose mammograms at a very young age, you accumulate a rather significant dose if screening is done annually."

That, of course, is not what the radiologists and others in the mammography field want to hear.

Miller's major study found that mammography can certainly detect more tumors in their earlier, smaller stages, but it does not decrease death rates, thus calling into question the cancer establishment's longstanding claim that early detection is the key to surviving breast cancer. The trial, involving women in 15 Canadian cities, was divided into two parts. The first, the largest ever of its kind, sought to measure the value of annual screening among 50,430 women aged 40 to 49 — a combination of mammography, physical examination by a doctor or trained nurse, and breast self-examination. It found no evidence that screening for breast cancer is "effective" for these women, confirming other recent studies that drew the same conclusions.

The second part of the trial, studying women aged 50 to 59 having an annual mammogram plus a medical exam, concluded that these women don't do any better than women who already have their breasts examined each year by a doctor. In a commentary accompanying the studies, Toronto epidemiologist Dr. Antoni Basinski writes: "For mammography, the salient question is, does the treatment of disease detected by mammography prolong life or does detection by mammography prolong the burden of living with the disease? That an increased rate of detection leads to an increased lifespan has not been shown."

Dr. Christopher Adey, director of radiology for the Ottawa-Carleton region of the Ontario Breast Screening Program, said the Miller study was "grossly" flawed and should be ignored. "It's just infuriating. Numerous other studies have clearly demonstrated that routine screen mammography reduces disease and death for women over 50 if they have these cancers picked up early."

Adey said the study was flawed because substandard equipment was used, saying mammography technology has been revolutionized since the mid-1980s when the study was conducted. Miller counters that improvements in radiation were incorporated into the study. In addition, studies that the advocates of regular mammography use to support their position were conducted many years earlier on equipment considerably less sophisticated than that used by Miller and his team.

Another critic of the study was Dr. Linda Warren, executive director of the Screening Mammography Program of British Columbia, the only Canadian province that still advocates regular mammography for women aged 40 to 50. Speaking at the annual meeting of the Radiological Society of North America in a Chicago meeting in December 1992, Warren asserted that screening mammography does reduce the death rate from breast cancer, but it takes time to prove it. She said only 13 percent of the 455 cancers detected in the B.C. program had spread to the lymph nodes; of the 70 younger women, only 6 percent had lymph-node involvement. She said it takes longer than seven years, the duration of the study, to show a drop in mortality.

Not all her B.C. colleagues agree, however. Vancouver's Dr. Charles Wright, vice-president of medicine at Vancouver General Hospital, who has long argued that screening mammography is not cost-effective, told the Vancouver *Sun*, "There's no dispute that mammography picks up the disease much earlier than it would otherwise be picked up. The problem is, it doesn't help you any." Wright said the $5.2 million spent on breast screening by the B.C. government would be better spent on basic breast-cancer research. "To me, it's a dreadful tragedy that we should be pouring multi-millions of dollars into a non-solution. For God's sake, let's put some money into something that might bear fruit."

Miller, of course, was not the first person to scrutinize the true value of mammography. Just as mammography was reaching its peak as the latest technological answer to the unanswerable, it became the subject of a devastating critique entitled "False Premises and False Promises of Breast Cancer Screening" in the August 10, 1985, edition of *The Lancet*. In the article, Peter Skrabanek of the department of community health, Trinity College, University of Dublin, Ireland, argued that "the evidence that breast cancer is incurable is overwhelming. The philosophy of breast cancer screening is based on wishful thinking that early cancer is curable cancer, though no-one knows what is 'early.' Unable to admit ignorance and defeat, cancer propagandists have now turned to blaming the victims: they consume too much fat, they do not practise self-examination, they succumb to 'irrational' fears and delay reporting the early symptoms. It would appear that no woman needs to die of breast cancer if she reads and heeds the leaflets of the cancer societies and has her breasts examined regularly. Adherence to these myths and avoidance of reality undermines the credibility of the medical profession with the public."

More recent studies confirm Skrabanek's findings.

The December 1992 *Annals of Internal Medicine*, the journal of the American College of Physicians, editorialized that "groups recommending routine breast cancer screening in women under age 50 should review their recommendations . . . medical scientists and physicians do not do modern women a service by promulgating a screening practice that medical science has not been able to substantiate after so many tries."

At that time, most European countries had already opposed regular mammography for women under 40 because there is no scientifically demonstrated benefit, leaving the United States, and the Canadian province of British Columbia, as almost the only jurisdictions where it was being recommended. Indeed, the American Cancer Society recommendation was a baseline mammography at about age 35, followed by regular mammography every year or two at 40 and an annual mammography at 50 and older. Charlotte Gray, a contributing editor to the *Canadian Medical Association Journal*, wrote in the February 1993 edition that part of the resistance to Miller's mammography study had little to do with science, but much to do with the fact that "screening for breast cancer is a multimillion dollar industry here, and younger women are the best customers." She cited a *New York Times* interview with Dr. Larry Kessler, chief of applied research at the National Cancer Institute, saying as many as 40 percent of women in their 40s have the test regularly, which costs $50 to $100. That compared to 35 percent of women in their 50s, 27 percent in their 60s and fewer than 20 percent in their 70s having regular mammograms.

"Telling all those 40-something women that a mammogram is not going to affect their chances of dying of breast cancer, despite endless glossy magazine articles urging them to be screened, would shrink the mammography market dramatically," Gray wrote.

She also quotes Esther Rome, a member of the Boston Women's Health Book Collective and co-author of *The New Our Bodies, Ourselves*, saying, "I think some of the resistance to the Canadian study springs from the attitude among doctors here that they must do something, particularly if they have the technology, even if they cannot affect the outcome of any condition they diagnose."

Rome says that for any women whose mammogram found cancer, the program is worth every cent. "But it isn't so great for the woman whose mammogram revealed a suspicious lump, and who has gone through the anxiety, costly surgery and scarring only to discover that the lump was not cancerous."

Although mammography is the only practical test to detect breast cancer before it is palpable, early detection does not guarantee cure. It merely leads to longer survival times due to the lead-time bias. According to Peter Skrabanek of the University of Dublin, "this is often confused with better prognosis and lower mortality." For example, the "improvement" in five-year survival rates between 1950 and 1975 of about 10 percent in 97 percent of cancers "can be explained by the fact that cancers are diagnosed an average six months earlier." Thus, he argues, mammography is very expensive: $195,000 per cancer detected according to a 1981 Philadelphia study, or £80,000 per life saved according to a 1985 British study.

For mammography, Skrabanek says, "Informed consent should be the rule but it is rarely sought." He adds that screening programs, "with accompanying propaganda from cancer societies and media, may heighten the level of cancerphobia in society, with little to show in return. This could have an adverse effect on the credibility of the medical profession. . . . The profession has become a prey to its own wishful thinking."

As a result, the cancer/medical establishments don't exactly trumpet the down side of treatments, which makes it difficult for women to make informed decisions. Take for example a six-page brochure entitled "Commonly Asked Questions About Breast Health," published by the Canadian Cancer Society (CCS) and currently distributed to women across the country. Among several questions on mammography, and consistently reassuring answers, the CCS asks: "Is radiation exposure from a mammogram dangerous?" The answer: "There is no risk at all to women who have mammograms done with new state-of-the-art equipment which delivers very low doses of radiation." Their advice to women under 50 is to "consult with their family physician as to when or if a mammogram is recommended."

In February 1993, two major consensus conferences were held to assess the value of screening mammography for women under age 50 — with two distinctly different results.

In Paris, the European Society of Mastology recommended that regular screening mammography be reserved for women over 50. In New York, however, the American Cancer Society reaffirmed its traditional support for screening women, beginning at age 40.

Dr. Michael Baum, professor of surgery at the Royal Marsden Hospital, London, and Ismail Jatoi, a clinical fellow at the same hospital, wrote about this disparity in the December 4, 1993, edition of the *British Medical Journal*. They pointed out that mammography can be harmful for younger women and that these women "must be properly informed about the potential for harm as well as for benefit before screening." Unfortunately, that rarely happens.

The two writers wanted to explain why the Europeans and the Americans would hold such different positions, given that they both studied the same scientific data.

"Putting aside any uncharitable suggestions concerning profit motives and a return on the capital costs of mammographic equipment, and assuming that the data are understood equally well we must conclude that the responses are fuelled by culture differences on either side of the Atlantic.

"American culture seems to dictate that some sort of medical intervention is better than nothing, and Americans are reluctant to accept the conclusions of clinical trials which fail to support a commonsense view. Europeans are more willing to accept these trials at face value and in the case of screening mammography evidence so far shows no significant benefit for screening women under the age of 50. But although evidence of benefit is lacking the greater concern is whether screening younger women does more harm than good."

They also underscore another serious danger, rarely discussed by physicians, about the impact of mammography on women carrying the gene for A-T (ataxia-telangiectasia), a rare nervous-system disorder that affects both sexes. It occurs in about one in 100,000 people, but one in 5,000 is a carrier of the gene. In 1991, four University of North Carolina researchers announced that women who are carriers of the gene are six times more likely to develop breast cancer when exposed to even low doses of radiation than carriers who were not exposed. Because up to 1 million American women may be A-T carriers, the investigators estimated the gene may account for 7 to 14 percent of all U.S. breast-cancer cases. Baum and Jatoi write that women with a family history of the disease "should seek alternatives to mammography, but most carriers have no family history."

Probably the only unrealistic aspect of Baum and Jatoi's academic paper is their suggestion that profit may not play a major role in the continued promotion of mammography in the United States. It is unlikely, for example, that they have been to Los Gatos, an affluent California town of 28,700 on the northern slopes of the Santa Cruz mountains, 52 miles south of San Francisco. The town's largest employer is a private hospital with 700 employees.

Los Gatos is also home to Mammography Plus, a private clinic established by 65 physician-investors in 1988, and boasting three X-ray rooms equipped with the most up-to-date General Electric technology and ultrasound equipment and employing a staff radiologist. An estimated 12,000 X-rays are performed each year at Mammography Plus for a basic fee of $135 for a mammogram of both breasts.

"We have patients come to us from as far away as Oregon because we provide such a good service," explains Tricia Baker, the clinic's business manager. "We had a patient just the other day who was born in 1899. She was very sweet."

Just three months after it launched its fee-for-service trade, the physicians who had invested in Mammography Plus received their first dividend cheques, totalling $300 per share. This represented "approximately 50 percent annualized return on your investment" according to a quarterly business report distributed to shareholders. The dividend cheques were accompanied by a detailed account of how many patients each physician-investor had referred to the clinic in its first 90 days of operation, and an enthusiastic letter that urged doctors to boost the traffic for mammograms at the clinic.

"One physician has referred 115 patients during the first quarter," the letter stated. "A fine example for us to follow." Business partners in the clinic were also cautioned that 20 percent of their fellow investors had ordered just five or fewer mammograms at the clinic, while another 20 percent had referred ten or fewer. They were all urged to increase the number of patient referrals. "The long term goal of this partnership is the responsibility of each of us."

Dr. Donald Cariani, one of two obstetrician-gynecologists who co-authored the letter to the investors, is now retired and, along with the 65 physician-investors associated with the clinic, refused an interview for this book. But in 1989, Cariani told the *San Jose Mercury News* that physician-investors who referred patients to Mammography Plus had always conformed with American Cancer Society guidelines on the use of mammograms and breached no ethical guidelines. "We were not encouraging over-utilization," he said. "If people order mammograms according to the American Cancer Society guidelines, then we'd like them to refer to our center."

Tricia Baker said the doctors don't want to be interviewed because, "Nobody wants to be misquoted. In the past, people have been interviewed and the words that were printed in the newspaper were not what our doctors had said."

Then again, California physicians who have profited handsomely from patient referrals to private clinics like Mammography Plus have cause for hesitation in encouraging public scrutiny of their practice.

Since 1985, California has joined what has evolved into a national campaign to regulate the trade in patient referrals to clinics in which physicians have a financial interest. Initially, the state adopted legislation that obliged doctors to disclose significant financial interests to patients when referring them to an outside clinic. But effective in January 1995, California will adopt a much tougher measure, including a $5,000 fine, restricting the practice altogether. The passage of these restrictions followed a long and often bitter campaign of opposition by the state's mighty medical establishment.

Proposed restrictions on patient referrals to private clinics were initially defeated on the floor of the state Senate in 1992 after what the bill's chief sponsor, Assemblyman Jackie Speier, described as "powerful and persuasive" opposition from the California Medical Association (CMA).

The CMA spends about $2 million a year lobbying Sacramento lawmakers to restrict their activities to consideration of agreeable legislation. The association remains one of the largest contributors to political campaigns in California, and has generously rewarded friendly legislators with large donations while stripping funds for those state officials considered to be enemies of the CMA. What did the CMA think of restrictions on patient referrals? The association's chief Sacramento lobbyist denounced the proposal as excessive, while a former CMA president and physician-investor in a Santa Monica clinic told the legislators to, "Come on. Get off my back."

Speier, now serving her fourth consecutive term, became the first woman to be elected in the 19th Assembly District (San Mateo County) in November 1986. Her husband, a prominent physician, was tragically killed in a traffic accident early in 1994. During her first election campaign, the CMA was the only special-interest group that supported her. And in the 1990 election, it gave generously, contributing $7,806 to her campaign. By 1992, however, because of her support for the physicians' self-referral bill, the CMA chipped in only $380, enough to buy memberships for a couple of doctors in a breakfast meeting club Speier holds in her district.

Speier, born in San Francisco, the daughter of a German immigrant father and an Armenian mother, is no stranger to confrontation. As legal counsel to California Congressman Leo Ryan in 1978, she accompanied

Ryan on a fact-finding mission to Guyana to prove the activities of cult leader Reverend Jim Jones. Ryan was murdered by Jones' followers and Speier was hit by five bullets while fleeing the site of the Jonestown Massacre. Later that day, 911 cult members died at Jonestown.

While the 35,000-member CMA didn't use live ammunition or spike her drinks with poison, she did face what she called "adamant" opposition from them. In a September 14, 1993, letter to California Governor Pete Wilson, Speier wrote, "War is like politics, except in war you can be killed only once — in politics, many times over."

In a November 1993 speech to the California Clinical Laboratory Association, a group that supported her legislation, Speier said, "Within the CMA I have been described as a draconian 'expletive deleted.' I have received calls from physicians who told my secretary to strap me to an examining table and do a pap smear and have me wait for the results from an outside lab." Her office was sent a crude caricature depicting a helpless physician impaled by a "Jackie Spear." It had been publicly posted in a state hospital. Her husband was "hounded as he worked in the emergency room" by fellow physicians who accused him of "sleeping with the enemy." She described the CMA as an "800-pound gorilla" and accused the association of waging a "systematic campaign of misinformation" against her legislation.

State Senator Daniel Boatwright, chairman of the Senate's Business and Professions Committee, vehemently opposed Speier's bill. He received $18,318 from the CMA as a campaign contribution in 1992, a fact disclosed by an advocacy group friendly to Speier's initiative. And, in pushing for support for legislative reforms in committee, Speier flourished an April 11, 1991, confidential letter in which Nick Thurmond, the director of the now-defunct Thurmond, Federal, Bartok Radiology & Imaging Medical Group, Inc. in San Francisco, offered a physician a Lexus 400 for patient referrals. "If your mind is definitely made up and nothing will change it, then so be it," Thurmond wrote. "It goes without saying, everything stays strictly confidential between us — including the offer of a new Lexus . . ."

In her September 1993 letter to Governor Wilson asking for his signature on the Physician Ownership and Referral Act of 1993 — which, after losing the first round now becomes law — Speier referred to a Consumers Union report that California wastes at least $17 billion on unnecessary medical treatment and inefficient administration, and one of the chief examples cited "as a cause of squandered resources was the massive proliferation of physician owned 'joint ventured' facilities in California."

About the same time, the state's Inspector-General found that doctors in California who owned clinical labs ordered 45 percent more lab tests for Medicare patients than for non-physician-owned labs. In 1992, Maryland Center for Health Policy found that physician-owned MRI (magnetic resonance imaging) joint ventures in California resulted in a 5 percent increase in testing — at an extra cost of about $215 million a year.

A November 19, 1992, article on joint ventures in radiation therapy by Dr. Jean M. Mitchell and Dr. Jonathan H. Sunshine, which appeared in the prestigious *New England Journal of Medicine*, strongly recommended "legislation to ban ownership of joint ventures by referring physicians." The authors concluded that joint ventures have adverse effects on patients' access to care and "appear to increase the use of services and costs substantially." Studying the situation of free-standing radiation-therapy centers in Florida, the authors found that for every 1,000 Medicare enrollees the submitted charges for radiation therapy exceeded the overall U.S. average by 42 percent ($13,290 vs. $9,752) and that the number of procedures at these clinics was 58 percent higher than in the rest of the country.

In her letter to Wilson, Speier pooh-poohed the argument offered by her opponents that physician-owned facilities improve access to technology for patients who might otherwise be inconvenienced by unavailable equipment. "Nothing could be further from the truth. . . . To date, there are 413 MRI units in our state which represents one MRI for every 57,000 persons living in California. To put this number in perspective, there are some 25 MRI machines in all of Canada, one machine for every 1.5 million persons." She said one southern California radiologist recently reported that in the ten-mile radius in which he works in Los Angeles, there are 37 MRI clinics. Each machine costs about $2.2 million. "In other words, the MRI clinics are purposely located in the most profitable and densely populated locations in the state to guarantee a high volume of utilization. They are not being established in the more remote locations because of medical need as some opponents have led many to believe.

"California is not alone in this abuse. Most American cities are now awash in MRI machines. Indeed, the U.S. has 3,200 of the 5,800 MRI systems worldwide. The number of scans administered in the U.S. has risen to 7.5 million from 2.9 million in five years." Germany, whose health system is generally considered to be among the most advanced and efficient systems in the world, has about 800 of the MRI machines — about one-quarter the U.S. total.

A 1983 study by the Michigan Blue Cross and Blue Shield comparing price and usage of 20 doctor-owned labs versus 20 independent labs showed that the average payment for physician-owned labs was $44.82 — almost 80 percent higher than the average at independent labs. In addition, the average number of tests per patient was 3.76 at the independent lab and 6.23, or almost double, at the physician-owned labs.

A March 1, 1989, article in the *Wall Street Journal*, headed, "Doctor-Owned Labs Earn Lavish Profits In a Captive Market," documented the case of William Birnbaum, a radiologist in Irvine, California, who in 1985 was confronted by a colleague suddenly demanding a share of his profit. When Birnbaum refused he was told his colleague and other physicians in the same medical building would stop referring patients to him for X-rays and other tests. Three years later, in a building next door, these doctors created a separate radiology practice in which they each owned shares. Practically nonexistent just a few years earlier, these arrangements rapidly spread across the United States. The *Journal* quotes Terrance Gill, a consultant who helps set up such deals, bluntly describing the phenomenon in a tape-recorded seminar for physicians a few years earlier. "Stickup, extortion, bandit[ry], anything else you want to call it, but it's a reality out there, folks." Physicians were soon supplementing their incomes with profits from their interests in laboratories, X-ray centers and other medical facilities where they sent their patients. They earned up to 100 percent and more a year on investments of $5,000 to $100,000. Physicians who bought partnership shares in 1986 at $25,000 each in the MRI of Elizabeth, New Jersey, for example, received a financial report last June showing a six-month return of $248,442, or almost $10,000 a share. This amounts to an annualized return of nearly 80 percent after just two years of operation.

Many physicians get involved in such ventures in an attempt to close the income gap between themselves and surgeons and other specialists.

In 1990, according to the American Medical Association, the median income for general family practitioners was $93,000. For pediatricians, it was $100,000. That seems not bad at all until you consider that the median income for surgeons and radiologists was $200,000. And according to a study by the Medical Group Management Association, cardiovascular surgeons in group practice averaged about $500,000 in 1990.

In December 1991, the American Medical Association (AMA) Council on Ethical and Judicial Affairs said, "In general, physicians should not refer patients to a health care facility outside their office practice at which they do not directly provide care or services when they have an investment interest in the facility." In June 1992, however, the AMA's House of Delegates adopted a new policy allowing doctors to make such referrals if patients are first informed of the doctor's financial interest in the facility and of any available alternatives.

As things stand, many doctors are still reaping the benefits of such arrangements, but the situation may be short-lived. At least 20 states have adopted "physician-referral bans" or have similar legislation pending.

Individual physicians looking for profits are not the only promoters of frequent mammograms. The process first gained national popularity in the United States during the 1970s as a result of increased funding earlier in the decade sparked by President Richard Nixon's declared "War on Cancer." Breast cancer in particular sprung to national prominence with the highly publicized news that Betty Ford and Happy Rockefeller had the disease. At the time, there was limited scientific justification for expanding mammography, although a few small, early studies did conclude it was helpful in early detection. Others, which showed no particular benefit, were ignored. This heightened interest in the disease combined with widespread American faith that science and technology could conquer all — a fall-out from the manned moon landing — resulted in a situation where public sentiment was running high that the magic cure for cancer was just around the next corner. This public excitement sparked the Breast Cancer Detection Demonstration Project (BCDDP), which the organizers later admitted "was not originally designed as a research or investigational project; no provision was made for systematic collection of data."

Still, over 280,000 women were recruited for this project with no warnings about the potential risk of induction of breast cancer by the test that was supposed to detect it, particularly in the early days when much higher doses of radiation were used. Early on, the U.S. National Academy of Sciences warned that the women were being exposed to doses that could cause more cancers in the long run than could be prevented by the program, but it took considerable time to force the industry to dramatically reduce the levels of radiation doses. What isn't known is how many women lost their lives as a result of that shameful exercise in public relations. It should, however, serve as a sobering reminder that at any given time the accepted wisdom of the medical establishment isn't necessarily in the best interests of the patients.

But the die was cast and, possibly because there was nothing that offered any more hope, mammography quickly shot into the public consciousness and sparked the introduction in several countries of national screening programs. Over the years, a whole series of major clinical trials have offered a mixed bag of results on mammography.

The first randomized trial, the Health Insurance Plan (HIP) was conducted in New York during the 1960s and followed the participants for 18 years. It involved 62,000 women, half of them chosen at random to receive mammography and physical examination. Four annual screenings were scheduled for each participant, and after five years, an encouraging 40 percent reduction in breast-cancer mortality was seen in women aged 50 to 64. For those under 50, no reduction was seen until much later, and researchers still can't agree whether the difference was significant. While the HIP study sparked considerable growth in the process, some researchers now believe that because it was conducted in the early stages of mammography, as much as 70 percent of the reduction in mortality rates resulted from the physical examination component of the screening.

The aforementioned BCDDP came next, followed by two major Swedish trials — the two-county study, involving more than 133,000 women, and the Malmö trial, studying about 42,000 women. In the over-50 group in the two-county study, a 40 percent reduction in breast-cancer mortality was found after seven years, with no change for those under 50. At 10 years after initiation of screening in the Malmö trial, the reduction in mortality for women aged 55 to 69 on entry was 21 percent. In a trial started in Stockholm in the early 1980s, where 40,000 women were screened every two years and 20,000 allocated to a control group, an 8 percent reduction was seen in mortality rates for women aged 50 to 64, but again, no reduction was seen for those under 50.

Around the same time, the U.K. Trial of Early Detection of Breast Cancer Group conducted a nonrandomized study for women aged 45 to 64. It included an annual physical examination and biennial mammography for some, breast self-examination teaching by classes for others and no screening for still others. One component of the study found lower breast-cancer mortality in the sixth and seventh years, in the mammography and physical examination groups. But the Edinburgh component of the U.K. study, a randomized trial involving about 45,000 women, found little difference in mortality between the screened group and the control group after seven years.

In addition to the controlled studies, case-control studies took place in two cities in the Netherlands — Utrecht and Nijmegen — and in Florence, Italy. All of them showed some evidence of mammograms reducing mortality rates in women over 50, but not in younger women.

In the United Kingdom, where breast cancer remains the leading cause of female death (15,000 a year), the government got on the screening program bandwagon after the 1987 publication of findings of the Forrest Committee, led by Professor Sir Patrick Forrest. Although Forrest pointed out that "mammography is not a good screening test," the report went on to say that despite problems associated with it, "screening mammography can prolong life to a greater extent than any other change in the management of breast cancer." On the strength of this analysis, the United Kingdom set up a national breast-screening program. The Forrest Committee was set up in June 1985. The final report was completed in 1986 but not published until February 1987 when Secretary of State for Social Services Sir Norman Fowler announced the government had decided to provide for screening every three years for all women aged 50 to 64 in the United Kingdom. "Breast cancer is a major scourge. We believe that these measures will achieve a substantial reduction in the mortality from this disease among women of this age group," said Fowler.

By the mid-1980s, both the American Cancer Society and the American College of Radiology recommended that all women have a baseline mammography at the age of 35 to 40 with follow-up examinations annually or biennially until age 50, and annually thereafter. By that time, the two-county Swedish study had shown great promise, a 31 percent reduction in mortality from breast cancer and a 25 percent reduction in the proportion of Stage 11 or more advanced tumors in the group offered screening mammography every two to three years as compared with those not screened.

Dr. Ferris M. Hall of Beth Israel Hospital in Boston foresaw problems with the increased biopsies that would result from a nationwide screening program in the United States. He wrote about his concerns in the *New England Journal of Medicine* in 1986. The rapid implementation of a nationwide screening program would mean yearly mammograms for almost 50 percent of adult women — eight examinations per radiologist per working day. For surgeons, he said, mammographically suspicious but nonpalpable breast lesions are common. Because of this, however, the number of biopsies at his hospital had already increased to seven a week from just one four years earlier. "Is it reasonable to perform 100, 50, or even 25 breast biopsies, and the accompanying preoperative radiologic breast-localization procedures, in order to discover one nonpalpable carcinoma? In most instances I think not."

Hall concluded that "screening mammography deserves the accolades it has received. It saves lives and I heartily endorse the ACS/ACR recommendations for its use. However, screening mammography is still in its infancy, and we would all like to see it grow in a responsible manner."

Dr. Ruth Berkelman of the Centers for Disease Control, in a letter in the May 29, 1986, *New England Journal of Medicine* gave this response to Hall's article: "Currently available data, however, do not adequately demonstrate a benefit of periodic screening with mammography for women under 50." And Dr. John Spratt of the University of Louisville School of Medicine wrote in the same issue, "Any blanket recommendations about screening must contain disclaimers that recognize the extreme biologic variations in the lethality of breast cancers, the extreme variations in growth rates, and the imperfections in screening techniques. Without these disclaimers, there is a risk that the effectiveness of the screening programs may be exaggerated fraudulently, particularly when any universal benefit is applied."

Others too questioned the widely accepted notion that mammography would save thousands of lives. Dr. Maureen Roberts, who, until her own death from breast cancer, was director of the Edinburgh Breast Screening Project, wrote in an article published posthumously in 1989 in the *British Medical Journal* that "screening is always a second best, an admission of failure of prevention or treatment . . . What can screening actually achieve? Two randomized trials, the Health Insurance Plan and the Swedish two-county trial showed a reduction in mortality of 30 percent in women offered screening. Other trials such as the Malmö, United Kingdom and Edinburgh . . . trials, found a non-significant reduction in mortality. We cannot ignore them and it is not enough to say that our techniques weren't good enough a few years ago but are adequate now.

"We all know that mammography is an unsuitable screening test: it is technologically difficult to perform, the pictures are difficult to interpret, it has a high false positive rate, and we don't know how often to carry it out. We can no longer ignore the possibility that screening may not reduce mortality in women of any age, however disappointing this might be."

Too late. Nobody wants to hear that kind of cautious talk about the wonders of mammography. The United Kingdom was the first country in the European Community to introduce a nationwide breast-screening program, but programs were soon introduced in the Netherlands, Finland, Sweden, Australia, New Zealand and several other European countries.

In Canada, the Canadian Cancer Society, Health and Welfare Canada and the National Cancer Institute of Canada hosted a workshop March 16–17, 1988, with representatives from every part of the country to discuss and develop a Canadian consensus on an early detection program, which includes mammography, physical examination of the breasts by a health-care professional and the teaching and monitoring of breast self-examination through a series of dedicated screening centers. There was little dispute for women aged 50 to 69. For women under 40, however, screening was not recommended. The *Canadian Medical Association Journal* reported the consensus was there was no conclusive evidence that mammography, physical examination or breast self-examination, or any combination of these, can reduce the rate of death from breast cancer in this age group.

In spite of these negative reports, on May 8, 1989, Ontario Health Minister Elinor Caplan announced a screening program for Ontario, Canada's most populous province, saying she could reduce breast-cancer deaths in women aged 50 to 64 by 40 percent by 1995 when the province hopes to have 300,000 women participating. In doing so she had made the typical political response to activism from breast-cancer victims. Under pressure to act, to do something, politicians have seen breast-cancer screening programs based on mammography as a way to point to real spending on breast-cancer prevention without really addressing the cost in human terms of the response.

One person who is highly skilled at calculating human costs is well-known activist Rosalie Bertell, president of the International Institute of Concern for Public Health in Toronto. A former Grey Nun of the Sacred Heart with North American native people in India, Malaysia and the Marshall Islands, Bertell has a doctorate in mathematics as well as two additional post-doctorate degrees. She has written for 97 publications and is author of the 1987 book *No Immediate Danger: Prognosis for a Radioactive Earth*. That same year, in recognition of her 25 years in the cancer prevention and environmental health fields, she was awarded the Right Livelihood Award, the alternative Nobel prize, supported by the Swedish Parliament, Greenpeace and the U.N. Disarmament Commission.

In a paper on the Ontario mammography program entitled "Comments on the Ontario Mammograph Program," Bertell wrote it "should be immediately abandoned as an experiment on human beings, namely 300,000 Ontario women. It should be replaced by a massive educational program for physicians and the public on monthly breast self-examination. There should also be an ethical committee to review such programs in Ontario before they reach the economic and political commitment of the Breast Screening program. All simply routine X-rays should be banned, with decision making on a case by case basis made by the physician and patient."

Calling it "a deliberate program to reduce breast cancer deaths by increasing breast cancer incidence" due to radiation exposure of sensitive breast tissue, Bertell said the exposure "will result in between 15 and 40 breast cancers, 7 to 18 of which will be fatal. . . . About 163 women will have unnecessary breast surgery due to the program, and roughly 10,000 women will have re-tests because of false positive mammograms (where an apparent tumor turns out to be harmless). Roughly eight or nine women will be significantly benefitted by the program because of early detection of a Type A tumor. About 300 women may benefit indirectly because of the educational and consciousness raising aspect of the screening program."

She said the program, "while well intentioned, is ill thought out and likely to cause more harm than good."

In another article on mammography in the Summer 1992 edition of *Mothering*, Bertell wrote that "the public relations effort behind mammography conveys a false sense of benefit, security, and control, and it does so by glibly overlooking the core question: How much X-ray exposure is too much?"

Montreal journalist and breast-cancer activist Sharon Batt, herself a victim of the disease, wrote in the June-July 1992 edition of *This Magazine* that the debates over mammography and breast surgery illustrate how women get caught between warring factions of professionals.

"Before menopause, when one-third of breast cancers occur, breast tissue is dense, so mammograms aren't very accurate. Even after age 50, many mammogram-detected lumps are beyond today's treatment methods. An estimated 30 percent of breast cancer deaths in women aged 50 to 70 could be prevented with detection through mammography every two years. That's a significant number, but hardly justifies the reverence women have been taught to have for this imperfect technology.

"Basic mammogram politics are fairly obvious. The most vocal advocates of routine mammograms for women under 50 are radiologists and companies that make mammography equipment. Provincial governments (who pay for the screening), and many public health groups, cite studies that show regular mammograms don't benefit women in this age group and may cause cancers in hormonally active breast tissue."

Another critic of government-sponsored breast screening, Dr. Richard J. Epstein of the Breast Evaluation Clinic, Dana-Farber Cancer Institute and Department of Medicine, Harvard Medical School, has shown that these programs are not cost-effective. In November 1992 he published a chilling article in the *European Journal of Cancer* entitled, "Does the Breast Cancer Dollar Make Sense?"

Epstein measured the cost-effectiveness of four increasingly common breast-cancer activities: screening mammography in women under 50, breast-conserving therapy, adjuvant chemotherapy for node-negative premenopausal women and management of metastatic disease.

He said the recommendation of the American Cancer Society, the American College of Radiology and the National Cancer Institute for regular mammograms every one to two years for women aged 40 to 49 at an average cost of $125 per two-view mammogram plus $50 to $80 for a follow-up visit to the physician, could cost more than $3 billion a year. "Although the evidence that screening improves the natural history of breast cancer in women aged less than 50 is weak, increasing numbers of lawsuits are being waged and won on the premise that insufficiently vigilant attempts at early detection have prejudiced the outcome of subsequent clinical disease. The Physicians' Insurers Association of America recently reported that alleged delay in breast cancer diagnosis (DBCD) is the single most expensive and second most common cause of medical litigation in the United States, accounting for 27 percent of all cancer-related claims at a mean cost of $211,000 per claim.

". . . Hence, unwittingly or not, the American legal system may be transforming mammography of younger women into a de facto form of life insurance subsidised by health care payers. Mammography works. But does it work well enough to justify current American screening recommendations?"

Clearly the NCI didn't think so. In October 1993 it announced it would no longer recommend regular mammograms for women under 50. Instead, these women should "discuss the appropriateness of a screening mammogram individually with their physicians, taking into account individual risk factors," and continue to have a physical breast exam every year.

As usually happens in medicine, the advocates of mammography for younger women stood firm while evidence against their position continued to mount. In March 1993, a team of New Zealand scientists reported at an NCI meeting that an analysis of international studies on the subject fully supported the conclusions of the controversial Canadian study by Dr. Anthony Miller. That's because in younger women, breast tissue is denser, making it hard to pick up a potential tumor. As women get older, their breasts grow less dense and mammograms are easier to read and more likely to catch a malignancy.

It is ironical, then, that advocacy for mammography has had more effect among younger women than older women. Put another way, women in their 40s, who shouldn't be getting regular mammograms, tend to be more assertive in what they see as prevention, while women in their 60s, who are at much higher risk, are often unaware that they should be having mammograms.

A study on this point published in the June 15, 1992, *Canadian Medical Association Journal* by Dr. Heather Bryant, director of Alberta's screening program, and her research associate Zeva Mah, concluded that more education is needed. They want a change in the behavior of women and physicians to increase the use of breast self-examination, clinical breast examination by a health-care professional and mammographic screening. Quite apart from the obvious self-interest in their conclusions, they discovered in telephone questionnaires with 1,284 Alberta women that "older women believed they were less susceptible to breast cancer than young women and were less likely to have positive attitudes toward screening." They also cited a 1989 U.S. telephone survey of urban women aged 45 to 75, where just 50.8 percent of women aged 60 to 69 reported having ever had a mammography, compared to 56.8 percent of those women aged 45 to 49. Similarly, a mixed rural and urban 1991 U.S. telephone survey showed more women in their 40s had had mammograms than those in their 60s. And a 1990 population survey in Rome showed that more women in their 40s than women aged 50 to 64 had undergone mammography.

In an article in the same issue of the CMA journal, Dr. Cornelia Baines argued that perhaps a main barrier to knowledge, attitudes and behavior in older women, who are at higher risk of breast cancer than younger women, is "a media focus on the young and media-generated fear.

"That older women's attitudes are as they are is no surprise: the media bombard them with breast cancer information that is targeted at the young. In 1991 *Time* featured on its front cover the profile of a young woman's nude torso, the breast highlighted as the target zone; on the contents pages another nude young woman was featured, in a half-page frontal view, also in color. Feature articles on breast cancer — all focusing on the young — have appeared by the dozens in magazines such as *Flare, Glamour, Self* and *Cosmopolitan.* Breast cancer 'survivors' (the younger, the greater the impact) appear in television documentaries, sending a message that the young are vulnerable to the breast cancer 'epidemic.' Pictures are worth a thousand words, and the juxtaposition of breast cancer with the young and beautiful may well send a message to older women that breast cancer is not really their problem."

Even in Ontario, home of Dr. Anthony Miller and his team who were responsible for the landmark Canadian study, the unabashed hucksterism of mammography continued apace. The Summer 1993 edition of *Connection*, a newsletter for volunteers in the government-funded Ontario Breast Screening Program, which has screened more than 100,000 women, published the following under a section entitled "myths and facts" about mammography and breast cancer:

"Myth. Mammography is unsafe.

"Fact. Virtually all experts conclude that women over 50 will benefit from regular breast screening. Mammography is a safe, simple, effective examination of the breast."

This isn't entirely true. There are, in fact, circumstances where mammography has been shown to be unsafe and cause unnecessary pain and suffering and expense. False positive results are only discovered by a biopsy, for example, and that carries its own risk of infection and bleeding. And radiation, although relatively low in dosage, is cumulative and can be unsafe for some women, particularly those carrying the ataxia-telangiectasia gene. The second sentence also implies that mammography is safe for everyone, when in fact it isn't safe for everyone under age 50.

Another example:

"Myth. I don't have any symptoms. I don't need a mammogram.

"Fact. Mammography can detect very small breast cancers before there are symptoms, often two to four years before it can be felt."

Again, the "fact" is only part of the true story. First, it makes no distinction in the age of the woman. And second, it doesn't make the salient point that finding tumors early often has no bearing on survival at all. What's more, if mammography were given to every woman in her 40s who had cancerous tumors too small to feel, nearly 40 out of every 100 cancers would be missed. Even in women over 50, a single mammogram fails to detect cancer 13 percent of the time.

The last of the sixth "myths" is easily the most pernicious.

"Myth. There is no history of breast cancer in my family, so I don't need to worry about it.

"Fact. It is every woman's responsibility to protect herself from breast cancer. Most women who develop breast cancer have no history of the disease."

True, most women who develop breast cancer have no history of the disease. But to say it is every woman's responsibility to "protect herself" from breast cancer is to blame the victim for her own misfortune. It's one thing to advocate sensible precautionary measures, but it's unconscionable to promote the notion that if a woman gets breast cancer it's her own fault. It isn't. After all, the 20-year-plus, trillion-dollar war on cancer still hasn't uncovered the secrets of this disease.

Not everybody was plugging into the propaganda, however. The May-June 1993 edition of *Ms* magazine argued that baseline mammograms "should be abolished" and that mammograms "should be done only when there is a clinical reason or she is postmenopausal."

And a Swedish study published in the October 20, 1993, *Journal of the National Cancer Institute* on the long-term impact of radiation therapy concluded that "a statistically significant increase in the incidence of breast cancer following radiation treatment of various benign breast diseases was observed even among women older than 40 years at the time of first treatment . . . These findings need to be considered when weighing the relative benefits versus risks of generalized screening of younger women for breast cancer by mammography."

Some governments and cancer-research organizations finally began to listen. About that same time, an NCI advisory board recommended retention of regular screening for women 50 and older, but said the NCI should rescind the guideline for women aged 40 to 49. The Division of Cancer Prevention and the Control Board of Scientific Counselors heard scientists and members of professional, community, advocacy and volunteer groups debate the evidence. In the end, the NCI proposed new guideliness recommending screening every year or two for these women and against routine screening for women under 50.

In fact, several significant groups had already recommended an end to routine mammography for women under 50, including the American College of Physicians, the National Women's Health Network, the U.S.

Preventative Services Task Force and the American Academy of Family Practice.

Mary Ann Napoli, associate director of the Center for Medical Consumers, New York, told the meeting that "mammograms do not prevent breast cancer, do not cure breast cancer, and, alone, do not reduce breast-cancer mortality by one-third. The value of mammography seems to have taken on a life of its own," she said, showing a *New York Times* ad that claimed that nine out of ten breast-cancer deaths could be saved by mammography. "Those who promulgate guidelines have an obligation to tell women about the risks as well as the benefits."

In November 1993, Quebec Health Minister Marc-Yvon Côté announced that the province would spend $7 million to improve radiography equipment and training of technicians in an effort to convince 100,000 more women aged 50 to 69 to have mammograms each year, a move he suggested might reduce breast-cancer mortality by 40 percent by the turn of the century. At the same time, the province launched an education campaign to encourage breast self-examination as well as increasing chemotherapy and radiation-treatment programs across the province.

While pressure was building to change mammography guidelines, the NCI decision did not stop the debate. While some governments and organizations viewed their mammography policy more soberly, at least part of the establishment was still circling the wagons against discouraging women under 50 from having regular mammograms. Eleven members of the 18-member National Cancer Advisory Board in Bethesda, Maryland, sparked by Miller's Canadian study, which had appeared a year earlier, and the subsequent international workshop sponsored by the NCI in February, introduced a resolution asking the NCI to "defer action on recommending any changes in breast cancer screening at this time." The motion was introduced by board member David G. Bragg, a radiologist, chairman of the Department of Radiology at the University of Utah School of Medicine. The motion's supporters wanted more time to evaluate and research, saying that changing the old (1987) guidelines would confuse women and — getting to the real issue — threaten insurance and government reimbursement for mammography. Despite growing scientific evidence against them, the American Cancer Society, the American College of Radiology, the American College of

Obstetricians and Gynecologists, and the National Medical Association all lined up against changing the guidelines for women under 50, arguing the case still had not been proven.

Despite a series of scientific studies recommending against regular mammography for women under 50, including the NCI scientific advisory board decision a month earlier, Janet Rose Osuch, a Michigan breast surgeon, chairman of the breast cancer advisory committee for the American Cancer Society and the American Medical Women's Association, was quoted in the *Washington Post* saying the studies on mammography screening for women in their 40s had been poorly designed and conducted. Osuch said it is "important to understand that no good data exist disproving the benefits of mammography."

In December 1993, the Food and Drug Administration began to take some of the criticisms of mammography more seriously. The FDA announced new regulations, the first mandatory national program, to create quality control standards and a certification system for most of the 11,000 medical facilities that perform and interpret mammography in the United States. "The bottom line," said FDA Commissioner David Kessler at a Chicago meeting of the Radiological Society of North America, "is that 10 months from now, no mammography facility that fails to obtain federal certification will be allowed to operate." Under the new rules, either a state's health agency or the American College of Radiology (a long-time advocate of more widespread mammography) would be responsible for accrediting clinics. Congress had already approved the Mammography Quality Standards Act in the wake of reports that many tests were poorly conducted and misread, and President Bill Clinton, whose mother was suffering from breast cancer herself, had promised to intensify the fight against the disease.

Dr. Samuel Epstein, professor of occupational and environmental medicine at the University of Illinois Medical Center in Chicago, a prominent critic of radiological practice, said the FDA rules should have gone further and made a distinction between mammograms for postmenopausal women and those for younger women, where it is a less effective tool and not worth the potential risk of radiation exposure.

The next day, December 3, the National Cancer Institute released a statement announcing its revised guidelines:

"There is a general consensus among experts that routine screening every 1 to 2 years with mammography and clinical breast examination can reduce breast cancer mortality by about one-third for women aged 50 and over.

"Experts do not agree on the role of routine screen mammography for women ages 40 to 49. To date, randomized clinical trials have not shown a statistically significant reduction in mortality for women under the age of 50."

The NCI statement was advisory only. It does not enjoy legal or regulatory standing, and it still didn't convince the American Cancer Society. Spokeswoman for the society Joann Schellenbach told the *Washington Post*, "The NCI issued not a guideline but a statement, which doesn't give advice. Women still need guidance. The American Cancer Society will continue to advise women to get routine mammography screening beginning at age 40."

The NCI's new position received another blow with the appearance in March 1994 of a 20-year study by doctors at Thomas Jefferson University Hospital. In this study, nearly one-third of 3,752 women given biopsies as a result of suspicious mammogram findings were found to have cancer. All the women had no symptoms and no lumps detectable to the touch. Principal researcher Dr. Gordon Schwartz said that in nearly 30 percent of the cases, the cancer was caught before it spread beyond the breast and could often be treated without mastectomy or radiation. "Without access to mammography, these women would be denied this earliest detection," he said. About 25 percent of the women in the study were under 50. Schwartz, a professor of surgery and specialist in breast diseases, said, "Failure to screen women under 50 would be a great leap backward in the early detection of breast cancer."

About the same time, medical technology got another boost with a *Health* magazine report on the latest toy, a new technique called high resolution digital ultrasound. It had been tested by doctors on 10,777 women in Europe and the United States who had a breast lump or abnormal mammogram, and judged about 400 of the masses to be non-cancerous. It was right in all but five of the cases, a 99 percent accuracy rate. Of the masses it labelled worrisome, 60 percent turned out to be malignant. As things stand, 80 percent of breast masses detected by mammograms turn out to be benign, but the biopsies needed to confirm this often cause bleeding, infection and scarring. It is hoped the new detection technique can reduce biopsies by as much as one-third. Ultrasound focuses on a small area of the breast and therefore can't replace mammography. But researchers argue that women whose mammogram raises suspicions could ask about getting a high-resolution ultrasound scan before a biopsy.

On the negative side of mammography, a group of researchers at the Royal Jubilee Hospital in Victoria, B.C., in a letter in *The Lancet*, wrote that "compression (of the breast) during mammography can rupture cysts, and dissemination of cancer cells as a result of compression might occur." Citing earlier studies that found trauma to the breast could cause small cancer cells to burst and then spread, the letter, signed by J.P. van Netten, said that "some of the reported risk increase for breast cancer mortality in younger women undergoing mammography could be caused by trauma associated with this procedure in the in-situ component."

As always happens when anybody questions the benefits of mammography, the radiologists get immediately exercised. This time it was Dr. Roberta Jong, a radiologist with the Ontario Breast Cancer Screening Program, who told *The Toronto Star* that "it's quite clear [by] this gentleman's theories [that] he's really done no research into justifying his thoughts. There's no scientific evidence for what he's theorizing."

On the other hand, if mammography is as effective as its proponents say, and can save the lives of up to 40 percent of women with breast cancer, why haven't mortality rates dropped with the widespread use of mammography? And how much of the debate has little to do with science and much to do with raw politics and with profiting from the suffering of others?

And so it goes. The mammography muddle continues and many women are caught in the middle, not certain what they should do.

Sadly, the debate will go on until a cure for cancer is found.

7 Men Are Not Immune

IN EARLY JANUARY 1993, 59-YEAR-OLD
English Professor Jim Wilcox was at work at
Ottawa's Carleton University campus when he suddenly fell on a
slippery tiled floor.

"I fell on my chest and didn't think anything about it at the time,"
said Wilcox. "It was a hard fall, and I was perturbed I wouldn't be able
to go skiing as I had planned that weekend. Little did I know I had
another surprise waiting for me."

Three weeks later, while taking his morning shower, Wilcox found a
lump on his breast. He had a tumor. The flesh around it had hemor-
rhaged when he fell, so he went to an Ottawa surgeon and had it
removed.

"I always worried about my wife or daughters," he said. "Until then,
I didn't even know men could get breast cancer. I guess the doctor I went
to didn't know about it either."

That's not too surprising. In Canada, about 16,300 women will get breast cancer in 1994. But what most people don't know, and don't hear about, is that more than 100 men will also be diagnosed with the disease, and about 40 of them will die.

In the United States, where some 183,000 women will be diagnosed, more than 1,000 men will get breast cancer this year. It will kill more than 300 of them.

Since one man gets breast cancer for roughly every 100 women who get it, that means that worldwide, with more than 1 million women suffering from the disease, some 10,000 men will have breast cancer and about 4,000 will die from it.

While the overall numbers are small compared to those for women — and compared to lung or prostate cancer in men for that matter — the men who do get breast cancer have fared worse than women, largely because they tend to be older at the time they get it. Also, since it doesn't occur to most men that they can get breast cancer, their disease tends to be further advanced than is the case for women when they do show up for treatment.

In addition to men getting breast cancer, however, this chapter also explores two other often neglected aspects of medicine. The first is the devastating emotional toll on men, and their children as well, when their spouse is diagnosed with the disease. While the woman with breast cancer, of course, has top priority, there is precious little emotional support offered to her friends and family; this need is particularly critical when the woman dies. And, more often than not, physicians do not come clean with men and tell them when their spouse is dying.

The second aspect is another controversial experiment. Just as women are being asked to take part in the tamoxifen trials, men, too, are being recruited for an experiment with a popular prostate pill that hasn't lived up to its early promise of a cure.

Jim Wilcox certainly didn't think he had breast cancer. Indeed, after his lumpectomy, Wilcox was so optimistic he was in good health that he prepared to leave for China on a six-month teaching exchange program. The night before he was scheduled to leave for Beijing, a doctor telephoned him at home with the shocking news that the tumor was malignant.

Wilcox said he had been "fairly optimistic that somehow I did not have cancer," but the news from the doctor was "a bit of a downer."

Even so, he went to China on his contract, where doctors determined that the cancer had spread to ducts in his lymph nodes. They performed a mastectomy and lymphectomy and he spent more than ten weeks in hospital in Beijing. His Chinese surgeon told him he had only a short time to live.

"These guys will tell you that you have one or two years," he said. "Since then, I have learned to tell the experts to go to hell."

After returning to Canada, Wilcox began radiation therapy, which he continues, and embarked on a personal program of meditation, acupuncture and other alternative treatments to maintain both his immune system and his good spirits.

"So much of fighting cancer is in the mind," he says. "You can fight this thing. You may lose, you may win, but you can fight it."

Wilcox has also taken to delivering speeches on male breast cancer "to demystify this disease for people. The more men know about it, the better. No one tells a man to examine his breast. . . . But the danger for men is, there is not much breast for the cancer to develop in, so it can be spread to the lymph nodes much faster — and be heavily spread by the time it is detected."

Even though breast cancer is generally considered a woman's disease, Wilcox says, "I see nothing embarrassing about this. I wear my scar with pride. The fact I have it shows I survived."

Not all men feel the same.

Ernest, a Wisconsin businessman, was diagnosed with breast cancer in 1992 at the age of 63. For fear of being ostracized by his business associates, he agreed to be interviewed only if his true identity and home city were disguised.

In the spring of 1992, he discovered a lump in his right breast. "I had misgivings about this, and my wife suggested I see someone."

So he consulted two physicians — one of whom told him that the lump was "probably nothing" — before he found a competent surgeon and underwent a modified mastectomy in November 1992.

"There was absolutely no history of this in my family," he said. "And I mean the men and the women. It was completely baffling.

"I wasn't stoic at all. It was like the end of my life. I have been an extremely healthy guy all my life, and when I was told I had breast cancer, my God, I can't even begin to tell you how it hit me. I was really upset. The word cancer has all these connotations. Even now, I worry about it. I have a wonderful family and enjoy my work, but every now and then a dark cloud passes by.

"The only thing I regret is that I didn't act faster. Most men would leave it until it might be too late. I think it is really important to let men know they are at risk."

Ernest said that although he has recovered, "There is no question you can tell I have had a mastectomy. I probably wouldn't give a damn, except as it relates to the work I do. But at the gym, you'll never see me without a towel covering my breast."

Dr. William Donegan, professor of surgery at the Medical College of Wisconsin and chief of surgery at Milwaukee's Mount Sinai Medical Center, is one of the world's leading authorities on male breast cancer, author of a definitive medical text on breast cancer and a researcher who has conducted extensive studies on the disease in men.

During 30 years of practice in Missouri and Wisconsin, he has treated 20 men with breast cancer.

"I think men are more stoic about it than women," says Donegan. "Breast cancer does not have the same sexual implications as it does for women. The fact a man may have what is supposed to be a 'women's disease' doesn't seem to be particularly upsetting for many of my patients. I have even had patients who seemed to treat the news as a curiosity.

"A woman's sexuality is primarily based on the breast, and the public and media tend to play that up. A mastectomy is not as devastating for a man. Even a radical mastectomy in which the nipple is removed and there is scarring does relatively little damage for a man."

Donegan says that just as breast cancer in women is linked to estrogen, "the same pattern occurs in men."

In fact, male breast cancer is almost identical to breast cancer in women, except that it is much less common — accounting for only about 0.6 percent of cancer in men — and tends to occur at a later age than is the case with women, most frequently affecting men in their late 60s or older.

Donegan says, "Men tend to present themselves in later stages of the disease. I think there has been less awareness a man can even suffer from a malignancy of the breast."

Even so, in a chapter on male breast cancer in their 1988 book *Cancer of the Breast*, Donegan and Dr. John S. Spratt of Louisville attempt to dispel the widespread ignorance about the disease. They wrote that male breast cancer "is fundamentally identical to breast cancer in women except for being less frequent, occurring at an older age, arising regularly beneath the nipple, and being more hormonally sensitive." It was known to Fabricus Hildanus (1537–1619), a famous Italian surgeon who helped found modern embryology. In 1927, American Dr. J. M. Wainwright was able to document 418 cases of male breast cancer reported before that time. The incidence is highest in Britain and North America. In the United States it accounts for 0.3 to 1.5 percent of all cancers in men and only 0.6 to 0.9 percent of all breast cancers. Although it has been reported once in a five-year-old boy in 1972, and ages generally range from 25 to 93 years, it is extremely rare in younger men. "For obscure reasons, cancer of the male breast appears almost a decade later than cancer of the breast in women," writes Donegan, author of that particular chapter, with patients predominantly in their seventh decade of life, with median ages 61 to 65. The incidence rises from 0.1 per 100,000 men aged 30 to 34 to 6.5 at 85 and older.

As with female cancer, of course, the cause of the disease is unknown. Because of the small numbers involved, research into male breast cancer has been limited, but the research that has occurred has produced the following findings:

- Exposure to medical radiation at a young age has been linked to male breast cancer in some cases;
- In the United States, according to a major 1985 U.S. study, Jewish men tend to be at higher risk than white men of other religions;
- It occurs at an older age in men than in women;
- It appears to be more hormonally sensitive than female breast cancer.

One study found that men who had suffered injury to the breast and testicles, and men with undescended testes, tended to be at higher risk.

157

Other studies have found an association with men who showed signs of genetic "feminization." And cancer of the breast has occurred in male transsexuals who take estrogen, a hormone that promotes development of female characteristics.

As with female breast cancer, some studies have also drawn a connection between male breast cancer and exposure to electromagnetic fields (EMFs). In 1989, Dr. Genevieve M. Matanoski and two colleagues from the School of Hygiene and Public Health at Johns Hopkins University studied 50,582 New York telephone workers and discovered six cases of male breast cancer. Telephone workers who were actively employed in a statewide company from 1976 to 1980 were matched to the cancer registry of the state. Four of the cases were not counted in the study because the men were either too old or not working for the full 1976–80 study period.

In a March 23, 1991, letter in *The Lancet* explaining the study, Matanoski, Patrick N. Breysse and Elizabeth Elliott explained that the study found a different pattern of EMF exposure for men working in the central office switching environment from that for cable splicers and other telephone lineworkers. "Until the 1980s, the predominant technology in telephone switching offices was electromechanical switches. The rapid on and off switching of this machinery produced a complex field environment. For example, adjacent to these switches a directional compass was erratic and spun at times." The conclusion for all this was that "the excesses of male breast cancer which have been observed in workers potentially exposed to EMF may fit theories that EMF exposures . . . lead to changes in the incidence of specific cancers."

In a presentation at the 23rd Annual Meeting of the Society for Epidemiologic Research in Utah in June 1990, the Fred Hutchinson Cancer Research Center in Seattle, Washington, reported six times the expected rate of male breast cancer among electricians, power station operators and telephone linemen.

In December 1990, Tore Tynes and Aafe Andersen of the Cancer Registry of Norway in Oslo discovered a doubling of male breast cancer among a group of 37,952 men exposed to EMFs with railroad and tram drivers experiencing four times the expected incidence. In a report in the December 22–29 *Lancet*, Tynes and Andersen say the results of their study "seem to support the justification of further studies on the association between breast cancer and occupational exposure" to EMF fields. The largest single group were electricians (16,242), but they also studied railroad engine drivers, tram drivers, radio telegraphists, railway track walkers, power plant operators, radio-TV repairmen, fitters and powerline workers. Because the numbers are small, the authors say, "The results should be interpreted with caution." Even so, these results fit into the pattern of other studies indicating at least a prima facie case of the connection between EMFs and male breast cancer.

In May 1994, a report in the journal *Nature Genetics* from a group of researchers in the United States, Britain and Holland revealed that the breast-cancer gene BRCA1 that scientists recently isolated is not involved in male breast cancer. The study discovered strong evidence that, in families in which breast cancer is common and at least one male member is affected, only a small proportion are linked to the gene, adding weight to the theory that there are genes other than BRCA1 that predispose people to developing breast cancer. Nevertheless, family history has not been linked directly to male breast cancer.

Donegan and Spratt report that a 1985 U.S. case-control study that found Jewish men at higher risk than white men of other religion also found that "a familial relationship is difficult to document, although a number of observations suggest it." Breast cancer in sisters or mothers of men with breast cancer "has been observed in 11 percent of cases, approximately the same as expected for female patients." One study reported two brothers with breast cancer and another observed two families in which several men had the disease. There are also two known cases where both father and son were affected. While it's rare, cancer of the breast also occurs in men treated with estrogen for prostatic cancer.

The two authors also report that male breast-cancer victims often have a history of trauma to the breast "but the relevance is not clear. A [1980] case-control study . . . found that, compared with controls, men with breast cancer had more often graduated from college and held professional or managerial positions, had a history of gynecomashia, mumps, orchitis, testicular injury, and undescended testes and had married at older ages and failed to have children, most of which suggests an associaton with hormonal factors." There is also a slight predominance of the disease in the left breast, just as there is with women. But unlike women, where from 7 to 10 percent get cancer in the second breast as well, both breasts are rarely involved for men. However, as many as 21 percent of men have another kind of cancer either before or after being diagnosed with breast cancer. It's unusual for the disease to be discovered during routine physical examinations, "probably because the breasts of men are not always examined carefully."

Another parallel between men and women is that radical mastectomy used to be routine for men, but modified mastectomies are replacing it, no doubt influenced both by earlier diagnosis and the results of clinical trials in women showing favorable results for the less radical surgery. Between 1949 and 1976, a modified mastectomy was performed in just 9 percent of the cases of male breast cancer. That jumped to 40 percent in another study between 1961 and 1981, and to 54 percent from 1967 to 1981. One study found no significant difference in five-year survival rates between 19 men treated with a radical mastectomy (76 percent), and 18 men treated with modified mastectomy (80 percent). "A frequent observation," wrote Donegan, "is that men fare more poorly than women, particularly in the presence of metastases in axillary lymph nodes, but the evidence is growing that cancer of the male breast is as curable when the disease is of comparable stage."

Donegan added that men who cannot tolerate major surgery or have a locally advanced tumor "usually are managed with simple mastectomy or local excision combined with postoperative irradiation to the chest wall and regional nodes." He said the success of adjuvant chemotherapy in women "translates to men with some uncertainty." It's sometimes used, but "the fund of available information is fragmentary and inconclusive." Hormone treatment with tamoxifen has become increasingly important for treating male breast cancer with chemotherapy playing a secondary role.

For men, of course, breast cancer does not rate as a major cancer killer. Lung cancer, for example, will kill more than 90,000 men in the United States alone this year. (Only about 300 men will die of breast cancer.) The second leading cause of cancer deaths in men is in the gender-specific prostate, a small, walnut-sized gland that weighs about one ounce and is loosely attached to the bottom of the bladder. The American Cancer Society estimated that 165,000 American men would be diagnosed with prostate cancer in 1993 and about 35,000 would die from it. That compares to about 170,000 new cases of lung cancer in the United

States in 1993, and 182,000 of breast cancer. More than 75 percent of prostate cancer cases are in men aged 65 or older, and the disease affects about half of all men by age 80. The death rate for American blacks is more than double the rate of white American men. Overall, the rate of prostate cancer jumped 16 percent from 1989 to 1990 and an astounding 30 percent the next year, the fastest rise in cancer detection ever recorded. It is now the most common cancer among American men, and growing to epidemic proportions in Canada and Northern Europe as well.

It is a popular refrain among breast-cancer activists that if more men had breast cancer, we'd have a cure by now. Not necessarily. Prostate cancer, as the most common cancer among American men, has attracted considerable publicity, although not as much as breast cancer in women. Jim Wilcox says that for every four women who die of breast cancer, three men die of prostate cancer. Yet six times more research money is available for breast cancer as for prostate cancer in the United States. Yet this has not generated a cure either. On the other hand, male breast cancer has received almost no public attention, and men also find themselves sidelined in the search for support groups to help them cope with their emotional trauma when they lose their loved ones to breast cancer. Indeed, one thing women with breast cancer and men with prostate cancer do share is the reality that the drug companies and the rest of the medical establishment have exploited their fears of these diseases. Radical surgery and faith in wonder drugs have been more prevalent than treatment that is sensitive to the patient or than a real emphasis on prevention techniques.

A May 1993 study published in the *Journal of the American Medical Association* showed that surgery for prostate cancer has increased almost sixfold in recent years, yet most men enjoy little or no benefit from the operation and often suffer considerable harm. Within a month after surgery, about 2 percent of men over 75 died and 8 percent had major complications such as heart attacks. Using data from 11,000 medical files between 1984 and 1990, Dartmouth researchers found the rate of radical prostatectomy — the removal of the entire gland — was 5.75 times higher in 1990 than in 1984. The operation sometimes works, but it often causes impotence and incontinence — and the death rate for this kind of surgery is higher than for other kinds.

Nearly 150 medical journal articles on prostate cancer were published since 1966, yet for all that, there had been only one small study, involving just 111 men, that randomly assigned patients to either surgery or "watchful waiting," where doctors monitor the cancer to make sure it doesn't spread or treat only serious complications, such as pain or urinary blockage. That study found no difference in survival between surgery and watchful waiting. A January 1994 article in the *New England Journal of Medicine* came to a similar conclusion. A research team headed by Dr. Gerald Chodak of the University of Chicago determined after analyzing 828 cases of men in several studies of prostate cancer in older men from 1985 to 1992 that "watchful waiting" was the best treatment in the early stages of the disease. At least 30 percent of men over 50 who develop prostate cancer die of other causes. Despite these studies, however, which clearly cast doubt on the wisdom of routine surgery, doctors continue to recommend the surgical option for most men with prostate cancer.

On March 4, 1994, *The Toronto Star* reported on some closely guarded scientific research that showed that the rate of castration for Ontario men stricken with prostate cancer had jumped 56 percent over the previous decade, even though more moderate therapies were available. The rate of orchidectomy (castration), which is the surgical removal of the testicles, increased from 67 per 100,000 in 1981–82 to 104 per 100,000 in 1991–92, with huge differences in various parts of the province. The number of prostate-cancer cases in Canada had risen steadily since the 1960s and was quickly overtaking lung cancer as the most frequently diagnosed cancer in men.

In the March-April 1994 edition of *Natural Health*, Dr. Adriane Fugh-Berman, an outspoken critic of the tamoxifen trials on women who are considered "high risk" but don't have breast cancer, underscores the point about the chemical exploitation of men as well.

"Lest it be thought that only women are to be hormonally manipulated," she wrote, "the National Cancer Institute has begun recruiting for a study in which 9,000 men over the age of 55 will be given Proscar, a drug that inhibits the body's conversion of testosterone to dihydrotestosterone, which plays a role in prostate cancer. As the side effects of Proscar include impotence and decreased libido, recruitment to this trial may require uncommon salesmanship.

"The tamoxifen and Proscar trials point to an alarming fact: Doctors now are suggesting that simply being a man or a woman puts one at sufficient risk for pharmaceutical intervention."

When the New Jersey-based pharmaceutical giant Merck & Company received FDA approval in 1992 to market the drug finasteride under the brand name Proscar — a drug that costs more than $50 a month and must be taken every day indefinitely to remain effective — it immediately launched a massive newspaper and magazine advertising campaign to push the new miracle drug onto the massive male market and, to promote it even more, simply gave away 30-day supplies to physicians as samples. It worked. In October 1992, two drug firms — Merck & Company and American Home Products Corp. — announced they enjoyed double-digit increases in third-quarter earnings. Merck had introduced Proscar to the United States and Britain late in the second quarter, and had since introduced it to Canada, Italy, Finland, France and Sweden. Merck said it earned $644.5 million compared with $552.4 million a year earlier, a 17 percent gain. Proscar sales were not as high as the company had forecast, but new prescriptions for August still totalled 22,000. In Canada, the *Medical Post* greeted the introduction of Proscar with a front-page story and a banner headline: "Prostate Pill," heralding the news that the new drug approved by the federal Health Protection Branch "represents a significant new treatment option for the common disease that affects men over 50." It quoted Dr. Ernest Ramsey, a leading Canadian urologist from Winnipeg, saying, "The beauty of this drug is that it has little or no side-effects."

Then an editorial in the October 22, 1992, *New England Journal of Medicine* on the prospective blockbuster drug announced that men with enlarged prostate glands who took the drug in a study showed no significant improvement over surgery, which is called, "quicker, more effective, less costly, and safe." It cited John D. McConnell, who directed the Proscar clinical trials at the University of Texas Southwestern Medical Center at Dallas, saying that short-term therapy with Proscar "has very limited benefits in small numbers of men" and shouldn't be used by men with mild symptoms. "This certainly isn't the panacea people were hoping for several years ago when it was first developed." News of the prestigious journal's conclusions caused Merck's stock to drop $2.125 to $42.125 on the New York Stock Exchange that day.

In events precisely paralleling the promotion of tamoxifen by the British drug firm ICI Pharmaceuticals, the National Cancer Institute on October 20, 1993, announced the Prostate Cancer Prevention Trial using — you guessed it — Proscar. The plan was to enlist 18,000 healthy men aged 55 and older to see whether the drug prevented prostate cancer or not, even though its effectiveness as a cancer drug on patients diagnosed with cancer was already questionable. News of the study prompted more than 7,500 calls to the NCI's Cancer Information Service between October 13 and 15, which even surpassed the 4,000 calls the NCI received from women for the Breast Cancer Prevention Trial in the two days immediately following its April 1993 announcement.

This trial, like the better-known Breast Cancer Prevention Trial, was at the cutting edge of a new — and some believe dangerous — frontier of using drugs designed for disease on healthy individuals, all in the name of disease prevention. But according to a report in the November 17, 1993, NCI journal, it's an approach that the Clinton administration heartily endorses. The report quotes U.S. Assistant Secretary for Health Dr. Philip R. Lee saying that his boss, Secretary of Health and Human Services Donna Shalala, "is steadfast in her insistence that NIH-based prevention research be part of the health care reform package."

Another parallel with the breast-cancer movement is that the rapid increase in incidence of prostate cancer in Europe and North America has generated considerable political activism, although that activism has not been as effective so far. Historically, men have been more reluctant than women to discuss such personal diseases in the open. While women grow up with doctors inspecting their most intimate areas, men generally don't experience that until they get much older. Even then, men regularly refuse routine rectal exams as part of annual check-ups. But just as the increase in breast cancer sparked lobbying by a myriad of activist organizations lobbying for more research money and greater recognition, the increase in prostate cancer has inspired similar organizations for men.

One of those organizations, featured in the May 11, 1992, *U.S. News and World Report,* is the Patient Advocates for Advance Cancer Treatments, PAACT, a 10,000-member nonprofit foundation incorporated in 1987 by retired engineer and prostate cancer survivor Lloyd Ney of Grand Rapids, Michigan. Among other things, Ney helped convince

Washington to approve a hormonal treatment that saved his life. Clinical trials were set up at 204 U.S. sites, and in addition, Ney raised about $150,000 from PAACT members to sponsor the group's own clinical trial to test a tumor-permeating antibody called TNT.

Like many women breast-cancer advocates, Ney drew the comparison between federal funding for cancer research and for AIDS research. Both diseases received roughly the same amount — about $1.3 billion — but cancer kills half a million Americans each year compared to about 33,000 for AIDS. "If they can get that kind of money for AIDS, more power to them," said Ney. "Just as long as we get equity."

The largest and perhaps best-known group lobbying for prostate-cancer victims, called "Us Too," was formed in February 1990 by Edward Kaps and four other men. Kaps, 68, former director of industrial relations for General Motors, was first diagnosed with the disease when he was 52. After having the tumor radiated, the cancer returned ten years later. The July 5, 1993, issue of *Forbes* reported that Us Too — with U.S. Senators Robert Dole and Ted Stevens as honorary chairmen — had 40,000 members in 43 states. "Although prostate cancer has become the most common cancer in men, Washington has earmarked only $37 million for prostate cancer research this fiscal year (ending Sept. 30). By contrast, nearly $400 million in federal money will be spent on breast cancer research in 1993, thanks in large measure to the political clout of the National Breast Cancer Coalition. It includes 170 different organizations with millions of members."

Kaps explained that "women have just done a better job of getting funds. They speak more freely with their doctors, while men are pretty macho. But that's starting to change."

One of those changes has been the recruitment of several celebrity victims of prostate cancer, such as Senators Jesse Helms and Alan Cranston, Wall Street wizard Michael Milken, rock star Frank Zappa and even the King of Belgium. Another prominent American, U.S. Operation Desert Storm hero Gen. H. Norman Schwarzkopf, 59, underwent surgery for prostate cancer at the Walter Reed Army Medical Center in Washington on May 25, 1994. Another change that has heightened male awareness and interest in the disease was the availability of a simple, inexpensive (less than $50) PSA (prostate-specific antigen) blood test that measures the level of a protein produced by the prostate and tips physicians off about the likelihood of the disease. Senator Dole became a believer in 1991 when a routine PSA test revealed he had prostate cancer. In his words, "Early detection saved my life." He not only got involved in Us Too, but also sponsored a prostate cancer screening booth during the 1992 Republican Convention, and has broadcast commercials urging all men to seek regular prostate exams.

Just as regular mammography is recommended for women over 50, the American Cancer Society now advocates annual PSA tests for all men beginning at the same age, and even earlier for black men and men with a family history of the disease. Like mammography, however, the PSA test has its serious critics. One cited in the *Forbes* article was Gerald Chodak, co-director of urologic oncology at University of Chicago Hospitals. He opposes widespread PSA testing. "I don't believe we know it is the right thing to do," he said, "and until we do know it's the right thing, I don't think we should do it." Chodak's concern is that many men, especially those over 70, will test positive, undergo the follow-up ultrasound or biopsy tests, and then suffer unnecessary surgery or radiation treatment for cancers that are not threatening their lives. Consider the fact that about one man out of every three over 50 has prostate cancer, but fewer than three out of 100 will die from it. And of those deaths, many will come at advanced age when death from other sources is likely. Barnett Kramer, the NCI's associate director of early detection and community oncology, summed the situation up by saying, "Many more men die with prostate cancer than of prostate cancer."

The problem is that either the cancer grows quickly and kills or, in the vast majority of cases, it grows too slowly to do any harm since men tend to be older when they get it. The PSA test can identify the prostate cancer, but not whether it's the killer variety or not. In the United States in 1990, prostate-cancer treatment cost $5 billion. Yet about 90 percent of men who chose surgery, and half those who undergo radiation to fight it, become impotent. That too can be treated, but at a cost of about $10,000 per patient. In the United States alone, the 1990 census found that there were about 23.4 million men aged from 50 to 75. If they all had annual PSA tests and the follow-up treatment, the overall cost to society would be astronomical and the overall benefit minimal. Still, as in breast cancer for women and other diseases, when physicians acquire a tool, there's a demand to use it, even if it isn't necessarily the most scientifically sound approach.

In a June 1993 meeting on the subject, the National Cancer Institute expressed public concern because prostate cancer was being diagnosed at record rates and as a result, more men than ever were undergoing surgical removal or radiation. The problem, they said, was that because of advanced diagnostic techniques, prostate cancer was being caught at an earlier and more treatable stage. But there is no evidence that catching the disease earlier improves survival rates, so overall, there's a greater risk in the treatment than in the disease itself.

Dr. Larry Kessler, NCI director of research on cancer detection, told the *New York Times* that testing would pick up between 20,000 and 30,000 more men who have no symptoms and would otherwise have gone unnoticed. "This is clearly a major public health issue," he said. "Yet we don't know if treating them is advisable or whether a lot of the surgery is proper."

Proper or not, Medicare data show the number of operations to remove cancerous prostates for men 65 and over increased by between 500 and 600 percent from 1984 to 1990. The death rate from the operation is 1 percent among men aged 65 to 74 and 2 percent for those 75 and over. Some 63 percent of men are incontinent after the surgery and between 60 and 90 percent are impotent afterwards.

While prostate-cancer treatment is still controversial and, like female breast cancer, needs considerably more research and clinical trials to sort out, another area that has been largely ignored is the impact of breast-cancer deaths on the surviving family and loved ones. While women's support groups have been around for years, men's support groups are just beginning to spring up across North America, offering solace and practical help to the men, and often the children, who have lost a wife or partner or daughter.

Barry Toghill, a member of a Hamilton, Ontario, support group told his story to a March 30, 1992, meeting of a special parliamentary subcommittee on breast cancer, 16 months after his 45-year-old wife Karen lost her four-year battle with the disease.

The point I want to make here is that during this entire period of, basically, her last three weeks of life, there wasn't any real contact

167

with doctors. *I don't believe any human being who is losing a loved one should have to be running around trying to find out this information. I think good medicine is done, but I think, like that old maxim — something about the law must be seen to be done — good medicine must not only be practised, but it must be seen to be practised.*

After Karen died, Kimberley (their daughter, then 14) and I went home and I realized then the circus had left town. It had folded up the tents and gone, because Karen had dealt with a couple of specialists . . . for four years and after she'd died there wasn't even a phone call to say, gee, I'm sorry to hear it. I realized then that what was missing and had been missing from day one was mental or emotional support.

Stage one of the support finished when Karen died and it wasn't there — and stage two never arrived. I knew then we were basically on our own. I realized, too, the system operates in a non-communicative way. Unfortunately, patients and their families go with the system, often not knowing what is being done and why.

For example, Karen was a very slim person and we were not prepared for what the steroids would do for the brain tumor. No one ever told us this would give her a moon-like face, and she wasn't only handling her cancer then, but she was handling her looks and no hair.

I think the one thing I will never forgive the system for . . . Karen and I really never said good-bye. One of the last things she said to me was, 'I didn't know it would end like this.'

In my opinion, cancer clinics do not treat the disease as a family concern, but rather as a one-on-one patient and doctor. I read with interest in The Spectator *about two of the oncology people . . . who designed this wheel with the options and the risks . . . the nurse discusses it with the cancer patient. If the cancer patient has a question, the doctor will come in and answer it, and then if she wants, she can take it home — or a little version of it — to discuss with her husband and family and her general practitioner. I'm sorry, why isn't the husband there at the time it's being discussed?*

I can't understand that. Why would a woman take that home? A woman who is trying to handle a cancer. I think the husband has to be there to discuss it — not to take this home.

The second thing is that patients find treatments are changed without any explanation from the doctor. My wife was taken off tamoxifen. We don't know, to this day, why. . . . At one time she was supposed to have had radiation treatment. As she was on the table waiting for the radiation treatment, it was cancelled by another oncologist who said no, we are going to give you chemotherapy. The chemotherapy did not work . . .

There's little communication. At one time she was seeing a bone specialist, a radiation oncologist, a chemo oncologist and a general surgeon, and none of them was communicating with the other.

I believe the cancer treatment treats the disease but not the patient. It comes across as a not-caring system, right to the last day of life, and I saw this firsthand. Cancer is a traumatic mental, physical and emotional problem for the patient and her family. It has to be made as easy as possible to handle and it is not being . . . The system lets the patient down and, as importantly in my opinion, it lets the family down.

. . . there is a need for the family to be involved with this decision-making from day one, especially the husband. You know, we always talk about good marriages being founded on communication between husband and wife. I would think good marriages between the medical profession and a patient are also founded on communication, except this time we're talking about a doctor, a husband and a wife, and perhaps the children.

If the medical profession cannot learn to involve men in this, I think the men have to start demanding.

You know, when the wife . . . [at this point in his testimony, Toghill tried to say "dies," but couldn't] . . . and, as we know, many do, it's the husband who has to pick up these pieces. Unfortunately, you'll often hear that one of the biggest problems for a man who loses his wife is support. Women, if they lose their husbands, will talk on the phone with their friends. There are umpteen support groups. *There aren't support groups for men. I'm very fortunate that there is a little support group. There is a support group for my daughter, which she is going through. The men have to be helped here, and the men have to help as well; otherwise we are just going on. We can spend millions and millions of dollars, but some of that millions of dollars, perhaps a very small amount, has to be used for educating the men. They are part of the solution. Their wife's problem is their problem as well and the problem of their children. . . . I can get rid of my fear and my sad feelings from time to time. I know how to handle it. Kimberley doesn't know how to handle it. It will suddenly come up when she sees one of her friends out with her mother. Kimberley will say, 'My mother's not there.'*

. . . from 48 hours before Karen died, I had no contact (with doctors). My last contact was with a neurosurgeon who — again I can't say anything but good for the man as far as his handling of Karen is concerned — was very attentive, but no one ever said to me or to Karen, 'You're dying.' Karen was a strong enough person that she could have handled this.

As her husband, unless Karen has indicated she doesn't want anyone to know, if she's asked for that prognosis, I think I'm entitled to know. I think a doctor has to be able to make a value judgment. Should this person be told that they have only three months or three weeks to live? I think if Karen had been told that she had three weeks to live, it would have put a different perspective on what happened. But that was not to be, and as I say, that is perhaps the thing that I shall remember for the rest of my life, that nothing I do or say can bring my wife back, whom I loved very much. We never said good-bye. . . . You find out that death doesn't end as it does in the movies, but death should not end where the wife's husband is running around trying to find someone who can tell him.

One active survivor of male breast cancer who is also doing his best to raise men's consciousness of all aspects of the disease is Ottawa's Jim Wilcox, who has read everything he can find on the subject — most of the literature, of course, about female breast cancer.

His message is quite simple: "Men get breast cancer too."

8 Dancing in the DDT

WHEN TERRY PENDER WAS A LITTLE girl growing up in Ottawa, she could hardly wait for spring. Not just because it signalled the end of another long, cold Canadian winter, but because with spring came the DDT truck, winding its way slowly through the city's neighborhoods, spraying the weeds with its deadly cargo.

"I'd run along behind the truck and dance through the mist," she said. "A lot of the kids did. Nobody thought anything of it then. I loved the smell."

That was about the same time Rachel Carson was publishing her breakthrough epic, *Silent Spring*, which for the first time focused widespread attention on the health effects of chemicals in North American society. "The chemical agents of cancer have become entrenched in our world in two ways . . . ," she wrote, "first, and ironically, through man's search for a better way of life; second, because the manufacture and sale of such chemicals has become an accepted part of our economy and our way of life." Carson herself died of breast cancer a year after her book was published.

She also wrote, "As the tide of chemicals born of the Industrial Age has arisen to engulf our environment, a drastic change has come about in the nature of the most serious public health problems. For the first time in the history of the world, every human being is now subject to contact with dangerous chemicals, from the moment of conception until death."

DDT (or, dichloro-diphenyl-trichloro-ethane) originates from the work of a German chemist in 1874, but it wasn't until 1939 that the Swiss Paul Muller discovered its effectiveness as an insecticide. Muller won the Nobel Prize for his efforts, and DDT instantly became a panacea in the battle against insects. Nobody thought it was deadly to other forms of life. It was considered so safe, in fact, that it was commonly used during the war to dust soldiers, refugees and prisoners to combat lice.

So it's not surprising that Terry Pender and everybody else her age were in frequent contact with DDT. Few households didn't have a pump-action DDT spreader to spray every corner of their houses to kill those pesky flies, mosquitoes and other bothersome bugs.

Now, 30 years after dancing in the mist of the DDT, at age 38, and two decades after DDT was formally banned, Pender has undergone a mastectomy and endured poisonous chemotherapy. A mother of two, Pender believes her early exposure to DDT is a factor.

"Long before I knew I had breast cancer or knew anything about breast cancer, I told people if I ever wrote my biography it would be called 'Dancing in the DDT,'" she says. "Somehow I knew this was a significant event in my life. I've never had any doubt there's a relationship. Nor am I simplistic enough to think that that's the only thing. I understand the complexity of cancer, and everybody else on my street was dancing in the DDT too. But that doesn't mean it wasn't the main contributing factor in my case."

She's not alone. A growing body of evidence suggests that chemicals, pesticides and other environmental hazards are major contributors to the breast-cancer epidemic.

What isn't certain, however, is just which chemicals, how many breast cancers they cause and, for that matter, how they actually do it.

At an April 1994 forum sponsored by Breast Cancer Action Montreal, renowned scientist Dr. John C. Bailar III, chair of the Department of Epidemiology and Biostatistics, McGill University, said, "I am convinced that certain chemicals do cause breast cancer, particularly synthetic organic chemicals. . . . But I'm not convinced this makes up a large percentage of the total cancer load. This is not to say these should be ignored. We need to find the causes and root them out. But the hunt for chemical causes must not be allowed to divert us from the search for other sources [of breast cancer] which in the long run will likely be more harmful."

On the other hand, San Francisco activist Judy Brady, editor of *One in Three: Women with Cancer Confront an Epidemic*, argued that cancer is for the most part a preventable industrial disease. Brady said breast cancers have risen dramatically since World War II, "and most of them are an effect of pollution . . . but the question is not whether the rise in breast cancer is due to the environment. . . . The question is, if we know about the connections at this time, why has nothing been done about it? . . . Even if we find a cure and don't stop spewing out these poisons, it's a bit like going out to fight a forest fire with a garden hose in one hand and a gasoline can in the other. It just doesn't make sense."

And Dr. Devra Lee Davis, an epidemiologist, resident scholar at the National Academy of Sciences and senior adviser for the Office of the Assistant Secretary of Health in Washington, D.C., said breast cancer "is the most common cancer in women in modern countries and it appears to be growing for reasons we don't really understand. . . . One thing they have in common is they are all tied to total lifetime exposure to estrogen. . . . These environmental factors don't cause all breast cancer, but even if they only cause 20 percent of the disease, that represents an enormous number."

While scientists and activists debate the true impact of environmental factors on breast cancer, what they do agree upon is that only a minuscule amount of research is being done to find the answers to questions about these and other environmentally induced cancers. Breast-cancer action groups are demanding changes to this reality, and powerful corporate interests are fighting the activists.

Pender, an alternative health practitioner before her breast cancer prevented her from working, has little hope that things will change quickly.

I breast-fed both my children. I'm under 40, premenopausal, with no family history of breast cancer. I eat a whole food diet and live an outdoors life. I have no risks. Yet, I have breast cancer.

I don't feel individual practitioners are out to get me. It's just the way the entire cancer enterprise is organized. . . . Oncologists have no recommendations to make to me because there is no clinical research on these questions. They really need a 20-year trial before they can say anything. Well, I may not have 20 years, but research into these things is not being paid by the pharmaceutical companies and the chemical companies.

Right now I'm told there are 25 different clinical trials going on around the world about whether it's best to take tamoxifen before chemo begins or at the end of the chemo treatment. Just on that alone. Why not divert some of those funds and study other things? It's because the companies who finance research will pay to study drugs, but they won't finance other things, such as diet, lifestyle and environmental questions.

If a major factor turns out to be organochlorines, for example, look at what we're up against. I'm not optimistic I'll ever see it in my lifetime. Look at the pressures the tobacco companies put up before they finally had to admit their product causes cancer. It was obvious for years, yet they fought it every step of the way. And that's just one industry. Think of the size and clout of the chemical industry. I feel completely completely helpless in this situation.

She has a point, but still, there are some encouraging signs.

In 1991, when she learned she had breast cancer, Lorraine Pace of West Islip, New York, decided there had to be a reason why so many women living on Long Island were getting the disease. She and a group of her friends formed Breast Cancer HELP (Healthy Environment for a Living Planet) and, meeting in Pace's basement, began to canvass its neighborhoods with questionnaires and prepare a huge cluster map showing heavier-than-average concentrations of breast cancer in the area.

Other groups sprang up too, such as 1 in 9, the Long Island Breast Cancer Action Coalition, and the Long Beach Breast Cancer Coalition.

What they knew was that in the 1980s, there were 110.6 cases of breast cancer for every 100,000 women living there, compared to the national rate of 94.7. And they believed the high rate was related to local environmental factors, such as toxic materials at waste-disposal sites, auto emissions, electromagnetic fields, polluted drinking water and the more than 800 chemical plants in the area, 200 of which are still operating.

The women demanded action, but a federal study conducted by the Centers for Disease Control in Atlanta concluded that the higher incidence of breast cancer could be explained by known risk factors, such as heredity and the higher-than-average median age of women living on Long Island. Acting on the recommendation of a panel of epidemiologists, the National Cancer Institute determined that the incidence rate in Nassau County, New York, 20 percent higher than the state rate, could be explained by the known risk factors, so they wouldn't finance a study. In adjacent Suffolk, the rate of 107 per 100,000 women is also well above the state average of 96 per 100,000.

The women's groups, attacking the findings as a typical example of the medical establishment dismissing concerns about the cause and prevention of the disease, then recruited political support from Senators Alfonse D'Amato of New York City, Tom Harkin of Iowa, N.Y. State Senator Michael J. Tully of Roslyn Heights and others. In November 1993, federal health and environmental officials reversed themselves and announced they were launching a series of comprehensive studies on Long Island looking at such things as radiation released by everyday appliances, pesticide levels in the dust in household carpeting, and chemical contamination in drinking water to see if the high incidence rates were connected to something in the soil, water or air. About that time, the NCI awarded a $1.26 million grant to Dr. Lee Caplan, an epidemiologist at the University Medical Center at Stony Brook, New York, to study whether pesticides or electromagnetic fields from appliances or overhead transmission wires were related to breast cancer. The NCI, along with the National Institute of Environmental Health Sciences, also began soliciting proposals for a larger environmental investigation called the Long Island Breast Cancer Study Project.

At the time, Pace, 52, a real-estate saleswoman, whose group Breast Cancer HELP had documented hundreds of cases of breast cancer in her community of 28,000 people on Long Island's South Shore, told the *New York Times*: "We know how to increase our chances of getting lung cancer. But we do not know what we did to increase our chances of getting breast cancer. And we feel, as women, we have the right to know."

A conference at New York's Adelphi University on breast cancer and the environment — the first of its kind in the United States bringing together scientists and grassroots women's groups to discuss research on the subject — was told that about 30 percent of the cases of breast cancer can be explained by known risk factors. "What we're really asking is, What are the risk factors of the other 70 percent?" said Dr. Devra Lee Davis, co-chairwoman of the conference and now a leading advocate in the fight to study the connection between breast cancer and the environment.

The other co-chairwoman of the two-day symposium, Dr. Susan Love, director of the Breast Center at the University of California in Los Angeles and also a major voice in breast-cancer action in the United States, said, "We don't really have a clue as to what the factors are. What we're trying to do is broaden the question to ask, What is wrong with a society that causes this?"

Well, at least some clues to those questions were discovered in the release of the Long Island study on April 12, 1994, when the New York State Health Department announced that women living near large chemical plants there ran a significantly greater risk of developing breast cancer after menopause than women who didn't live near the plants.

Scientists cautioned that the study did not establish a specific cause-and-effect relationship between chemical pollution and breast cancer, but their conclusions sure suggested a possible link. In Nassau County, according to the Health Department study, 14.5 percent of the women with breast cancer lived within one kilometer of plants that produced chemicals, rubber and plastics between 1965 and 1975. That compared to 9.5 percent of the women in the control group who lived near the plants but did not develop breast cancer. Statistically, that meant women living near a chemical plant had a 62 percent higher risk of breast cancer than those who didn't live near one, about the same heightened risk of women with a family history of the disease. And the risk of breast cancer increased with the number of chemical plants near a woman's home.

State Health Commissioner Mark R. Chassin told the New York Times, "If this association proves to be real, it will be the first time that an environmental risk factor that is avoidable has been identified."

Chassin said those factors could account for as much as 5 percent of breast-cancer cases on Long Island, although it's still possible that other known risk factors were responsible.

The study examined the records of 793 women living in the area for more than 20 years whose breast cancer had been diagnosed between 1984 and 1986, and compared them with a control group of 966 cancer-free Long Island women chosen from motor vehicle records for the same period. Researchers divided Long Island into five-kilometer grids to study traffic patterns around women's homes and into one-kilometer grids to study their proximity to industry. Since researchers believe estrogen production is a critical factor in the development of breast cancer, and since exposure to pesticides and some chemical pollutions has been linked with estrogen production in laboratory animals, both traffic pollution and chemical pollution were studied. While the incidence rates were high for postmenopausal women living near the chemical plants, they were no higher than average among women living near busy highways or nonchemical industries.

Geri Barish, co-chairwoman of 1 in 9, the Long Island Breast Cancer Action Coalition, was pleased with the findings. "My first thought was, they're really acknowledging the fact that there's something wrong here." And Mary Lou Monahan, president of the Long Beach Breast Cancer Coalition, said, "I'm so happy that they're looking at it, that they're finally doing studies that are environmentally linked."

Dr. Mary S. Wolff, a professor of Community Medicine at Mount Sinai Medical Center in Manhattan, whose own 1993 study concluded that women with the highest exposure to DDT have four times the breast-cancer risk of women with the least exposure, said the state study was "the first credible report of its kind. This doesn't establish a link between the chemicals and breast cancer, but it casts suspicion in that direction, and that has to be followed up with more research."

Which is precisely what Dr. G. Iris Obrams is about to do. In a five-year study for the NCI, she hopes to find specific causes for the high rates of breast cancer on Long Island. "I don't think it [the state study] changes our opinion that air and water quality are extremely high priority questions for Long Island," she told the *New York Times*, "but these earlier analyses will guide us toward the kinds of industries we will focus on. It's a very timely study."

Lorraine Pace of Breast Cancer HELP said that while the state study didn't offer any specific answers, she believed the NCI studies would. She said every time she looks at Long Island's Great South Bay it strengthens her belief that ecology plays a role. "You used to be able to go out and fish in the bay; you could walk across the bay from clam boat to clam boat. You can't do that now. I think that whatever happened to the clams is now happening to us."

There's no doubt women are interested in the issue. Release of the New York study sparked a record-breaking 600 calls to the state's toll-free environmental health number. It also prompted activists in states throughout the Eastern Seaboard to begin taking a closer look at their own backyards. In New Jersey, for example, where some areas have even higher breast-cancer rates than New York, Felice James of the state's Breast Cancer Coalition said her group would likely focus more on potential environmental links. "We don't have that strong political sense that got Long Island started," she said. "But I don't feel our environment is any safer here." However, by focusing on environmental links, her group will also be venturing into the political realm.

Dr. Obrams confirms James' assumption: "The whole Northeast is an area that's in need of study." The NCI study she will oversee will include a series of separate ecological tests on Long Island, along with studies in New York, New Jersey, Connecticut, Massachusetts, New Hampshire, Rhode Island, Vermont, Maryland, Delaware and Washington, D.C. It's the first major breakthrough in what promises to be a long, costly and politically charged battle in determining the extent of the link between industrial pollution and breast cancer.

While New York State may have earned some kudos for its Long Island study, the problem of toxic waste in the area has been known for many years, and the state has done little about it. In 1986, New York state voters approved a $1.2 billion bond issue to clean up toxic waste sites, yet by May 15, 1994, a *New York Times* article pointed out only $257.7 million had been spent. The state has the power to proceed with a cleanup and recover the cost later either through negotiations or, if that fails after nine months, in court. But it's an option the state has rarely chosen.

Benjamin A. Marvin, a spokesman for the State Department of Environmental Conservation, told the *Times* that the state's approach was working. He said steps were being taken to clean up 80 percent of the 561 known toxic waste sites in the most serious category, and in up to 70 percent of those cases, the private companies responsible for the pollution are paying, thereby saving taxpayers $1.5 billion.

"Anybody can find a couple of sites and say, 'Here the state isn't doing anything, and here's proof," Marvin said. "The criticism fails to point out where the state has done work on hazardous waste sites."

But the newspaper points out that the state's own figures show that only 14 percent of the 561 sites are actually being cleaned and capped, while another 14 percent have cleanup plans under preparation. That leaves 403 sites that are either being negotiated over, studied or cleaned on an interim basis just to stop further contamination. The New York Public Interest Research Group estimates that 54 percent of known or suspected hazardous dumps on Long Island, and 43 percent in New York City, have been on the state Superfund cleanup list for more than a decade.

Journalist Diana Jean Schemo in a story in the *New York Times* tells of one 25.3-acre site in the City of Glen Cove on Long Island, New York, which is not only an example of hazardous dump sites, but a study in governmental stupidity and delay. That particular site was sold to Village Green Realty for $1.1 million in 1981 for a large (328 units) condominium project, despite the fact the site had been a city dump for more than 20 years and Nassau County health officials warned that hazardous chemicals dumped there could endanger people who lived in the condominiums. Not to worry, the City Council approved the project in 1984 with the absurd condition that no apartments could be built on the ground floor in case methane seeped from underground. Two years later, with toxic chemicals in groundwater exceeding acceptable levels, the company had to halt construction. In 1988, Village Green and Old Court Savings and Loan of Maryland signed a consent order to correct the problem. But radioactive waste was discovered the next year, traced to Li Tungsten, a defunct manufacturer of tungsten for light bulbs, high-speed drill bits and artillery shells during World War II. Discovery of the radioactive waste meant that cleanup costs skyrocketed, and by September 1990, both the real-estate company and its bank had gone into receivership.

In 1991, the state asked the Environmental Protection Agency (EPA) to add the site to the Federal Superfund cleanup list. Five months later, the state was asked to forward all its information about the site, and it took the Department of Environmental Conservation about 18 months to assemble the material. In 1994, the EPA hired a consultant to investigate the site independently. EPA spokesman Richard J. Cahill told the *New York Times* that the consultant would likely begin the investigation in the summer and the agency would likely not decide whether to add it to the Federal Superfund list until 1996, five years after the state had suggested the idea, and 15 years after the site had been sold for a condominium project against the advice of local health officials.

Throughout this torturous delay, the contamination continues its inexorable spread into surrounding areas. And it is just one of several hundred sites representing a continuing and serious health hazard to the people of Long Island.

Concern over environmental factors, while excruciatingly slow in developing, isn't exactly new. In 1775, Sir Percivall Pott, a London physician, noted that scrotal cancer was commonplace among chimney sweeps and concluded that the disease had to come from the soot that accumulated in their bodies. There were other indicators of the cancer-chemical connection as well. Copper and tin workers in Cornwall and Wales, constantly exposed to arsenic fumes, were plagued by skin cancer and uranium miners in Bohemia were found to have high rates of lung cancer, although it wasn't recognized as cancer at the time.

Today, it is known that certain areas have much higher incidence and far more deaths from cancer than other areas. New Jersey, for example, which has roughly the same rate of tobacco sales per capita as Wyoming, has a 36 percent higher female cancer death rate than that state. In fact, the five highest cancer death rates in the United States, for both men and women, are all in the Northeast, historically the country's most heavily industrialized area, while the five lowest are predominantly in rural western and southern states with relatively little heavy industry. For women, the combined cancer death rate for the five highest states is 38 percent higher than the five lowest. There's an even larger discrepancy (45 per cent) for men.

The same is true for Europe, where maps of cancer incidence range from the highest rates in the world in parts of England, to exceptionally low rates in southern Italy. According to a 1993 World Health Organization report on cancer incidence and mortality, the incidence rate per

100,000 women aged 30 to 74 in 1985 in European Community countries ranged from a low of 89.8 in Zaragoza, Spain, to a high of 154.6 in heavily industrialized Hamburg, Germany. Even wilder fluctuations appeared in non-European Community countries, ranging from 61.7 in Szabolcs-Szatmar, Hungary, to 152.3 in Geneva, Switzerland. Although incidence rates are much lower in Asia, they still range from a low of 43.3 in Shanghai, China, to a high of 69.8 among Indians in Singapore. Among Filipinos in Hawaii, the incidence rate was just 90.6, compared to 206.4 for native Hawaiians and 204.3 for caucasian Hawaiians.

In Canada, breast-cancer rates in the westernmost province of British Columbia are about 100 per 100,000, some 40 percent higher than those in Newfoundland, the easternmost province. By the same token, a few cities — particularly Toronto; Montreal; Sydney, Nova Scotia; and Brantford, Ontario — also have higher than average rates, and tend to be heavily industrialized urban settings.

In his book, *The Politics of Cancer*, Dr. Samuel S. Epstein cites a January 1978 report by the American Industrial Health Council, an organization created by the chemical industry to fight against regulation of carcinogens in the workplace, which tries to explain away the continuing rise of cancer incidence and deaths.

"If we use the turn of the century as a time against which to compare today's cancer problem," the report says, "there has indeed been an increase in the incidence of cancer . . . but the increase is predominantly attributable to (1) greater longevity (the incidence of cancer increases with age), and (2) pandemic cigarette smoking." The council argues that no more than 5 percent of all cancers in the United States are attributable to industrial chemicals. It claims that when lung cancer is excluded, overall death rates are down. Epstein counters that even the council's own data show that most cancers are increasing, but there have been large decreases in two sites — the stomach and the cervix. He says the decline in stomach cancer remains unexplained, but the dramatic drop in cervix cancer "is due in part to widespread Pap screening programs which detect and treat precancerous conditions, not to the disappearance of its possible environmental causes."

Epstein adds that "most cancer is environmental in origin and is therefore preventable. The striking increase in cancer death rates in this century cannot be accounted for by aging alone and cannot be due to genetic changes in the population, which would take generations to propagate throughout the population. Furthermore, a series of epidemiological studies have concluded that environmental factors cause from 70 to 90 percent of all cancers. Such estimates are derived from a comparison of cancer incidence and mortality in different countries all over the world."

Epstein goes on to write that "the low priority which the NCI has accorded to research on environmental carcinogens in the past has been an important factor in limiting possible regulatory initiatives for cancer prevention and control. The absence of adequate information on carcinogenicity testing of suspect carcinogens and on epidemiological [epidemic-related] investigations on environmental and occupational carcinogens is one of the most common arguments used by industry to oppose regulatory controls."

While the establishment remains reluctant to pursue the impact of chemicals on the human body, chemically induced health problems appear to be getting more acute with the appearance, along with the standard chemicals, of a whole new class of organic chemicals that are much more persistent in the environment.

Epstein explains. "We are living in a new era of organic chemicals, not just familiar ones, but exotic ones which have never previously existed on earth, and to which no living thing has previously had to adapt. Organochlorines are nondegradable or poorly degradable, persist in the environment and in the body, and are fat soluble and have accumulated and concentrated in the food chain. As a class, they also contain a disproportionately high number of carcinogens. . . . Literally thousands of them are being released into the environment, and not in lots of a few pounds or gallons but by the millions and billions of pounds and gallons. The intricate biochemical defenses that living beings throughout evolution have developed to cope with their environment are now being constantly violated by foreign materials introduced into the environment in petroleum products, synthetic organic chemicals, and organic pesticides."

In April 1993, Mary Wolff, a chemist at the Mount Sinai School of Medicine in New York, published the findings of her study in the *Journal of the National Cancer Institute* showing that women with the highest exposure to DDT have four times the breast-cancer risk of women with the least exposure. Wolff and her team measured levels of a DDT breakdown product in the blood of 58 women with breast cancer and 171 women without it. Women with levels in the top 10 percent had four times the risk of women in the bottom 10 percent. Wolff said that even though DDT was phased out in 1972, because it was common in meat and dairy products and is stored in the body for decades, most North Americans still carry DDT residues. Children are exposed to it through their mother's milk. "Breast cancer is the most common cancer among women, and a lot of the risk is unexplained," she said.

Pointing out that U.S. breast-cancer incidence rose 8 percent between 1973 and 1980 among women under 50, Wolff showed that it rose 32.1 percent for those over 50. She and her team said the increase can be explained in part by increased screening, but "the upward shift is also consistent with the historical pattern of accumulation of organochlorine residues in the environment; i.e., older women who had the greatest potential cumulative exposure to DDT between 1945 and 1972 may now experience a higher risk of breast cancer than women much older or younger who were not similarly exposed."

Wolff and her team also studied a link between PCBs and breast cancer but could find none.

Dr. Devra Lee Davis called it "the best-designed study yet conducted to investigate the link between toxic chemicals and a major disease in women . . . [and] should be regarded as a very serious message to all of those concerned with figuring out how to prevent cancer — which is something we have not paid enough attention to in the past."

Even the American Chemical Society was beginning to notice. An article about the same time in its *Chemical and Engineering News* reported the growing concern that the chemicals "are causing cancer in adults and adverse health and reproductive effects in the off-spring of both humans and wildlife." The article pointed out that DDT levels in Great Lakes fish dropped sharply after 1972 but are increasing again, likely because DDT used elsewhere is being transported by atmospheric currents and dropped into the lakes. It also noted that atrazine, now the most widely used pesticide in the United States, has been linked to an increased risk of ovarian cancer.

A small 1976 pilot study in Israel measured tissue levels of PCBs and organochlorine pesticides in cancerous breast tissue, adjacent non-cancerous breast tissue from the same women and breast tissue from a control group of cancer-free women. It found PCB levels were 3.3 times higher than adjacent normal tissues and 3.1 times higher than tissue from women without cancer. In addition, p,p'-DDT was three times higher in cancerous tissues than adjacent tissue and 26 percent higher than in cancer-free women.

A 1990 Finnish study of 44 women with breast cancer and 33 without the disease found that the women with the cancers had 50 percent higher concentrations of the pesticide beta-hexachlorocyclohexane (b-HCH) in their breast fat than women without breast cancer.

Between November 1991 and May 1992, 41 of 42 women aged 40 to 69 who had a biopsy for a breast mass in a Quebec City hospital volunteered for a study. In addition to a questionnaire on age, weight loss, parity and breast-feeding, researchers collected breast adipose tissue from the biopsies for organochlorine analysis. Four of the women were excluded for various reasons, and of the remainder, 20 were case patients and 17 had benign breast disease and served as a control group. The study, conducted by a group of seven scientists at Laval University's Faculty of Medicine and published in the February 1, 1994, edition of the *Journal of the National Cancer Institute*, concluded that the study "supports the hypothesis that exposure to estrogenic organochlorine may affect the incidence of hormone-responsive breast cancer."

The evidence continued to mount with a study at Hartford Hospital between May and September 1987. Published in the March-April 1992 edition of the *Archives of Environmental Health*, the five-member research team discovered "mean concentrations of PCBs and p,p'-DDT were 50 to 60 percent higher in tissues of women who had breast cancer." They called for further study. "In light of increasing rates of breast cancer and our limited knowledge of the causes, investigation of carcinogenic environmental chemical exposures is a promising avenue to explore . . ."

Famous activist Dr. Rosalie Bertell, president of the Toronto-based International Institute of Concern for Public Health, addressed the issue in the Summer 1992 edition of *Mothering*. Bertell wrote that exposure to estrogenic compounds (chemicals that imitate the female hormone estrogen) and to electromagnetic fields (EMFs) increase breast-cancer risks. "Pregnant women who took the estrogenic drug diethylstilbestrol

(DES), popular from in the late 1940s until the early 1970s, showed a definite hike in breast cancer 20 years later," she wrote. Bertell also worried about radiation exposure from X-rays, fluoroscopy and mammography, and recommended women who use a VDT have it checked for EMF emissions, buy a shield, sit 26 inches from the screen "and avoid sitting behind and to the left of another person's terminal." For women who use electric blankets, Bertell advised them to turn the blanket on before bedtime then turn it off when they get into bed.

One of the major problems for humans from organochlorines is that they resist breaking down and therefore accumulate in the environment, to be spread around the world through the air and water, exposing humans to these poisons in food, groundwater, surface water and a host of products such as pesticides, dioxin and PCBs. A 1987 U.S. study identified 177 organochlorines in the fat, breast milk, blood, semen and breath of the general population of the United States and Canada. They are passed from one generation to the next through the placenta and breast-feeding, and sometimes cause damage to genetic material in the sperm or ovum, which is then handed down to the next generation.

The environmental group Greenpeace, in a major 1992 report on chlorine and human health, wrote: "No industrial organochlorines are known to be non-toxic. A growing body of evidence links persistent organochlorines to large-scale ecological disruptions and effects on human health."

Marti Mussell, coordinator of the Women's Environmental Network (WEN) told the Breast Cancer Action Ottawa annual meeting on April 11, 1994, that "we produce 40 million tons a year of organochlorines. It doesn't go away. There is no away. It's time to act, time to phase out these poisons in our environment." But another panelist, Dr. Ivo Hynie, who spent 12 years as director of medical biochemistry for the Canadian government, said that environmental factors are involved in breast cancer, "but there is no proof organochlorines are involved . . . to say clearly this is organochlorines is to jump to an unscientific conclusion . . . yes, we are certain there is a connection between [chemicals] and breast cancer, but we are not certain which ones . . . there are several hundred organochlorines and several thousand other chemicals."

Dr. Eva Tomiak, a medical oncologist at the Ottawa Regional Cancer Clinic, told the Ottawa meeting there is "no firm proof yet" linking breast cancer and organochlorines, criticized Greenpeace for having "underestimated the possibility of other dietary factors" and said she was "disappointed" that some activists were boycotting the American Cancer Society. "Everyone has to work together if we're going to beat this thing," she said.

Her colleague, Dr. Shail Verma, agreed that while the subject needs more study, it is "premature to relate a cause to a single chemical or group of chemicals." Later, he acknowledged that most of the funding for therapeutic research comes from the pharmaceutical companies. Asked what he would tell his wife and daughters about the dangers of organochlorines, Verma said, "I'd get rid of them. I think there is enough emerging data to justify that. I'd tell my wife and daughter to avoid them."

Dr. Howard Morrison, an epidemiologist with Health Canada's Laboratory Centre for Disease Control, Cancer Division, said a group of women, asked at a Montreal forum what they thought was the major cause of breast cancer, chose stress first and pesticides second. "A couple of people in the U.S. have been strong advocates of the [environmental] thesis and have received considerable publicity," he said. "The evidence is intriguing and it is certainly worth pursuing, but it is not as strong as these people would have you believe. The science on it isn't convincing at all."

Morrison said some of the evidence "scares the hell out of you, and if it pans out in the long run, then we've got a major finding here. But some people prefer to find risk factors for breast cancer that don't reflect your lifestyles. They prefer to blame the environment. That may sound cynical, but it's true. For example, if you have a baby before aged 18, that lessens the risk. But what are we going to do with that knowledge? Have a baby? I don't think so. If you find that abortion increases the risk, as some studies do, well, that's a hot potato. What are you going to do about that? Or if menarche begins early, yes, that's a risk factor, but there's not much you can do about that, is there?"

The explosion of industrial chemicals began in earnest after World War II. In the United States alone, production of pesticides skyrocketed from 259,000 pounds in 1947 to 637.7 million pounds in 1960. A chart in the 1971 article "The Closing Circle" by Barry Commoner, director of the

Center for the Biology of Natural Systems at Queens College, Brooklyn, New York, illustrates the point dramatically. It shows that from 1945 to 1970 alone, the increase in production of synthetic fibers increased by 5,980 percent, while plastics production went up 1,960 percent, nitrogen fertilizers, 1,050 percent, synthetic organic chemicals, 950 percent, and organic solvents, 746 percent. Commoner also said in another article, "The best way to stop toxic chemicals from entering the environment is to not produce them."

Industry began producing small amounts of chlorine and organochlorines around the turn of the last century, but it wasn't until World War II that large-scale production began, primarily prompted by military use. About 40 million tons of chlorine are manufactured each year. There are now about 11,000 organochlorines, including plastics, pesticides, refrigerants, solvents and other chemicals. Thousands more are formed as by-products of chlorine-based industrial processes, such as bleaching of pulp and incinerating waste products containing chlorinated materials, along with a group of extremely toxic and hormonally active chlorinated dioxins, furans and related compounds. Chlorine used to sterilize drinking water represents just 1 percent of the amount of chlorine being manufactured.

Chlorine does occur naturally in ordinary salt and poses no environmental threat. But when industry splits the salt molecule to make chlorine gas, which is not a natural substance, that creates environmental problems. When the chlorine gas comes into contact with organic (carbon-based) matter, that's when organochlorines are formed.

One of the legacies of World War II industrial plants and a continuing by-product of heavy industrialization is hazardous waste sites. Industry produces a lot of them. The problem is how to get rid of hazardous waste safely. Even that wasn't a serious concern with industry and government until pressure was brought by the burgeoning environmental lobby during the past two decades. But the fact that hazardous waste and human beings don't match appears indisputable.

A scientific paper on cancer mortality in U.S. counties containing hazardous waste sites (HWSs) and groundwater pollution published in the March-April 1989 *Archives of Environmental Health* demonstrated that environmental problems lead to higher death rates in various cancers in both men and women, particularly breast cancer. The study was published by the U.S. Environmental Protection Agency (EPA) and conducted by Drs. Jack Griffith and Wilson B. Riggan, along with Dr. Robert C. Duncan of the University of Miami School of Medicine's Oncology Department, and Dr. Alvin C. Pellom of the Northrop Corporation, Research Triangle Park, North Carolina. They identified 593 waste sites in 339 U.S. counties in 49 states that had analytical evidence of contaminated groundwater. In all cases, the groundwater was a sole source of water supply — for drinking and other uses. They also enumerated HWS and non-HWS counties that showed excess numbers of deaths for various cancers and found "significant associations" between excess cancer deaths and hazardous waste sites.

The study pointed out that since the late 1950s, more than 750 million tons of toxic chemical wastes had been discarded in 30,000 to 50,000 hazardous waste sites in the United States. Throughout October 1984, the EPA inventoried almost 19,000 uncontrolled HWSs. "The disposal of toxic waste creates a major pollution problem and a potential for increased risks to human health," the paper concluded. "It is clear that chemical wastes can leach from disposal sites into community water supplies. . . . Ground water provides 50 percent of the drinking water in the United States, and is reported to be the primary source of human exposure to chemical pollutants."

For breast cancer, the rates were particularly high in what they called EPA Region 1, which encompasses Connecticut, Maine, Massachusetts, New Hampshire, Rhode Island and Vermont. In the end, the paper argued that because so many other factors could be involved, "it is clear that more definitive studies are necessary to assess the magnitude of any adverse health effects associated with waste sites and polluted ground drinking water. It appears from our data, however, that HWS locations may be used as an initial index of possible exposure to toxic chemicals."

Health problems related to the environment are linked to far more than just the proximity of hazardous waste sites. A considerable body of science has been accumulated to show that it's not just where you get your water from, but where you work that could be deadly.

On October 10, 1991, *The Lancet* published a German study by the Centre for Chemical Workers' Health, Hamburg Department of Health, on cancer mortality among workers in a chemical plant that produced herbicides, including processes contaminated with dioxin (TCDD). The mortality results were compared with a similar group of gas workers. The authors of the study collected vital statistics for 1,537 workers hired between 1952 and 1984. During this period, 367 deaths (313 men and 54 women) were recorded, with cancer the underlying cause of death in 93 men and 20 women. Only 7 percent of the women worked in the high-exposure locations in the plant (compared to 39.6 percent of the men), but even so, "breast cancer mortality was raised." In addition, eight of the women still living had cancer, five of them breast cancer.

The Hamburg-Moorfleet plant was operated by Boehringer-Ingelheim, where herbicide production began in 1951. But public concern over potential hazards from disposal of waste products contaminated with TCDD and other higher chlorinated dioxins led to its closure on June 18, 1984.

The study showed that the rate of death from cancer was lower among employees who began work after 1954 than among those who began before. "During 1951–54," the study said, "high concentrations of TCDD were present as a contaminant of TCP. . . . In women we found an increase in breast cancer mortality. In a Danish study in the context of herbicide exposure there was no such increase, but those women were exposed mainly to 4-chloro-2-methyl-phenoxyacetic acid, which is not thought to be contaminated with TCDD."

Another 1991 study, conducted by Dr. Nancy Hall of the New Jersey Department of Health and Dr. Kenneth Rosenman of Michigan State University's Department of Medicine, published in the *American Journal of Industrial Medicine*, studied New Jersey occupational patterns to assess potential associations between workplace exposures and cancer incidence. Its aim was to attempt to identify specific jobs that create an added risk of various cancers, including breast cancer.

Using occupation and industry information on 17,621 cases routinely collected by the New Jersey State Cancer Registry between 1979 and 1984, Hall and Rosenman set up four categories: white males (10,824), white females (4,248), black males (1,957) and black females (592). The results showed "an elevated proportion of breast cancer both in the chemical industry . . . and in its subcategory, pharmaceutical products" for black women. A study of white pharmaceutical industry employees in 1979 had also reported an excess of breast-cancer rates in that industry, while a 1986 New York State analysis showed high breast-cancer mortality for white women in the electrical and printing industries. The New Jersey study also showed a high mortality rate for black women in those industries. It also found higher rates of uterine cancer for women in several manufacturing industries, including rubber and plastic products, apparel and electrical equipment.

These studies have forced governments to act and industries to change their practices some, but not a whole lot.

The evidence between cancer links and the environment is too strong to be written off as mere coincidence. But as you'll read in the next chapter, women continue to die of breast cancer while the battle between maximized profits and environmental responsibility goes on.

9 The Clan

IN HER MOVING 1991 BOOK, *REFUGE*, author Terry Tempest Williams, a breast-cancer survivor who became the matriarch of her family at age 34 because cancer had killed most of the women in her family, opens the epilogue with this:

"I belong to a Clan of One-Breast Women. My mother, my grand-mothers, and six aunts have all had mastectomies. Seven are dead. The two who survive have just completed rounds of chemotherapy and radiation."

Part of a Mormon family with roots in Utah since 1847, where the "word of wisdom" dictated healthy living — no coffee, tea, tobacco or alcohol — and where most women finished their childbearing by age 30, only one had breast cancer before 1960. By all standards, her family should have been at low risk. Is her family a cultural anomaly? she asks. Or is it something else? Williams argues it's definitely something else — specifically the above-ground nuclear testing in Nevada from January

27, 1951, to July 11, 1962. That was during the Cold War days when public health rated below national security and when deadly winds blew north in Utah covering what the federal security officials called "low-used segments of the population" (bureaucratese for low population densities) with nuclear fall-out and leaving sheep dead in their tracks. As a result of this, Williams writes of "children growing up in the American Southwest, drinking contaminated milk from contaminated cows, even from the contaminated breasts of their mothers, my mother — members, years later, of the Clan of One-Breast Women."

On May 10, 1984, in a suit against the United States brought by Irene Allen of Hurricane, Utah, Judge Bruce S. Jenkins awarded damages to ten plaintiffs. It was the first time a federal court had determined that nuclear tests had been the cause of cancers. Three years later, however, the Tenth Circuit Court of Appeals overturned the ruling, not on the science, but on the ground that the United States was protected from suit by the legal doctrine of sovereign immunity, a centuries-old notion left over from the days of the absolute English monarchs. In January 1988, the Supreme Court refused to review the Appeals Court decision. "To our court system," writes Williams, "it does not matter whether the United States government was irresponsible, whether it lied to its citizens, or even that citizens died from the fallout of nuclear testing. What matters is that our government is immune: 'The King can do no wrong.'"

While strong anecdotal evidence, along with scientific studies on the environmental link to breast cancer, was beginning to pile up in the academic world, the issue itself was still not capturing much public attention, largely because the cancer establishment and the industries implicated in the problem — industries inextricably linked with the establishment — were systematically discrediting the claims of environmental researchers.

Still, the activists persisted. The May-June 1992 *Resist Newsletter* wrote that in the United States, one out of every three people will get some form of cancer and one out of four will die from it, adding that "extensive evidence exists to indicate that cancer is an environmental disease." They list four major factors that support the argument that environmental factors are critical.

- "The dramatic differences in the incidence of cancer between communities; i.e., incidence of cancer among people of a given age in different parts of the world can vary by a factor of ten to a hundred;
- "Changes in the incidence of cancer (either lower or higher) in groups that migrate to a new country;
- "Changes in the incidence of particular types of cancer over time;
- "The actual identification of specific (environmental) causes of certain cancers . . ."

Environmental Protection Agency regulations at the time allowed as many as 60 cancer-causing pesticides to be used in the most commonly eaten foods, albeit in small quantities, but some foods had 20 or more carcinogens in them. The newsletter cited Rachel Carson's 1962 book, *Silent Spring*: "This piling up of chemicals from many different sources creates a total exposure that cannot be measured. It is meaningless, therefore, to talk about the 'safety' of any specific amount of residues."

On the question of breast cancer, the newsletter pointed out that in the year 1992 alone, almost as many American women would die from the disease as American lives were lost in the entire Vietnam War. "Research suggests that the development of breast cancer probably depends on a complex interplay among environmental exposures, genetic predisposition to the disease, and hormonal activity. Research on actual identification of causal factors, however, is given low priority and proceeds at a snail's pace."

In November 1992, the radical environmental group Greenpeace released a controversial study as part of its Zero Discharge Campaign for the Great Lakes. It linked breast-cancer rates directly to chlorine pollution, setting off a firestorm of official criticism from industry and the cancer establishment, but helping finally to bring the environmental aspect of breast cancer into sharper public focus. The Greenpeace conclusion flew in the face of the conventional wisdom of the medical-scientific-cancer community, which traditionally argued that environmental factors played at most a minor role in cancer incidence.

Geoffrey Howe, director of epidemiology at the National Cancer Institute of Canada in Toronto, for example, was skeptical about the study. "In general, epidemiologists do not consider there is strong evidence for this type of [breast-cancer-pollution] relationship," although he did concede scientists don't have "an explanation" for the rising incidence. "I agree with that."

Greenpeace conceded the link cannot be "proven beyond a doubt" from existing research, but while calling for more research, it concluded that the weight of evidence "makes a strong case that organochlorines may make an important contribution to the incidence of breast cancer in industrialized nations." Pointing out that "alternatives are available now for all major uses of chlorine," it recommended a complete phasing out of both the production and use of organochlorines and the treatment of them as a class, since "it is not practical or necessary to regulate these thousands of substances one-by-one."

As things stand at present, chemicals must be reviewed one by one, and each one must be shown to be a hazard before action is taken against its use. Under this system, only 1 or 2 percent of the 80,000 synthetic chemicals in commerce have ever been subject to basic hazard assessments. What's more, industry produces thousands of new chemicals each year and thousands more organochlorines are formed as by-products of chlorine-based processes, so it is simply not possible to test these compounds on an individual basis.

Greenpeace, which operates in 30 countries on a budget of about $150 million, is no friend of industry. It never was. Nor is it without its own internal squabbles. Greenpeace's Canadian lawyer Brian Iler, fired earlier this year after 16 years with the organization, was recently quoted as saying that almost none of its donations reach environmental-campaign activities. Because Greenpeace relies on paid canvassers and direct-mail campaigns, as little as seven cents of every dollar donated goes to Canadian campaigns according to the critics.

All this, of course, gives critics plenty of ammunition to dump on the organization's work. But despite its own problems, and its well-known anti-industry bias, the Greenpeace report still raises some serious questions that can't be answered simply by bad-mouthing the source of those questions.

"Emerging evidence," says the report, "suggests that environmental organochlorine contamination is a health hazard to the general human population as well. . . . Scientists have begun to find that organochlorines may be a factor in hormonal disruptions, declining sperm counts, male infertility, abnormalities of the male reproductive tract, impaired childhood development, birth defects and low birth weight, and certain cancers in the general population."

One of those cancers, of course, is breast cancer. Greenpeace writes that at least 16 organochlorines have been shown to cause mammary cancer in rodents "despite the limited number of laboratory studies that have specifically investigated the relationship between these chemicals and this disease." While some of those compounds have been banned or severely restricted, many others remained in widespread use in both Europe and North America. One of those is atrazine, one of the most common pesticides in the United States, Canada and Europe. In the United States alone, between 70 and 90 million pounds of atrazine are used each year. According to one researcher at the National Cancer Institute, "Atrazine may play a role in human breast, prostate, ovarian, and endometrial cancer by inducing some hormones but inhibiting others."

Greenpeace argues, therefore, that governments should immediately "acknowledge the severe damage to health and the environment caused by the class of organochlorines . . . [and] establish a plan to phase-out the use of chlorine, chlorine-based bleaches, and organochlorines. Priority should be given to those uses that cause the most severe organochlorine pollution and for which alternatives are currently available: pulp and paper, solvents, plastics, and pesticides."

In 1991, the year before Greenpeace launched its anti-chlorine drive with release of this report, there were signs that those who were warning about the environmental impact of the chemical were gaining some significant allies. Both the National Research Council (NRC) of the National Academy of Sciences in the United States and the International Joint Commission (IJC), a Canada–U.S. body that overseas the Great Lakes Water Quality Agreement, were publicly backing away from the traditional approach that health hazards had to be absolutely proven through traditional epidemiological studies before any remedial action could be imposed.

The IJC argued that "as in solving a difficult crime, the weight of evidence together builds a basis for judgment. . . . But it does require new types of evidence and new ways of assembling evidence. Above all, it requires a willingness to act on an integrated body of evidence rather than to wait for irrefutable evidence of a cause-effect link."

The NRC's Committee on Environmental Epidemiology felt that traditional studies were unsuited for proving causal relationships and therefore it "must rely on a combination of evidence from different sources to reach any conclusion in accordance with its mandate to estimate health effects associated with hazardous waste."

Not surprisingly, the chlorine industry wasn't impressed by Greenpeace's work. On December 4, 1992, the industry launched a $5 million public relations campaign with a response prepared by CamTox, Inc., of Mississauga, Ontario, for The Chlorine Institute, Inc., Washington, arguing that the "premise and suggestions" of the Greenpeace paper written by Joe Thorton "are not valid . . . and are based on selective and inaccurate analysis of results from epidemiological studies." They even claimed that organochlorines are good for you because "toxicological studies show that PCBs, DDT and dioxin act via mechanisms that actually reduce or cause no increase in breast cancer." They argue that evidence of significant damage to human health should be considered valid only when scientists can prove "the specificity of the associations between specific chlorinated organic chemicals and reported adverse effects," adding that because organochlorines vary in their chemical and biological behavior, they must be assessed on a chemical-by-chemical basis.

In short, the industry claims "it is apparent that no causal association can be drawn between exposure to chlorinated organic compounds and risk of breast cancer," and things are just fine the way they are, thank you very much.

The widespread support among governments and the establishment for this approach might be understandable if there were no alternatives to organochlorines available. But that is not the case. There are safer alternatives available now — for all the major uses of chlorine.

As one 1993 Greenpeace publication put it, "Chlorine-free alternatives are available, practical, and proven effective. Twenty-seven pulp mills around the world are now producing high-quality, totally chlorine-free paper using oxygen-based bleaching or other methods. Dozens of European companies and municipalities have virtually eliminated the use of PVC (polyvinyl chloride) in construction, flooring, automobiles, furniture, and packaging."

In North America, however, PVC is more widely used than ever. It represents about one-third of chlorine use worldwide, the largest single use of chlorine. It's what those white plastic chairs are made of, and is routinely used by the plastics chemical industry as a cheap substitute for other traditional materials. Hospitals and municipal incinerators also burn substantial amounts of PVC, thereby creating serious dioxin problems.

On the environmental plus side, however, the Greenpeace report points out that "farmers around the world have achieved high yields and reduced expenses using organic farming methods instead of synthetic pesticides. Manufacturing firms and dry-cleaners are substituting chemical-free processes for chlorinated solvents. Even some chemical companies are using alternative processes to make chemicals that previously required chlorinated intermediaries.

"Alternatives are available now for all major uses of chlorine. But their implementation in North America has been slowed by the current regulatory focus on individual chemicals and acceptable discharges. In the end, one of the best reasons to phase out chlorine is because we can."

An April 1993 report written by Charles River Associates (CRA) for The Chlorine Institute estimates that the phasing out of all chlorines in the States and Canada would cost $102 billion per year. But because a few sectors that use only small amounts of chlorine account for the bulk of the cost of the phase-out, the CRA says eliminating 95 percent of chlorine would cost $20 billion. Compare that to the $75 to $150 billion annual health-care costs the International Joint Commission attributes to the effects of persistent toxic substances, and the phase-out sounds like a deal.

According to Greenpeace, it's even better than that. They say the CRA "drastically overestimates the cost of chlorine substitutes" in several major sectors by ignoring the economic benefits of chlorine-free technologies. In 1989, for example, the National Academy of Sciences found that farmers who eliminate their use of synthetic pesticides "increase their yields, lower their production costs, and have access to burgeoning markets for organic foods."

In some industries, such as dry cleaning, substituting chlorine processes actually creates more jobs. The "multi-process wet cleaning" technique, which is just as effective as traditional dry cleaning, does the job with greater numbers of skilled laborers using water, scrubbing, tumbling, steam and soap, along with relatively non-toxic spotting agents.

One of the strongest prima facie cases referred to in the Greenpeace report to link chemicals with breast cancer was a lengthy account of the extraordinary experience of an Israeli pesticide ban in the late 1970s. Three carcinogenic pesticides were taken off the market: a-BHC (benzene hexachloride, or hexachlorocyclohexane), y-BHC (lindane) and DDT. At that time in the United States, for example, a-BHC levels in milk averaged 10 parts per billion (ppb) on a fat basis, while mean concentrations in Israeli milk were about 1,000 ppb, and as high as 28,000 ppb. With lindane, the mean was about 17 times higher than the comparable U.S. value in milk and DDE (a by-product of DDT breaking down) was found in Israeli milk at levels 500 percent higher than in U.S. milk. At the same time, Israel's breast-cancer mortality rate among pre-menopausal women was about double the rate of that for other countries with comparable levels of fat consumption. This sparked a huge public outcry and a threat of Supreme Court intervention and prompted the government to begin an aggressive phase-out program of these pesticides in the spring of 1978. Within two years, breast-milk levels of the compounds fell dramatically. And astonishingly, between 1976 and 1986, at a time when breast-cancer rates were rising in every other country in the industrialized world, the national age-adjusted breast-cancer rates in Israel dropped by nearly 8 percent. Put another way, if the rate is compared to what would have been expected based on worldwide increases, the Israeli rate fell in effect by 20 percent.

The greatest reduction in breast-cancer mortality occurred among women under age 44, a 30 percent actual decline in mortality. No decrease was evident among women aged 65 and over.

In 1990 a scientific paper was published in the *Annals of the New York Academy of Science* by Drs. Jerome B. Westin and Elihu Richter of the Unit for Environmental and Occupational Medicine at the Hebrew University-Hadassah School of Medicine in Jerusalem to comment on the Israeli breast-cancer "anomaly." In the paper, Westin and Richter attribute the drop in breast-cancer rates to the ban on pesticides in milk.

An anomaly in the rates for the younger women, therefore, would suggest the influence of an especially potent environmental factor having a selectively greater effect in younger cohorts.

The dramatic drop [in breast-cancer deaths] . . . suggests the occurrence of a dramatic change in the environment or in life style, especially coming as it does, in the wake of a 25-year period of continually increasing rates. . . . The Israeli population had continually been shown to have relatively high levels of organochlorine pesticides in body fat in general, and in breast milk in particular. . . . The ban resulted in the precipitous drop (by two to three orders of magnitude) of BHC levels in cows' milk. By 1980, a 90 percent drop in the lindane content of breast milk in Jerusalem, as well as a 43 percent decrease in DDT levels, and an estimated 98 percent reduction in a-BHC had been recorded. The carcinogenicity of all three compounds has been clearly established . . . and the abovementioned three compounds in particular . . . have chemical characteristics that are linked to the heart of the biochemical explanation of breast cancer causality: estrogens and the cytochromes P450.

If we assume that DDT and/or BHC are causes of human breast cancer, could their elimination from the diet result in a dramatic drop in breast cancer rates? The evidence available would indicate that the answer is, yes.

Industry critics of the Israeli study say that the latency period for breast cancer is up to 30 years. Therefore, they argue, a chemical ban in the 1970s could not have had such dramatic effects in the 1980s. Greenpeace counters that the Israeli researchers examined all other known risk factors for breast cancer during the period of decline. "Organochlorines that promote the development of cancers through hormonal, immunosuppressive, or other mechanisms may require only a few years to cause their effects," wrote Greenpeace. "Organochlorines may thus contribute to breast cancer on both long-term and short-term scales."

All this was enough to convince the International Joint Commission that something was rotten in the state of our environment. It struck many of the same themes in both its 1992 and 1993 annual reports. But little progress has been made.

When the United States and Canada first signed the Great Lakes Water Quality agreements in 1978, both countries committed themselves to a policy of zero discharge of all persistent toxic substances to protect the Great Lakes. To date, efforts by the IJC to pursue its mandate have been met with little interest by either federal government or by the state and provincial governments along the Great Lakes basin, and the commission has encountered downright hostility from the pollution-producing industries. Even media attention on the toxic dangers of the Great Lakes has been sporadic at best.

Another problem is what is called the "prove-harm" approach. Rather than manufacturers having to prove their chemicals are safe before putting them onto the market, and hence, the environment, critics have to prove they are not safe before action can be taken against them. This is not always possible or practical. The IJC, which historically has been cautious about taking strong positions on anything, argues that that system is seriously flawed. In its Seventh Biennial Report on Great Lakes Water Quality issued in 1994, the IJC says taking firm action against a particular chemical could take several years, "by which time damage has been done. Even when injury has been established, the focus is on management and control of releases on a chemical-by-chemical basis, rather than on strategically preventing the formation of the persistent toxic substance in the first place." It adds that "current resources cannot hope to screen all the chemicals in use (variously estimated to be 60,000 to 200,000 in number) or even all the new chemicals."

The solution, says the IJC, is a three-phase approach: controlling releases, preventing use or generation, and establishing sustainable industry and product/material use. That would mean sunsetting and eliminating toxic substances now in common use, through a determined effort by all governments and industry.

In essence, the IJC wants chemicals treated as a class, rather than being assessed through the current chemical-by-chemical approach, and it advocates the eventual elimination of all toxic substances with a half-life in water of greater than eight weeks. (Half-life is the time required for the concentration of a substance to diminish to one-half of its original value in a given lake or body of water.) It argues that "the

use of chlorine and its compounds should be avoided in the manufacturing process."

In February, 1994, Brad Lienhart, managing director of the Chlorine
Chemistry Council, told the *New York Times* that "the IJC report is not
a sound-science approach to decision-making." And Dow Chemical
Company, the world's largest producer of chlorine, said, "There is
currently no evidence that would support a total ban on chlorine
chemistry, and the social and economic consequences of such a ban
would be disastrous for the public."

But the IJC's American co-chairman Gordon Durnil said the commission has been trying to discuss the issue for years with the chemical
industry so the social and economic consequences would not be disastrous. However, the industry has refused to get involved. "We're now
having a pretty good dialogue with lobbyists," he said. "But the chemical
industry has not brought forth any evidence that their views have any
merit. It appears to us that the weight of evidence says there is a danger
from organochlorides. You've got some really major problems going on:
increases in breast cancer, prostate cancer, endometriosis. You can, in
many cases, trace it to organochlorines."

It has to be traced to something. Consider the fact that in 1900, cancer
was responsible for only 4 percent of all deaths in the world. By 1958 it
had risen to 15 percent of deaths. And by the end of this century, about
40 percent of the human population will have some form of cancer and
it will cause 25 percent of all deaths. This is a frightening rate of increase,
even considering that people are living longer and that deaths from such
contagious diseases like tuberculosis and cholera have almost been
eliminated — at least in the world's industrialized nations.

In October 1993 the Ontario-based environmental group Pollution
Probe sponsored a Citizens' Biennial Review of Canadian and U.S.
government actions to protect and restore the Great Lakes. The review
cited a host of official statistics outlining the magnitude of the pollution
and consequent human health dangers in the lakes.

According to the EPA's 1990 Toxic Release Inventory, for example,
industries on the U.S. side dumped more than 5.8 million pounds of
toxic waste into the Great Lakes and their tributaries and sent another
45 million pounds to city sewage treatment plants. Another 630 million
pounds of toxic chemicals were released into the air. The U.S. General

Accounting Office reported that legally permitted corporate discharges into the Great Lakes that year totalled 7 million gallons of oil, 89,000 pounds of lead and 1,000 pounds of mercury. Each year, 92 million pounds of the solvent toluene are discharged from U.S. sources. Eastman Kodak Company alone releases 14.4 million pounds of toxics and BPCO Inc., 7.5 million pounds of toxics into Lake Ontario. The result of all this is that bottom sediments laden with toxic chemicals are one of the most important sources of continuous and growing pollution problems in the lakes.

As if the legal discharges weren't worrisome enough, in 1990 in Ontario alone there were 5,419 violations of discharge permit allowances, 111 reported chemical spills into Lake Ontario, 73 reported spills into the St. Clair River, 67 into the St. Lawrence River and 26 into Lake Erie. In Sarnia, where much of Ontario's chemical industry is concentrated, chemical producers had reported 550 spills into the St. Clair River over the previous six years. And a 1990 train derailment spilled 20,000 gallons of toxic chemicals into Lake Superior, sparking the largest spill-related evacuation in U.S. history when more than 30,000 residents near Duluth, Minnesota, had to flee their homes.

In February 1994, in Ottawa, Environment Minister Sheila Copps delighted environmentalists by announcing the federal government would soon move to set timetables and schedules for the sunsetting of "all problem chemicals" in the Great Lakes basin, a sweeping commitment that went well beyond previous promises by the Liberals and would mean the end of the tedious and ineffective chemical-by-chemical approach dictated in the Canadian Environmental Protection Act. Paul Muldoon of the Canadian Environmental Law Association said he was anxious to discover what Copps means by "problem chemicals," but he added, "The implications of what she's saying . . . are impressive and dramatic."

Only if she actually does it, however. And so far, she hasn't.

While the chemical industry itself was hostile toward the Greenpeace report, and governments offered little more than promises, the cancer establishment didn't exactly join the battle against toxic chemicals either. In fact, the American Cancer Society has long been criticized for dragging its heels on the so-called "War on Cancer." Apart from its work on the issue of smoking, the society has been oddly silent on other environmental issues. Unlike the American Lung Association, for example, the society did not support the Clean Air Act and in 1987 a coalition of public interest and labor groups issued a strongly worded statement criticizing the American Cancer Society for "doing nothing to help reduce the public's exposure to cancer-causing chemicals."

Greenpeace official Jay Palter in Toronto accuses the cancer establishment of echoing the chemical industry's response to the Greenpeace environmental report. For example, the industry called the Israeli study unreliable, citing disease latency periods, and before long, cancer officials were saying the same thing. Palter says he's not accusing anyone of a conspiracy, but "they're in the same power elite in society. Someone who thoughtlessly regurgitates [industry arguments] betrays something to me. My opinion is that there are large world views which are shared," adding that men, largely, who have the same background and experiences are at the top of both the cancer and the corporate hierarchies, and they share vested interests in the status quo.

According to Palter, the "so-called cancer establishment" is actually a barrier to progress and "will not succeed in preventing cancers in the future. . . . The same establishment that profits from cancer" has ties to those who are supposed to be preventing it. "The cancer establishment has been notorious for not examining what causes cancer." He says the tide is changing, "but it doesn't happen without activism and people pushing for change."

Part of that push for change occurred in October 1993 when a panel of researchers and consumer rights advocates told a congressional hearing that the scientific evidence linking pesticides to breast cancer and other human health problems is growing. They acknowledged that pesticides have not been proven to cause breast cancer, but pointed out that several studies indicate a strong relationship between the two. Representative Henry A. Waxman (Democrat-California) who chaired the panel of the House Energy and Commerce Subcommittee on Health and the Environment promised to introduce legislation requiring the EPA to tighten control of pesticides used in food protection. "The potential adverse health effects for hormonal pesticides are alarming, but they are not proven," said Waxman. "Instead of consumer panic and changes in the diet, what we urgently need is more investigation and crucial regulatory improvements."

Ana Soto, a cell biologist at the Tufts University School of Medicine, told the panel of her finding that endosulfan — about 2 million pounds of which are used on fruits and vegetables in the United States each year — has an estrogen-like effect, as potent as DDT. (Estrogen, a hormone that is an integral part of female sexual development, has been found in numerous studies to play a major role in breast cancer, although scientists are still uncertain exactly how it does.)

In 1980, thousands of gallons of a pesticide containing DDT spilled into Lake Apopka in Florida. After years of studying the alligator population in that lake, University of Florida researcher Louis Guillette discovered that male alligators' penises were only one-quarter the normal size and their testosterone levels so low they were probably sterile. Like the canary in the coal mine, who was used to tip off the miners when gas was building up, problems with animals often foretell similar problems in humans. Guillette then learned of another researcher who had found similar effects on lab mice exposed to DDE — the chemical formed when DDT decomposes. Guillette, testifying before a congressional panel in March 1994, said, "I think we have a problem here." As *Newsweek* explained it, "by 'we' Guillette didn't just mean alligators. Because people live in a sea of the same gender-bending chemicals. . . . [He] told a congressional panel, 'every man in this room is half the man his grandfather was.'" Despite that, however, Thomas Goldworthy of the Chemical Industry Institute of Toxicology said, "Much of the evidence [about estrogen mimics] is circumstantial."

Perhaps, but in February, the Clinton administration indicated it wanted to find out, ordering an 18-month study to investigate the health effects of dioxin and other chlorinated chemicals, along with the safety and availability of substitutes for chlorine in major industries. Most people already have dioxin levels in their body at or near the levels that cause prenatal and immune-system problems in laboratory animals, and up to 12 percent of the dioxin in the body can come from the first year of breast-feeding. Recognizing these environmental and occupational health hazards, the American Public Health Association called for an end to chlorines in the United States in October 1993.

The same month that Clinton ordered the study, *Scientific American*, in a story headlined "Dioxin Indictment," reported on the work of the University of Milan's Pier Alberto Bertazzi. In his examination of people exposed to dioxin, he found "compelling evidence that dioxin has carcinogenic effects in the human species." It has long been shown to be carcinogenic in laboratory tests, but the Italian study on humans resulted from a 1976 industrial accident that spewed dioxin into the air near the town of Seveso. Since then, scientists have been monitoring the health of about 2,000 families in the town. People in the second-most contaminated area were almost three times more likely to acquire liver cancer as the general population. In addition, a form of myeloma occurred 5.3 times more often among women, and among the men, some cancers of the blood were 5.7 times more likely.

On the other hand, occurrences of breast and endometrial cancers were below normal. "What is remarkable about these findings is that they reflect animal data almost perfectly," said University of Maryland toxicologist Ellen K. Silbergeld.

Clinton's initiative, however modest, was more than most governments or government agencies were doing. On February 17, for example, Barbara J. Balaban, director of the New York State Breast Cancer Hot Line, told a joint committee of state assembly representatives at the first of statewide hearings on environmental factors in breast cancer that "you guys had better get your act together and do what needs to be done."

Balaban and other prevention advocates said what needs to be done is to introduce measures to cut pesticide use in schools, parks, golf courses and lawns. Lorraine Pace, the woman whose work sparked the Long Island environmental study and was recently named a breast-cancer education specialist at University Hospital Center on Long Island, criticized the two-year reporting delay in the state's tumor-incidence list. "We need accurate local and statewide registries so that we know where we are. It's interesting that our tumor registering is two years behind each diagnosis and yet our state lottery is only seconds behind the picking of the numbers," she said.

While public pressure was building to at least cut down on the number of pesticides in use, the EPA apparently wasn't impressed. In March 1994, it outraged environmentalists by giving two major U.S. chemical firms — Monsanto Company and Zeneca AG — approval to mass market acetochlor, a carcinogenic herbicide for farmers to use around corn crops. Classified as a B-2 grade carcinogen, it has caused cancer hormones when used in high doses in rats and mice in the laboratory. Lyn Goldman, EPA assistant administrator for prevention, pesticides and toxic substances, who approved the registration, told the *Washington Post* that "other herbicides already used on corn in this country are also carcinogenic. We believe that this one puts the American public at less risk than the alternatives," because only half as much acetochlor is needed per acre compared to other herbicides. Arnold Donald, a Monsanto vice president, said the health risk is so negligible it shouldn't even be controversial. "A human would have to drink 1.7 million gallons of acetochlor a day for life for it to produce the kinds of toxic effects it had on rats and mice."

Environmentalists, who have heard such assurances from manufacturers and the EPA before, weren't convinced. "Given the cancer risk we are facing in this country, it's ludicrous for this administration to be registering a chemical which has carcinogenic effects for use by farmers," said Jay Feldman, director of the National Coalition Against the Misuse of Pesticides. "What they should be doing is trying to get farmers off the chemical treadmill."

The pressure against the chlorine industry, while concentrated in the United States and Canada, has also spilled over into Europe. Reports show that the $225 billion worldwide chlorine industry — with 500,000 jobs in western Europe alone, and 1.27 million worldwide — is also fighting the growing green movement there. Pointing to the chlorination of drinking water in the United States, which reduced the annual death rate from typhoid from 25,000 in 1900 to almost zero today, the chemical industry argues the world is a healthier place with chlorines than it would be without them. But critics counter that the chlorination of water represents only about 1 percent of the chlorine going into the environment and that reasonable — and healthier — alternatives to chlorine products already exist.

So far, European governments have not followed the lead of the U.S. and Canadian governments in promising at least some phasing out of the products. Environmental groups think they should. Ann Link, a scientist with the Women's Environmental Network (WEN) in London, England, recently told *The European* newspaper that the priority should be the phasing out of bulk uses of chlorine. "The amounts used to make drugs and to disinfect water are small," she said. "PVC production and the manufacture of solvents should be the main target."

Despite the lack of formal sanctions against chlorine-based products, however, their use in Europe is declining, partially as a result of pressure from the green movement in European political circles and partially because a few industries have developed economical and safer alternatives. It has already been eliminated from the pulp-bleaching industry in Europe, and the phasing out of chlorinated solvents has led to a 15 percent drop in Europe's chlorine consumption since 1988.

Political action, however, has been slow overall because of the social and economic implications of banning chlorines. What's more, many serious scientists do not believe the case has been made for such a ban.

Dr. Howard Morrison, an epidemiologist with Health Canada's Laboratory Centre for Disease Control, agrees that "theoretically, it [environment] probably does contribute a small amount," toward breast-cancer incidence. "It's a highly politically charged issue. The truth is, who knows where it lies? But I get a bit disturbed about the things some of the really zealous people say about the connection. It's basically a religion with some of these people. . . . Some people want all these compounds banned immediately. Well, there are serious economic implications to consider. If you ban something that is economically important and it turns out there is no breast cancer implication, what have you done? What have you accomplished? We need to study the issue more before we go out making broad pronouncements which only serve to frighten people but don't get us any closer to solving this terrible problem."

Morrison is right about one thing, the issue is certainly fraught with serious economic implications. The cost of cleaning up the mess — not to mention costs associated with closing down entire industries — would be stratospheric. Consider, for example, some estimates prepared by real-estate appraiser Bert Hielema on the price of saving one life by cleaning up contaminated real estate. Writing in the Spring 1994 edition of *The Canadian Appraiser*, Hielema argues, "Some regulations make sense. . . . For example, the cost of seat belts to society is only $100,000 for each life saved, while the asbestos ban [which he argues is highly overrated as a risk to society] has a price tag of $110 million and the UFFI scare has cost the U.S. $82 billion for risks that are negligible."

Arguing that environmental laws need to be relaxed to reflect more common sense, he cites a 1993 case where city officials in Columbus, Ohio, wanted to pave a small portion of a parking lot next to the police station, but city engineers discovered traces of chemicals in the dirt and learned the federal Hazardous Waste Law required a $2 million cleanup before the project could begin. He quotes a March 21, 1993, *New York Times* piece arguing, "Standards are such that, since some chemicals had shown to cause cancer in rats, the EPA set a limit low enough that a child could eat half a teaspoon of dirt every month for 70 years and not get cancer. So far the so-called Superfund has spent $7 billion to comply with similar 'dirt-eating rules,' as they call them. These rules apply even on remote industrial sites where no houses may even be built."

Hielema has a point. But it doesn't mean governments should not attack the problem. He does, however, make a good case for the intelligent use of federal resources to combat real environmental hazards, rather than the current willy-nilly approach to the problem.

An April 1994 *Business Week* story on the bureaucratic-industry-environmentalists wrangling that has stalled the Federal Superfund toxic cleanup program estimated that the bill for U.S. industry could run between $300 billion and $463 billion just for cleaning up the country's Superfund sites.

In the meantime, all the news isn't bad. Health Canada, for example, found that DDT levels in milk from nursing mothers fell from nearly 150 ppb in 1967 to less than 15 ppb in 1986, and that they are still falling. PCB concentrations in breast milk also fell from 30 ppb to about 5. And the EPA reports that PCB levels in the flesh of Lake Michigan trout dropped substantially from 23 parts per million in 1974 to 3 parts per million in 1993, although that is still above the FDA's safety limit of 2 parts per million.

There is general agreement that U.S. bans during the 1970s of DDT, PCBs, herbicides containing dioxin and other toxic insecticides account for some of the improvements. In addition, both Canada and the United States have forced industries to spend billions of dollars to control toxic pollution through tougher water and air pollution laws. And since July 1, 1994, Canadian chemical companies who want to import or produce a new chemical for commercial use must meet stringent new health standards. Rather than waiting for approvals after chemicals are already in use, the companies must seek pre-approval for new products.

Despite the positive signs, however, there are still more problems than solutions. In April 1994, Gordon Durnil, outgoing U.S. chairman of the International Joint Commission, said the people he thought would help — industries — are instead blocking the cleanup of the Great Lakes. Durnil and two other Republican appointees had joined the IJC more than four years earlier. "As conservatives we thought industry could handle the environmental problems much better than government," he said. But according to Durnil, industry is stalling by using paid lobbyists instead of sending chief executive officers to deal with the issues. "That's something that disturbs me as someone who is very pro-industry."

Durnil added that authorities demand too much proof of the dangers of chlorine-based pollutants before passing regulations to stop them. "I can't think of another element in life where we demand such certainty before we start exercising caution," he said. "It's really strange. . . . The chlorinated organics we know about are harmful to humans and wildlife. Why do we then presume the ones we don't know about are safe?"

In September 1994, the U.S. Environmental Protection Agency promised to propose tougher rules in 1995 to reduce the chance that people would be exposed to harm from toxic chemicals. The agency called the potential harm to human health from dioxin worrisome, but less dangerous than smoking. It argued that although dioxin was a potent cause of cancer in animals, the available scientific data on people is less definitive. "There is currently no clear indication of a disease burden in the general population attributable to dioxin-like compounds," the EPA report said. It did note, however, that epidemiology studies on groups of people exposed to high levels of dioxin, such as chemical workers, had found moderate increases in cancer incidence.

In the May-June 1994 edition of *Mother Jones*, San Francisco medical writer Michael Castleman, who won the 1993 American Medical Writers' Association Rose Kushner Award for his coverage of breast cancer, wrote that "statistics represent human tragedies without the tears." One of those statistics was his wife, Anne, diagnosed with breast cancer at age 38.

"Individual women with breast cancer almost never know whether environmental toxins played a role, even if they're certain they were exposed to them," he wrote. "In 1973, a few hundred pounds of polybrominated biphenyls (PBBS), close chemical relatives of PCBs, were accidentally mixed into animal feed in Michigan. More than 30,000 cattle, 1.5 million chickens, and thousands of sheep and hogs either died or had to be slaughtered, and some 9 million Michigan residents consumed PBB-tainted meat and dairy products. By 1976, 96 percent of Michigan's nursing mothers showed PBB in their breast milk."

Castleman and his wife, a family physician and assistant clinical professor at the University of California's San Francisco Medical Center, lived in Michigan at the time. The question is, Could the exposure have caused her cancer?

Dr. Harold Humphrey, a public health laboratory scientist for the Michigan Health Department's division of environmental risk assessment, told Castleman no. "Not based on what we know now." Humphrey is director of the state's ongoing study of 4,000 farm family members heavily exposed to PBBs. After 20 years, he says, "We've seen no unexpected increases in their cancer rate."

Yet Dr. Janette Sherman, a toxicologist in Alexandria, Virginia, and author of the book *Chemical Exposure and Disease*, told Castleman that PBBs may have contributed significantly to his wife's cancer. "When a late-life cancer strikes unusually early in life, you have to suspect an environmental insult."

This, of course, is the problem. Nobody knows for sure. Dr. Clark Heath, chief epidemiologist at the American Cancer Society's Atlanta headquarters, told Castleman that "low-level exposure to toxic chemicals has not been shown to pose a major cancer risk."

But it hasn't been shown that it doesn't pose a risk either. That's because the American Cancer Society, among others, has been reluctant to fund studies on the subject. Clearly the only way to resolve the issue is to study it, but the medical-scientific community is often painfully slow to act. It's not as if there isn't sufficient cause for concern. Castleman points out, for example, that "cigarettes were persuasively linked to lung cancer in the early 1950s, but it took more than a decade for the surgeon general to issue the first major call to quit." Even now, 40 years after discovering the cancer-cigarette link, the tobacco companies are furiously fighting calls for controls on their poisonous product.

10 Genes: Internal Lightning Rods

IN 1976, A MAN KNOWN TO THE PUBLIC only as John Q. checked himself into Boston's Beth Israel Hospital for surgery for malignant tumors in both kidneys. The condition is rare, occurring in only 1 to 2 percent of all Americans with renal cancer.

It almost never hits before age 50.

John Q. was 37.

Three years later, a medical team headed by Dr. Robert S. Brown published the results of their study of John Q. and his family history in the *New England Journal of Medicine*.

Incredibly, of 40 family members over three generations in his family, 10 had renal cancer, 6 of them in both kidneys. From blood cells, doctors discovered these cancer victims all had a particular defect in 2 of the 23 paired chromosomes in each cell. Part of chromosome 3 was attached to chromosome 8 and vice versa, something geneticists call "balanced reciprocal translocation."

At the time, Dr. Brown was quoted in *Time* saying: "What we found may be a breakthrough. The fact is we don't know how to use it."

Millions of dollars and untold hours of research have been expended since that time by medical researchers trying to determine that same question: which genes are responsible for which diseases and, once we know, then what?

There are roughly 100,000 genes in the human body. Researchers use genetic markers, or signposts, in their search for discovering exactly which gene, or genes, increases a woman's susceptibility to breast cancer. Everybody has his or her own peculiar genetic make-up, which is how they use DNA to identify people. A genetic marker is a recognizable genetic difference between people. Researchers look for particular genes, or markers, and if many people who have the same disease seem to have this particular marker, scientists can begin to make a correlation between the disease and the gene.

A December 1991 report from the U.S. General Accounting Office to a House Subcommittee on Breast Cancer found that 50 to 60 genes had been implicated in various kinds of cancer "and scientists now suspect that a mutant form of a particular gene, the p53 gene, may be an almost indispensable element in the cancerous transformation of a healthy cell to a tumor cell." The report said that while the p53 gene (the p is for the protein it produces; 53 is its molecular weight) can help block unruly cell growth as a tumor suppressor, irregularities of the gene have properties of an oncogene. An oncogene is a gene that can play a normal role or can allow (or cause) a cell to divide and become a cancer cell that multiplies wildly.

"Recent studies," said the subcommittee report, "have shown that the p53 gene is overactive in 15 to 20 percent of breast cancer tumors. The bearing of this discovery on breast cancer is not yet clear, but further studies are expected to increase the understanding of how a normal cell is transformed into a malignant cell."

In other words: Who knows?

Well, scientists nudged a little closer to the answer in 1990 when Dr. Mary-Claire King, a professor of genetics and epidemiology at the University of Berkeley, located the gene on the 17th chromosome — one of the 46 chromosomes that every person has — significantly narrowing the search to one region of the genetic environment. It still was not easy, however. Chromosome 17 contains more than 1,000 genes, and teams of scientists around the world were scrambling to discover the magic BRCA1 (Breast Cancer 1), the gene suspected of causing between 5 and 10 percent of breast and/or ovarian cancers.

A team headed by Dr. Steven Narod, a cancer geneticist at the Montreal General Hospital, narrowed that search even further when their studies of 150 families with a history of breast and/or ovarian cancers reduced the hunt to about 15 genes.

In April 1993, researchers from the University of Michigan and the Dana Farber Cancer Institute in Boston reported having used molecular markers on chromosome 17 to identify women in families with high rates of breast cancer, ovarian cancer or both, who have inherited the abnormal form of the BRCA1 gene. Cancer specialists currently believe that the inherited gene defects — carried by one woman in 200 to 400 — have an 85 percent chance of developing into breast cancer over the course of the woman's lifetime, and many of them develop the disease before the age of 50. By contrast, women in the same family who have not inherited the defect have a 10 or 11 percent lifetime risk, and the vast majority occur well after their 50th birthday.

At the Revlon/UCLA Women's Cancer Research Program, Dr. Dennis Slamon, a hematologist-oncologist, and his colleagues have taken another tack. They have isolated a gene, HER-2/neu, which is abnormal in 30 percent of breast-cancer patients. The suspicion is that the gene is involved in producing protein receptors on the surface of breast cells that send a signal to the cells to divide when growth-factor molecules bind to them. In some women, the gene is hyperactive, so researchers are hoping to find a way to destroy it with an antibody that will fit into the receptor but send no signal to the cells. The antibodies are manufactured by injecting the HER-2/neu gene product into mice, cloning the antibodies that are produced and genetically engineering them to be "human" so patients will not reject them. A preliminary study of 20 patients enjoyed some success, and larger clinical trials are just getting underway.

Researchers do not believe that damage to a particular gene is the sole cause of cancer, but evidence is mounting that it is perhaps the most responsible. An August 22, 1992, article in *The Economist* summed up the complex nature of the problem.

213

"Every day, the DNA in an average cell in your body suffers more than 5,000 mutations. Heat, radiation, chemicals and simple bad luck conspire to scramble the genetic code which controls the cell's operation and reproduction. Since it takes only a single, well-placed mutation to drive a cell cancerously berserk — causing it to multiply feverishly and destroy its neighbors — the wonder is not that cancer kills so many people, but that it does not kill everyone."

The article cites Dr. Jo Milner, a cell biologist at the University of York, England, who noticed that when mutant and normal p53 proteins join up, the ordinary protein begins to behave as badly as the mutant. Using mutants from lung-cancer tumors, she discovered that certain common forms of mutant protein promote rampant cell division at body temperature but suppress tumor formation when chilled. Her hypothesis is that normal p53 inhibits cell growth until it receives an outside signal (such as a growth hormone) telling the cell to divide. Then the protein changes shape and starts encouraging the cell to grow — just as the mutant forms do. If she is right, then treatment of some cancers might be successful simply by cooling the mutant proteins by 7 degrees Centigrade for a few hours without affecting the surrounding tissue at all. In addition, pharmaceutical companies are already studying the possibility of developing drugs that twist the proteins produced by mutant p53 back into the right shape, since Miller's work already identified a protein that seems to do this. For all the prospects of future success, however, the article concludes that in genetics, "there are still many more questions than answers."

To date, scientists have discovered about 100 special cancer-causing oncogenes. They all play a central role in the normal growth of cells, but when they are not functioning properly, cells can quickly grow out of control. Suppressor genes, which is what p53 is, normally keep a cell from growing out of control. But if a genetic accident causes the suppressor gene to be lost or inactivated, cells begin a rapid growth. This is why p53 is implicated in breast cancer. Antenna genes are also involved in breast cancer. These are cells that received their growth signals through proteins acting much like a radio antenna. Mutations in antenna genes, however, cause them to signal the cell to grow all the time, even when no growth signal is present.

These human seeds, or genes, are carried by everybody. Some genes are needed only during the time the fetus is growing into a newborn, but most genes are needed throughout life. Unlike classic genetic diseases, however, such as cystic fibrosis or hemophilia, cancer genes are not always passed along by the parent. In the majority of cancer patients, in fact, the bad gene was caused by something. Many lung cancers, for example, are caused by the chemicals in tobacco smoke affecting the genes. The big hope of genetic research is not only the ability to find specific genes, but to be able to do something about them once they're found. For the moment, at least, science is a long way from that stage, at least in dealing with breast-cancer genes.

Science did take a small step toward that goal in September 1994, when, after an international four-year race to isolate the BRCA1 gene, Dr. Mark Skolnick of the University of Utah Medical Center in Salt Lake City announced that his team of 45 U.S. scientists had discovered the gene. "It feels very, very good," said Skolnick, but he was quick to acknowledge that the gene is exceptionally complicated — about 10 times larger than the average gene. Skolnick said "it's going to be quite a challenge to develop a diagnostic test." The scientists were also surprised that the BRCA1 gene appears to play no role in those breast tumors that do not have a familial link. Dr. Harold Varmus, director of the U.S. National Institutes of Health (NIH) told a news conference in Washington that progress is also being made on another gene linked to breast cancer, BRCA2. But everyone involved in the discovery acknowledged that it could be a long time before scientists figure out how to put the knowledge to practical use.

Much progress has been made, however, since Drs. James D. Watson and Francis Crick discovered the structure of human genes in 1953, telling scientists how a gene carries hereditary information in the form of a chemical code inside our bodies. Genetic research since that time has become a huge enterprise. A significant part of that was the October 1989 inauguration of the 15-year, $3 billion Human Genome Project in the United States under the direction of Dr. Watson. A joint effort of the NIH and the U.S. Department of Energy, with active participation from Japan and a host of western European countries, the massive project was designed specifically to identify each human gene, as well as the 3 billion pairs of nucleotides, or bases, that constitute DNA, the genetic material of a typical human cell. To do this, scientists began devising two types of maps: a physical map, showing the distances between two genes in terms of the number of base pairs that lie between them; and a genetic map, which assigns locations on chromosomes of genes associated with particular diseases or physical traits on the basis of how frequently they are inherited together.

Some of those answers were first found in 1991 by the French Genethon, the industrial-scale gene factory near Paris that revolutionized gene research by focusing on "whole genome" mapping rather than chromosome-by-chromosome mapping and taking what is called a "big science" approach to genome research, i.e., a host of researchers with robots and computer facilities all working together, rather than a lone researcher toiling away by himself in a laboratory somewhere.

The U.S. Human Genome Project copied the French approach in 1992 when it awarded a five-year, $24 million grant to set up a large genome-mapping center in Cambridge, Massachusetts, headed by Eric Lander, a geneticist at the Massachusetts Institute of Technology's Whitehead Institute for Biomedical Research. It also opened a $13 million gene-mapping center at the University of Iowa. In February 1993, Japan opened its massive Human Genome Centre at Tokyo University's Institute of Medical Science, joining the Supercomputer Laboratory of Kyoto University in a huge computer network for handling genome data.

At about the same time, the British government's Office of Science and Technology commissioned a major report on the state of genome research in that country to study research and training related to the human genome along with the scope of, and barriers to, commercialization of genome-related technologies. Ethical questions were also to be examined. As an indicator of the economic potential of such research, the study committee included the research directors of four of Britain's largest pharmaceutical companies: Glaxo, ICI, SmithKline Beeham and the Wellcome Foundation.

Since the discovery of p53, gene research has exploded from about 50 researchers toiling in the relatively obscure field, to an international search involving some 500 laboratories. Or, as *The Economist* put it in August 1992, "The function — and dysfunction — of p53 has become the hottest topic in cancer research, and the number of papers on the subject has doubled every year since 1989."

The extraordinary explosion of genetic research is not surprising considering the results of recent studies suggesting that the mutated p53 is present in between 30 and 50 percent of breast cancers, as well as 75 percent of lung cancers, 70 percent of colon cancers and a majority of almost every other kind of human cancer. The p53 normally guards against cancerous cells spreading out into the body, but when *it* mutates, there is nothing to stop other cancerous cells from going forth and multiplying.

Even with the September 1994 discovery of the BRCA1 gene, however, it will not lead to a quick cure of breast or ovarian cancer — or, for that matter, to a cure at all. More than a year ago, however, Dr. Steven Narod, the researcher whose team at the Montreal General Hospital narrowed the search to 15 genes, told *Maclean's* magazine: "I subscribe to the belief that the more we know about cancer, the better we will be able to treat it."

He also subscribes to the traditional value system in the scientific community where competition is so fierce that things like prestige, fame — and yes, money — override such niceties as sharing information.

And so Narod's team was competing with scores of teams around the world to localize the elusive gene. Asked by journalist Lyn Whitham in a November 1993 documentary on CBC television's *Prime Time News* if he would share his information with other scientists, Narod said:

> "When people believe that they are very close to the gene, they are very reluctant to divulge all the information and all the data to other communities. But things could change. If in six months from now, the gene is not found, people may realize that it would be to the benefit of all the groups concerned to get together again and to share them and to see . . ."
>
> "How likely do you think that is?" asked Whitham.
>
> "I think that's going to happen."
>
> "Would you share your information with the British if you were close, in six months?" she asked.
>
> "It's difficult to say . . ."

"Not really," said Whitham.

"Well . . . I think, if we published, the information would be there for all . . ."

"But would you?"

"If you knew exactly where the gene was, and we felt that we were in a position to find the gene ourselves without any outside assistance within a six-month period, we would probably at that time be . . ."

"But it would be great," said Whitham, *"if Steven Narod of Montreal found that gene, wouldn't it?"*

"Yes, I think, yeah, certainly speaking from my interests in my career, that it would be the nicest outcome that would happen if we were to find the gene."

There is no reason to believe that Narod's attitude was any different from that of the other scientists trying to go down in history by discovering the breast-cancer gene, even if, by hoarding their information, they are prolonging the search and, perhaps, a cure for at least one of the more than dozen forms of breast cancer.

Dr. Narod and his team were facing some stiff competition, too. Dr. Mary-Claire King herself, who first isolated the rogue gene by analyzing chromosomes from women whose family members suffered a history of cancer, joined forces with famed gene hunter Dr. Francis Collins in her quest for the elusive gene. She hoped their search may ultimately lead to a simple blood test that could determine whether or not women are carrying the gene. Reacting to the 1994 breakthrough by Dr. Mark Skolnick and his team, King admitted she was disappointed that the discovery had not occurred in her laboratory. Congratulating Skolnick and his team, she said, "It's clear that what they've found is a very complicated gene . . . it's going to take a lot of work from everybody in the field to figure out how this gene works."

The massive research effort into genetics is bringing results. There was considerable public excitement generated in July 1993, for example, when scientists from Bristol-Myers Squibb, the giant U.S. pharmaceutical manufacturer, announced the development of a "smart bomb" or "magic bullet" against cancer. Researchers used the protein called a monoclonal antibody and combined it with doxorubicin, a common anticancer drug, to wipe out a variety of tumors in laboratory mice, including breast tumors that had spread to other organs. The antibody, acting as the guidance system homing in on the cancer cells, carried the drug as its lethal payload to kill the advanced cancer in mice. But previous success in mice has not led to much success in people, no matter how promising many of the drugs looked initially. Still, Dr. David Scheinberg, chief of the Leukemia Service at the Memorial Sloan-Kettering Cancer Center in New York City, told *Time* that "one of the problems that have held back the field for a long time is that we were never sure that well-established solid tumors could be eliminated. Now we know that that is indeed possible."

But Pamela Trail, who led the Bristol-Myers Squibb research team, cautioned against too much euphoria. "Obviously, we're tremendously excited by our data, but the true proof will be in the human trials."

A month earlier, the Recombinant DNA Advisory Committee of the NIH approved two protocols for human tests of a strategy scientists called "chemoprotection." Dr. Albert B. Deisseroth of the University of Texas, M.D. Anderson Cancer Center in Houston, told *Scientific American* that "this is a totally novel approach, but a natural extension of gene therapy." Deisseroth hopes to enlist 20 to 30 women whose late-stage ovarian cancer has already defeated standard surgery and drug treatment. The plan is to genetically modify their bone marrow cells so they can withstand more courses and higher doses of chemotherapy, particularly taxol, the highly toxic cancer drug derived from the bark of the Pacific yew tree. It kills cells that are dividing, but it also kills bone marrow cells, which produce the white blood cells of the immune system. To counter the destruction of healthy cells, human trials were also beginning then to test another gene-therapy technique that took the opposite approach: molecular surgery was used to send in genetic "saboteurs" that would make tumor cells susceptible to a normally harmless medicine. The molecular-surgery technique was spearheaded by Dr. Kenneth W. Culver of the Iowa Methodist Medical Center; Dr. Edward H. Oldfield of the National Institutes of Health; and Genetic Therapy of Gaithersburg, Maryland. The first human trial began in December 1992 at the NIH and Culver launched two more in November 1993, one at Iowa Methodist Medical Center, the other at Children's Hospital in Los Angeles.

The Truth About Breast Cancer

In December 1993, scientists made another breakthrough: they discovered the genetic flaw that causes up to one in seven cases of colon cancer, as well as other fatal cancers of the uterus and ovaries. Combined, those cancers account for almost 80,000 deaths a year in the United States alone. Dr. Francis S. Collins, director of the National Center for Human Genome Research in Bethesda, Maryland, called it "a stunning achievement. This is the advance that's going to push us into the era of genetic medicine. It's no longer in the future. Genetic studies are going to be an everyday part of medical practice."

The gene was discovered through the kind of competition that is typical of all cancer research, with two competing laboratories working night and day for six months. One team, led by Richard Kolodner of the Dana Farber Cancer Institute in Boston and Richard Fishel of the University of Vermont, reported its discovery in the journal *Cell*. Results from the second team, led by Bert Vogelstein and Kenneth W. Kinzler at The Johns Hopkins Oncology Center, was slated for the next issue of the journal. The breakthrough was announced at a joint news conference at the NIH, prompting Henry T. Lynch, president of the Hereditary Cancer Institute at Creighton University School of Medicine in Omaha to say, "This would be considered by many to be one of the most important medical discoveries of the decade. As far as hereditary cancer syndromes are concerned, this is probably the most common one of them all, so this discovery is absolutely exciting and mind-boggling."

The dream of geneticists, of course, is to be able to alter the genetic makeup of a patient's cells to remove the risk of a genetic disease. While the ability to do that with breast cancer is a long way off — if it ever happens — scientists in Philadelphia on March 31, 1994, did announce that they had partly corrected a serious cholesterol disorder called familial hypercholesterolemia, an extremely rare condition that leads to early heart-attack deaths. Their patient was a 30-year-old Quebec woman whose condition was checked when they gave her copies of an essential gene that she lacked. The paper, which represented the first report of the therapeutic benefits of human gene therapy, was published in the journal *Nature Genetics*, almost two years after the woman received gene therapy at the University of Pennsylvania Medical Center. She had suffered a heart attack at age 16 and undergone coronary bypass surgery at 26. The researchers said they had cut her harmful cholesterol levels by almost 20 percent, but they cautioned that her cholesterol levels remained more than double the normal range, and they were not sure whether their gene therapy would prolong her life.

Gene therapy and the prospects for scientific fame and fortune have already sparked some scientific horror stories in the West. According to the January 5, 1994, *Journal of the National Cancer Institute*, for example, Dr. Gary Chase, a professor in the Department of Dental Hygiene at Johns Hopkins University, characterized an experimental gene-therapy treatment for an incurable form of brain cancer as "a truly awful experiment." Chase was a member of a federal advisory group of the National Institutes of Health Recombinant DNA Advisory Committee (RAC), which rejected the experiment by a 10 to 5 vote, citing a lack of preclinical data and insufficient information on the one patient previously treated with it. In December 1992, the patient's physicians, Ivor Royston and Robert Sobol of the San Diego Regional Cancer Center, won a "compassionate plea exemption" to begin treating the 52-year-old woman, who later died, after a direct appeal to then NIH Director Bernadine Healy and officials of the U.S. Food and Drug Administration.

The study was the first gene-therapy experiment to avoid public review by the RAC and the first involving only one patient. Dr. Robert Haselkorn, professor in the Department of Molecular Genetics and Cell Biology at the University of Chicago, criticized the two investigating doctors for conducting an experiment on a terminal cancer patient that "as I understand it, is not treatment or therapy." He said Sobol should not be called a gene-therapy doctor, but a gene toxicologist. "That doesn't sound so good, does it?" he quipped.

Even so, RAC approved another genetic experiment by the two doctors, this one involving colon cancer patients.

In the meantime, according to *The Economist*, Genetic Therapy in Gaithersburg, Maryland, has been working on patients with inoperable cancers, injecting what are called "producer cells" into the tumor. So far, more than a dozen patients have been treated. Although some have died, others have seen their tumors shrink significantly.

Advances in genetic research have also raised serious legal and ethical dilemmas. When the colon-cancer genetic flaw was discovered, U.S. Secretary of Health and Human Services Donna Shalala called it "a great day for science," but, in the middle of her administration's prolonged battle to institute a national health-care plan, she said it also illustrated the need for universal insurance coverage that does not penalize people with pre-existing health conditions.

A December 1993 report in the United Kingdom published by the Nuffield Council for Bioethics addressed that same issue, concluding that people should not have to divulge information about their genetic history to insurance companies unless it relates to a known family history of genetic disease or they are applying for an unusually large policy. The report, similar to one published shortly before the one issued by U.S. Institute of Medicine, was the first published by the council, which had been formed in 1991 to consider ethical issues raised by advances in biomedical and biological research in the United Kingdom.

Responding to the Nuffield Council for Bioethics report, Brian Sharp of the Association of British Insurers told the December 9, 1993, edition of *Nature* magazine (an international weekly journal of science published in London, England) that even though insurance companies do not ask applicants if they have had a genetic test, they expect to be informed if a test has been carried out. But Dame June Lloyd, head of the working group, and former Nuffield professor of child health at the University of London, said: "In the case of genetic screening, where there is still a lot of anxiety and fear, a genetic test result should not have to be divulged to insurers."

Another serious problem of confidentiality revolves around disclosure of test results to family members. Unlike standard medical records, the results of genetic testing can have a direct effect on the relatives of the person tested. Take the case of the Dickersin sisters profiled in the December 6, 1993, issue of *Newsweek*. Of the four women, just one, the youngest at 35, had not been diagnosed with breast cancer. Her three older sisters all had it. But take a family situation like that now that the breast-cancer gene has been isolated. Say the oldest sister has a genetic test and discovers she has the gene. Does she tell her other sisters? Does the doctor tell her other sisters? Do they really want to know? And if they do know, can they do anything about it?

And just think of what such information could do in the hands of an insurance company or an employer. Would an employer spend the time and money training somebody for management if he knew that person had a specific gene that would likely lead to an early death or at least incapacitation? Not likely. Would an insurance company insure some-body in that situation?

A 1992 March of Dimes poll found that 57 percent of those asked think someone other than a patient deserves to know that he or she carries a defective gene. Of that group, 98 percent believed a spouse should know and, surprisingly, 58 percent felt an insurance company should also be informed. Some 33 percent believed an employer should be told. In a separate study, reported in the June 1994 *Scientific American*, physicians themselves "disclosed a willingness to violate patient-doctor confidentiality in some cases: 54 percent said that, even over a patient's objections, they would tell relatives at risk about the results of a test for Huntington's chorea. Twenty-four percent said they would tell the patient's employer, and 12 percent would tell an insurance company."

A 1989 study found that just 12 of 330 Fortune 500 companies were monitoring or screening for any reason, but more than half the companies asked favored the idea of screening and 40 percent admitted a person's health insurance costs could affect his or her chance of employment.

In a paper at a 1988 Geneva conference on ethical and policy aspects of genetic screening, M.A.M. de Wachter argued that in the past "only with the person's consent was the doctor allowed to act on [information about the person]. Genetic medicine, however, is greatly expanding . . . views [of privacy and bodily integrity] into a wider concept of corporate ownership of familial and ethnic autonomy. It now seems that the totality of a person's physical existence exceeds the limits of a single person's body. Some already say that genetic information is the common property of the family as a 'corporate personality.' Are we then entering a new era of medicine . . . an era where information is governed not only by rules of individual confidentiality but also by the duties of common solidarity?"

The Privacy Commissioner of Canada produced a 1992 report entitled "Genetic Testing and Privacy," which also concentrated on the theme of the ethics of genetics. It cites Anthony Gottlieb's *The World in 1991*: "Beware of geneticists bearing discoveries. Their findings, perhaps more than any others in science, are likely to be abused and harmfully misrepresented in the near future. Danger usually comes from wherever you are not looking. Everybody is ready for the mutant viruses, plants and two-headed chimpanzees to crawl out of the ventilation shafts of biotechnology laboratories. That is not where the problem will come from. Everybody knows about the blue-eyed 'designer babies' who will be born quoting Aristotle. But they are not the real danger either. Look instead at insurance companies, personnel departments and the health pages of next year's women's magazines. That is where the trouble is brewing."

Then there was Janet C. Hoeffel, writing in the *Stanford Law Review*: "Imagine a society where the government had samples of tissue and fluid from the entire community on file and a computerized databank of each individual's DNA profile. Imagine then that not only law enforcement officials, but insurance companies, employers, schools, adoption agencies, and many other organizations could gain access to those files on a 'need to know' basis or on a showing that access is 'in the public interest.' Imagine then that an individual could be turned down for jobs, insurance, adoption, health care, and other social services and benefits on the basis of information contained in her DNA profile, such as genetic disease, heritage, or someone else's subjective idea of a genetic 'flaw.'"

The Canadian Privacy Commissioner argued that governments may one day "wish to test persons to see if they are genetically suited to have access to certain services (advanced schooling, immigration or adoption, for example) or benefits (disability payments). Private sector service providers (insurance companies, credit granting institutions) may wish to test to determine if a potential client might impose an undue financial burden because of a genetic disorder or related disease. . . . [I]n the United States, where health insurance is primarily a private sector concern, genetic testing to qualify for insurance might one day become widespread."

The report concluded that "governments have no monopoly on oppression or discrimination through the collection, use and disclosure of personal genetic information. And the private sector is subject to few of the legislative safeguards that help protect persons against government intrusions.

"Perhaps the private sector is largely benevolent, composed of good corporate citizens. But benevolence can be vulnerable to fear, prejudice, irrationality and the blind drive for efficiency. We have seen all these in the calls by some private sector employers for HIV antibody testing."

Many European countries already have laws and/or practices govern-
ing genetics and ethical questions, most of them currently related to the
reproductive process. In Austria, for example, genetic examination and
counselling services are publicly funded under the national health
insurance scheme for — among many other things — persons suspected
of having a genetic disease or chromosomal anomaly; for parents who
want children; and for parents expecting a second child, where a previous child has been born with a genetic disease, chromosomal anomaly,
an open neural tube defect or "other severe defect."

Many other European countries have variations on this theme, and
some are studying the prospects of branching out beyond pregnancy
issues into employment, insurance and genetic analysis for use in court.

In the United States, all states routinely screen all newborn infants
for PKU (Phenylketonuria, an inherited metabolic disorder that can cause
mental retardation) and hypothyroidism. Given advances in molecular
genetics, some scientists now envisage multiplex screening of the
newborn to identify 300 genetic diseases, actual or potential. This is an
exciting prospect for some, but it is frightening to others.

Not surprisingly, the United States has already felt the effects of well-
intentioned testing gone wrong. In the early 1970s, the United States
launched a screening campaign for sickle-cell anemia, a disease that hits
the African-American community. Responding to political pressure that
something be done to help, the federal government funded a program to
detect carriers of the sickle-cell gene, through a simple, inexpensive blood
test. Initially, the program was given wholehearted support. Members of
the Black Panthers were going door to door in black communities and
offering the tests, and heavyweight boxer Joe Frazier was one of many
high-profile blacks publicly promoting the program. At least 20 states
passed laws requiring sickle-cell screening aimed at newborns,
schoolchildren, marriage licence applicants and prison inmates.

The euphoria quickly wore off, however, as testing led to discrimination
by employers and insurers. The tests were often mandatory and given
without parental consent. The U.S. Air Force Academy rejected black
applicants who were carriers. Even some commercial airlines refused to
hire them as attendants, believing these people were susceptible to fainting
at high altitudes. (They weren't.) And prominent scientists argued that the

best way to solve the problem was for blacks carrying the gene to stop breeding, raising fears that science was being used as genocide against the black community. Since then, most state laws requiring sickle-cell screening have been repealed.

As an antidote to this kind of abuse, the Human Genome Privacy Act was introduced in the House of Representatives in September 1990, but it never got beyond the introduction. A year later, a modified version of the bill was introduced, aimed at protecting individuals through safeguards against invasion of personal genetic privacy.

A 1990 statement by the Boston-based Council for Responsible Genetics, not happy with the prospects of genetic fortunetelling, argued:

"As [genetic] tests become simpler to administer and their use expands, a growing number of individuals will be labelled on the basis of predictive genetic information. This kind of information, whether or not it is eventually proved correct, will encourage some sectors of our society to classify individuals on the basis of their genetic status and to discriminate among them based on perceptions of long-term health risks and predictions about future abilities and disabilities. The use of predictive genetic diagnoses creates a new category of individuals who are not ill, but have reason to suspect they may develop a specific disease some time in the future: the healthy ill."

The council added that basing employment decisions on genetic status "opens the door to unfounded generalizations about employee performance." In addition, it said, "Data banking increases the risk that genetic information will be used in ways that violate individual privacy."

Benno Müller-Hill, a molecular geneticist from the University of Köln, Germany, wrote in the April 1993 issue of *Nature* that the effects of the inevitable discoveries emerging from the U.S. Human Genome Project will be catastrophic for some, and that now is the time for preventative action. He defends the project but reminds people "of the past criminal misuse of human genetics in Nazi Germany."

One major problem he sees with the future ability to predict, say, that a healthy child will die in his or her 40s from Huntington's chorea, is that the time-point for the outbreak of the first symptoms will vary considerably — and other diseases may vary even more. "The predictions," he wrote, "will not be accurate in the sense that the severeness of the symptoms can be predicted for a particular time, but they will be statistically accurate. This concept is difficult to explain to patients and clients."

In July 1993, however, a talk given by John Maddox at the European Federation of Biochemical Societies in Stockholm was summarized in *Nature.* "The widespread fear of genetics cannot be justified," said Maddox. "On the contrary, the research community should speak out strongly to defend the good sense of what it is about." Maddox says, "Insurers already discriminate against people who smoke cigarettes, or who are infected with HIV; why should they not also discriminate against, say, people with the particular structure of the LDL receptor known to be responsible for early-onset familial heart disease? Second, would it not be beneficial that people carrying the heart disease gene should not be employed on heavy manual work (or better, that they should be steered towards drug treatment)? Third, there are practical problems: when 100,000 genes have been sequenced, how many will insurers or employers include in their genetic screens, and at what cost?"

As for references to Hitler, Maddox says, this is "common . . . but mistaken. What serious geneticist would at this stage advocate the artificial selection of a particular genome, throwing away the benefits of hybrid vigor and genetic diversity?"

Perhaps none would, but China has already introduced a law designed to eliminate "inferior births" by, among other things, forbidding people with a hereditary disease, such as hepatitis, venereal disease or mental illness, "which can be passed on through birth," from marrying, thus raising the spectre of a Nazi-style eugenics program. The policy also involves forced abortions for women carrying what is considered an abnormal fetus. And to illustrate that there's as much politics as science involved in this heinous policy, the Minister of Public Health Chen Minzhang told the Eighth National People's Congress Standing Committee in Beijing in December 1993 that births of "inferior quality" are serious among "the old revolutionary base, ethnic minorities, the frontier and economically poor areas."

None of these concerns, it seems, are having much real impact on the scramble for more genetic breakthroughs, including the mad dash leading up to the recent discovery of the breast-cancer gene. James Watson, said the search for BRCA1 was the most exciting quarry in medical science. Mary-Claire King, who first connected familial breast cancer to a single gene, was named one of *Glamour* magazine's "Women of the Year." King, completely caught up in the race for the gene, was reported in the December 6, 1993, issue of *Newsweek*, saying, "Sometimes, I think I'll wake up and find it's just the five of us [her original research team] in the lab again."

King's discovery was helped significantly by the work of biologist David Botstein, at MIT in the early 1980s, who conceived a new technique for analyzing genetic material. King, saying her colleagues "were very sceptical, and you know how sceptical boys can be. Scorn! Scorn! Scorn!," unveiled her findings at a conference in Cincinnati in the fall of 1990, and within minutes, despite a World Series game at nearby Riverfront Stadium, she had a roomful of those colleagues excitedly studying her seven pedigree charts. Within weeks, Dr. Gilbert Lenoir of the French-based International Agency for Research in Cancer began applying King's research to other high-risk families and discovered her results stood the test. By January 1991, he reported that his group had linked the new genetic markers to early breast cancer in three families and to ovarian cancer too. Before long, more than a dozen labs in the United States, Canada and Europe had joined the race. In studies of more than 200 high-risk families, researchers have found abnormal BRCA1 markers in more than 80 percent of those prone to both breast and ovarian cancer, and half of those with a tendency to breast cancer alone.

Most people inherit two copies of the BRCA1 marker in every cell in the body, one from each parent. If a breast cell loses one, the second copy can still prevent uncontrolled cell growth. Unfortunately, however, if a woman receives a faulty copy from one parent, damage to the cell's normal copy can be disastrous. In the families studied, a woman with a faulty BRCA1 marker has a 60 percent chance of developing breast cancer by the time she turns 50 and an 80 percent chance by age 65, assuming she lives that long.

Even having found the BRCA1 gene, there is little optimism that anyone will be able to repair defective copies. That would involve remaking millions of cells in the breast and ovaries. But scientists say the isolation of BRCA1 could lead to other kinds of therapy. "Understanding the gene may give us an important hand," Dr. Barbara Weber, an oncologist and molecular biologist, told *Newsweek*. "But first we need to know what it does."

For women who eventually discover they do carry the gene, well, King concedes: "We do not have a good option for women with inherited risk."

So what's the point, beyond scientific glory?

Well, discovering the gene may some day lead to a cure of that particular form of breast cancer, although everybody agrees that's a long way off. Women without the gene will get some relief knowing they don't have familial cancer, but that's small consolation, considering the fact that more than 90 percent of breast cancers are not inherited.

Even so, gene therapy and research is rapidly becoming big business. Several gene therapy centers have already been organized and more are on the way. The January 19, 1994, *Journal of the National Cancer Institute* cites gene-therapy pioneer Dr. Michael Blaese of the NCI saying, "There's an enormous amount of excitement out there. Every academic medical center in the country now wants to establish a gene-therapy center, with the feeling that otherwise they are far behind. But there hasn't been time for them to be behind. This field is only three years old."

Blaese says the nature of the research requires a multidisciplinary approach. "You need people with backgrounds in molecular biology, cell biology, probably immunology, virology, and oncology. Centers are one model that makes a lot of sense."

Certainly, Dr. Kenneth Culver of the Iowa Methodist Medical Center in Des Moines thinks so. Culver participated with Blaese and others in conducting the first government-approved gene-therapy protocol in 1990, and three years later set up his private, free-standing gene-therapy institute to do both lab and clinical research focusing on cancer.

"The treatment possibilities are more practical for cancer than for many of the genetic diseases," explains Culver. "Cancer is in a research tradition where phase 1 trials are very acceptable. It's a desperate disease. And although the technology of gene therapy is limited, what there is lends itself to cancer."

Dr. Nelson Wivel, executive secretary of the National Institutes of Health's RAC, also told the NCI journal that the large number of gene-therapy protocols directed at cancer is helping to shape development of the new programs. "Gene therapy centers are a natural evolution," he said, "because cancer centers have come to play a key role in chemotherapy clinical trials. We probably will see gene therapy trials for cancer set up along the lines of the chemotherapy trials conducted by NCI's cooperative groups. That is, there will be multicenter trials, where you can treat a whole lot of patients, relatively speaking, in a relatively short period of time."

The growth of these centers, of course, is fueled by far more than just the pursuit of science. Biotechnology companies have already moved in to the universities. Culver explains that "many of the universities are creating, along with a center, a for-profit biotech entity that hopes to commercialize technologies developed through its program." And Wivel says the vast majority of RAC-approved protocols involve collaborations between an academic medical center and a biotechnology company "because it's a complicated and expensive technology, and it's not easy to do yet. The company can do a lot of the necessary laboratory work, including preparation of vectors and packaging of cell lines. Then, of course, the patient care part takes place in the hospital." He said the arrangement allows university medical centers to cut expenses and defer some up-front costs. In exchange, the companies receive patent rights and other advantages.

"Advantages" is perhaps an understatement — as can be seen in a January 30, 1994, *Sunday New York Times* report on the Human Genome Project, pointing out that "in a rapid blurring of big science and big business, the effort has already created its first millionaires."

One of those is Dr. J. Craig Venter, who as a Federal employee at the NIH developed critical technology for spelling out long strands of genetic code. Then he left a little more than a year later to join a venture to commercialize the technology and, even before they had a product to sell, Venter and his backers raised millions of dollars by selling public shares of stock in their venture, Human Genome Sciences Inc. of Bethesda, Maryland. In January, his 766,612 shares in the project were worth $13.4 million.

"Depending on one's perspective," writes Lawrence M. Fisher, "Dr. Venter and his company typify the ideal link between Government-supported basic science and the entrepreneurial verve necessary for seeing that the fruits of the Human Genome Project make their way into the medical marketplace. But some scientists are uneasy — ethically and professionally — with the idea of their colleagues profiting from the research for which the Government has paid."

Dr. Francis S. Collins, who heads the genome project at the NIH, says he has no problems with the entrepreneurial efforts of former colleagues such as Venter. "I will be very surprised if we don't see products from some of these companies within four or five years."

As for Venter, he says all the work he produced at the NIH was published in scientific journals available to the public. Anyway, he says, the financing for his project "all had to do with my ideas, and an approach I developed — a whole new approach to doing the human genome. The real question is: while at the NIH I discovered 10 percent of the human genes; what happens to these genes if nobody proceeds with them?"

Other scientists are skeptical of the commercial prospects. The entire genome of the virus that causes AIDS is completely known, for example, but that hasn't led to a cure. In addition, the recruitment of leading scientists from publicly supported universities and federally backed genome centers "has stirred professional resentment among some geneticists, who argue that the rush to commercialize or patent pieces of the genome project will hinder the greater advances that can come when the scientific community freely shares its discoveries," writes Fisher. One geneticist called it "a quick and dirty grab — like the wild West, where everyone was trying to stake a claim. It's basically people with a lot of human genome money trying to cash in."

One of those in the *Times* piece is Kevin J. Kinsella, a venture capitalist with Avalon Ventures, head of Sequana Therapeutics Inc. in La Jolla, California, a company he helped set up. "This is my last biotech deal; this is the crown jewels," he said. The company had already raised $12 million and was negotiating with six large pharmaceutical companies about licensing its technologies. His standard sales pitch is: "Can you be competitive in the year 2000 without the disease genes in hand? Unequivocally, no."

And Mark Edwards, president of Recombinant Capital, a research company that tracks biotechnology investments, says, "This is groundbreaking, not only because of the Government involvement and investment [the U.S. Government pumps $165 million a year into the genome project], but because of how quickly and how richly it's been augmented by private investors." For example, a venture fund called the Healthcare Investment Corporation staked Venter $70 million in 1992 to create the Institute for Genomic Research, a not-for-profit lab. The company also founded Human Genome Sciences to commercialize the institute's findings and gave Venter stock in the company. The *Times* reported that although the company was "the first of its type to begin selling shares of its stock to the public, it is only one of a dozen human genome companies that has been set up with venture-capital funding or private funding."

Because the venture-capital community in Europe is less aggressive, many prominent overseas scientists have plugged into American companies, the biggest catch being Dr. Daniel Cohen, director of the Centre d'Étude du Polymorphisme Humain in Paris, commonly called CEPH, which, along with the United States, is regarded as the other recognized world leader in genomics. Cohen, who is a scientific adviser to Millennium Pharmaceuticals of Cambridge, Massachusetts, is joined at Millennium by Dr. Eric St. Lander, director of the federally funded Whitehead/MIT Center for Genomic Research in Cambridge, the largest genome center in the States. Lander's prominent role in the Human Genome Project has raised eyebrows in the genetics community but has also been a strong selling point for investors, including major venture capitalists Mayfield Fund and Kleiner Perkins Caufield & Byers. But Lander, before joining the advisory board, sought and received written permission from then NIH director Dr. Bernadine Healy. In addition, he says all his work at Whitehead/MIT was made public, without patents or other limitations.

Other major biotech companies in the cancer field include Genetic Therapy of Gaithersburg, Maryland, founded in 1987, and specializing in treatment of brain cancer. It currently has 135 employees and a market capitalization of $103 million according to the *Wall Street Journal*. The leader in the hot field of gene therapy, it has received approval for 31 human gene-therapy trials, more than any other company and nearly half the total authorized by federal authorities.

While profits continued to soar, some leaders in the medical community were getting worried. In March 1994, a high-level panel of scientists headed by Dr. Francis Collins, director of the NIH's Human Genome

Project, published a warning in the *Journal of the American Medical Association* against the use of newly developed gene tests that may detect susceptibility to a variety of human cancers. The panel argues that efforts to market tests to physicians and genetic counsellors are premature because the tests are not yet reliable and the specific genes that may trigger cancers have not been clearly identified. People relying on such results, they say, could face agonizing, and often dangerously wrong, decisions. Collins acknowledged that gene hunters have found evidence of genetic influences in various cancers, including breast, colon, brain, lung, bladder and esophagus, and that biotech companies have developed DNA test systems designed to show a person's risk of developing cancers that appear to run in the family. But he emphasized that scientists say no DNA test yet is specific or sensitive enough to accurately predict cancer risks. Nor do scientists know how many mutations of the genes exist, how frequently they occur or the true risk of disease when the genes are present.

Business ventures in genomics are high-risk and often bring enormous profits. But being on the cutting edge of a new scientific field also brings benefits. A research team at McMaster University in Hamilton, Ontario, led by Dr. Calvin Harley, for example, identified a telltale enzyme found in cancer cells, but conspicuously absent from most normal cells. If researchers can discover a way to disarm this enzyme, known as telomerase, they may finally have the magic bullet they have been searching for. Harley has taken leave from McMaster to work at Geron Corp. in Menlo Park, California, hoping to eventually find a drug that will block the action of telomerase. "The cancer cell," says Harley, "is already very old. If we can inhibit telomerase, we might cause the tumor to die after a few doublings." Better still, he says, the fact that cancer cells produce telomerase and normal cells (except sperm) don't "gives us hope that we may be able to develop a drug without serious side effects."

In May, a team of researchers led by Dr. John S. Kovach of the Mayo Clinic, Rochester, Minnesota, came up with a new anomaly: the genetic damage associated with breast cancer in rural white women is different from that in urban black women, and they do not know why. The team looked at patterns of damage in a gene linked to breast cancer in 53 white women from the rural Midwest, compared with samples from 47 black women from Detroit. "Our hypothesis was that if breast cancer is caused by the same events in all women, then the pattern of genetic damage would be the same in all women," Kovach told *USA Today*. But it didn't work out that way. "The kinds of damage are quite different," he said.

Black women have a lower rate of breast cancer than whites, but face a worse prognosis when they do get the disease. Scientists do not know why rates are lower among blacks, but their poorer survival rate is likely connected to economic and social factors.

That is just one of thousands of questions that remain unanswered in the whole field of breast-cancer research, and while genetic discoveries are changing the cancer landscape, and future discoveries will lead to banner headlines and celebrating scientists, at this point the field offers as many negative possibilities as it does positive opportunities.

In the June 1, 1994, issue of the *Journal of the National Cancer Institute*, Dr. Francis Collins warns: "If we think the dilemmas of testing are large now, just wait.

"As soon as we can do something about [the cancers for which we are finding susceptibility genes], the problem will be resolved," he said. "But for the next 10 to 20 years we will be in a situation where our ability to diagnose exceeds our ability to cure."

11 Desperately Seeking Survival

BEFORE SHE DIED OF BREAST CANCER in March 1994, Marjorie Markell tried a few things. "I never did chemotherapy," the dying Boulder, Colorado, woman told author Juliet Wittman. "No chemo, no radiation. This is minor and truly had nothing to do with my decision, but I had no money. They don't give out chemo for nothing. I'm being really clear telling you that it did not affect my decision but there are many people for whom it would have been hard.

"I didn't do visualization. Initially, I did radical dietary change. I worked with a naturopath. I went to Native American sweat lodges. When the cancer metastasized to my liver, my mind about it changed. I would have had to do more and more dietary things, which again required money. So I dropped it."

And Canadian broadcaster Jeannette Matthey, writing an article on her experiences several months before she too died of breast cancer at age 37, wrote that after being falsely reassured by doctors, cancerous cells were discovered in four lymph nodes under her arm.

I have since set out to make my body as inhospitable as possible. Having lost much of my faith in conventional medicine, I'm exploring as well the world of non-conventional treatment — plowing through books on a bewildering array of potions, herbal remedies, strange substances such as burdock root and shark cartilage, I'm learning about meditation, visualization, progressive relaxation. And I'm discovering that seaweed can be tasty as I embark on a low-fat macrobiotic diet.

But I feel like a lonely traveller between two solitudes. Many conventional practitioners look with indifference, sometimes disdain, upon the purveyors of alternative treatment. One nurse tells me many women do "the non-conventional thing" on the sly. They sneak acupuncture or aromatherapy in between chemotherapy sessions. They don't tell their doctors for fear of being scolded for straying from mainstream medicine.

I ask my oncologist what he thinks of macrobiotics. 'You can do them if you want,' he says. I think he figures it's some kind of exercise. I ask him about shark cartilage. That question draws a blank. How about Iscador? It's derived from mistletoe and is promoted by homeopathic doctors as an immune booster. My oncologist says it doesn't work. 'Forget it.'

But I won't forget it. Just as I couldn't forget the cyst that I was repeatedly told not to worry about. I'll continue to research, explore and experiment — arming myself for battle in my way. Knowledge is power, as they say. I wish I had known last August what I know now — that young, fit women do get breast cancer. And that doctors don't always get it right.

More and more breast-cancer patients are drawing the same conclusions. According to a 1990 U.S. survey published in the *New England Journal of Medicine*, about 10 percent of Americans spent $10.3 billion seeking the help of so-called "unconventional" medical practitioners — about one-quarter of them were cancer patients — and about one-third of American adults used some form of unconventional therapy that year.

No wonder. Conventional treatment — what breast surgeon and leading American activist Dr. Susan Love calls "slash, burn and poison" — does not work all that well for many breast-cancer victims. She recently told *People* magazine, "What drives me is the frustration of having patients and seeing them die. The best we have is not enough."

Despite years of practice and research, and untold billions spent on chemotherapy, radiation and surgery, the fact is more women are getting breast cancer and more women are dying from it. At best, many are living a little longer, but even some of that is because of technological advances that allow us to discover it sooner.

In November 1993, the Canadian government sponsored a three-day conference on alternative therapies, part of its new breast-cancer initiative, the first such conference of its kind in the country. A survey done for the conference by a coalition of Canadian health activists showed that 37 percent of the 1,150 women with cancer who responded said they had used some form of alternative treatment.

The most popular were vitamin therapy or visualization, a form of meditation where women close their eyes and imagine, for example, white knights picking up the cancerous cells and riding off with them.

One woman who said she "strongly believes" in alternative therapies was Mary Dover of Regina, Saskatchewan. She told a Canadian Press reporter at the conference that she was diagnosed in 1984 at the age of 34 and was given just six months to live in 1986.

"I tried acupuncture, visualization, I did massage, I went on a macrobiotic diet, I don't drink caffeine, I don't eat red meat."

Although the current science doesn't support it, Drover was still there six years after conventional medicine said she had six months.

And Nicole St. Denis tried carrot juice after she found a cancerous lump the size of an egg in 1986. She was 46. "I did juice therapy while I was having chemotherapy," she said. "The doctor couldn't figure out why I wasn't as sick as I should have been. I'm convinced that helped. I had surgery, radiation and chemotherapy, and I feel all these things sort of worked together. You cannot just treat the body, you have to treat the whole person."

Activist Pat Kelly said doctors have to be educated about the alternative treatments so they can be used in conjunction with traditional medical methods.

"Whether their physicians know about it, like it, encourage it or discourage it, it's a given that women are doing it," she said. "So are you going to make that easier for them or more difficult?"

Another measure of the popularity of unconventional medical care is the enormous success over the past few years of Dr. Deepak Chopra's New Age remedies. His book *Ageless Body, Timeless Mind: The Quantum Alternative to Growing Old*, sold almost 1 million copies, and another book, *Perfect Health: The Complete Mind/Body Guide*, quickly became a national number one bestseller. Chopra promotes such exotic-sounding healing methods as marma therapy and the bliss technique, formally called the Maharishi Ayurveda Psychophysiological Integration Technique, which he describes as "bringing the mind and body together."

Chopra, a native of India with a medical degree from the All India Institute of Medical Sciences in New Delhi, is a follower of Maharishi Mahesh Yogi, who bestowed upon him the title of Lord of Immortality. In *Perfect Health* he writes:

Laura Simons is a young woman with advanced breast cancer who has performed remarkably well since she began using the bliss technique in combination with conventional therapy. For several years, ever since she discovered that a suspicious lump in her left breast was malignant, Laura refused surgery. Fortunately, the tumor remained localized and continued to grow only very slowly. Eventually she made the painful decision to undergo surgery — a limited lumpectomy rather than a mastectomy — and began to employ the bliss technique during her period of chemotherapy. Most patients react to cancer surgery and chemotherapy with inevitable surges of fear and depression, accompanied by physical debilitation that ranges from mild to devastating. Even at the best of times, the treatment is an ordeal.

Laura, however, was actually able to find joy in the experience. As soon as she learned the techniques, she reported feeling more calm and positive. Sometimes she experienced a throbbing sensation, warmth, or even pain; most of the time, however, the pain in the affected breast would go away when she used the technique. The most dramatic result, subjectively, was her newfound awareness of

bliss in the midst of her illness. 'The experiences during the bliss
technique are not as profound as when I started one and a half
years ago,' Laura writes, 'but then there was such deep-rooted fear
and sorrow, a feeling of helplessness and intense anxiety, so the
contrast was quite great when I began to experience such joy and
bliss.'

A review of Chopra by Zina Moukheiber in the April 11, 1994, edition
of *Forbes* magazine cites Chopra's claim that "because the mind influences every cell in the body, human aging . . . can speed up, slow down,
stop . . . and even reverse itself." Moukheiber writes that there is "a
grain of truth in all this New Age fluff," as science shows "a positive
attitude does seem to increase survival chances for cancer patients."
Indeed, a 10-year follow-up study of women with metastatic breast
cancer published in 1989 by Stanford University psychiatrist David
Spiegel showed that women who joined support groups using mutual
support, self-hypnosis and guided imagery lived, on average, 18 months
longer than women in a control group who did not join such networks.
A Laval University study of 224 patients in Quebec also found that
women with breast cancer who confided in a friend about their disease
also lived longer. Researcher Elizabeth Maunsell found 80 percent of
women who confided in someone within three months of surgery were
alive five years after the operation, compared to 63 percent of women
who didn't tell anybody about it.

Science shows that diet, too, can be important. Some animal studies
suggest dietary fat can promote tumor growth in women by increasing
estrogen, a known breast-cancer risk factor, and several international
studies have found that there may be a correlation between a nation's
fat consumption and breast-cancer rates. Other scientists argue that the
carcinogen may be what is in the animal fat — the toxins used in food
production — rather than the fat itself. Still, the National Institutes of
Health Women's Health Initiative is testing 4,000 women to see if
cutting dietary fat in half lowers breast-cancer rates. They won't know,
however, until 2006.

Moukheiber's criticism of Chopra, however, is that when he was
pressed for scientific corroboration of his claims, he proclaimed he had
a medical degree and said, "I am not at all attached to the scientific

worldview at the moment. I see myself as a bum on the street who has a lot of fun writing."

A very wealthy bum, it seems. Besides the millions he has reaped from his books, Chopra is a former director of Maharishi Ayur-Ved Products International, which sells herbal products that claim to slow aging. Moukheiber also points out that Chopra is a consultant to the Center for Mind Body Medicine in San Diego, "where, for $1,125 to $3,200, you can get a weeklong 'purification' treatment of massages and herbal cures, plus lectures on ayurveda (traditional medicine from India). And he's an owner of Quantum Publications, which sells tapes on weight loss, insomnia and meditation."

There are, of course, many Chopras out there. Mystics, herbalists, faith healers, all peddling their own particular mantras and often their own products as well. Whether scientifically valid or not — and without controlled clinical tests, who can really say? — most can boast many public testimonials from believers, but like all nontraditional approaches to the problem, the cancer establishment has traditionally either scoffed at unconventional methods, dismissed them out of hand or, in some cases, worked actively to discredit them.

There is, it's true, a serious danger of quackery being sold in the name of alternative medicine. On the other hand, there are many skilled physicians and other trained health personnel practicing a host of alternative methods, some of which appear at least worthy of further exploration.

There has been progress.

It wasn't long ago that acupuncture, for example, was completely dismissed by the medical establishment. Not any more. Many anesthesiologists and others freely acknowledge its usefulness.

Perhaps the leading American exponent of a more internalized approach to cancer is New Haven, Connecticut, surgeon Dr. Bernie Siegel, president of the American Holistic Medical Association. Siegel's 1986 book *Love, Medicine and Miracles* sold more than 2 million copies and was number one on the prestigious *New York Times* bestseller list. Siegel began ECaP (Exceptional Cancer Patients) in 1978, which he defines as a specialized form of individual and group therapy based on "care-frontation," a loving, safe, therapeutic confrontation that facilitates personal change and healing and makes everyone aware of his or her own healing potential.

"Exceptional patients refuse to be victims," wrote Siegel. "They educate themselves and become experts in their own care. They question the doctor because they want to understand their treatment and participate in it. They demand dignity, personhood, and control, no matter what the course of the disease."

Siegel writes that acceptance by the physician "can help a patient achieve healing and peace." He cites the case of Bridget, an English woman who, under that country's national health plan, was assigned a physician. But she didn't like him, and never went back. She saw Siegel after moving to New Jersey and had a tumor "the size of a melon" in her left breast. Siegel listed the things he thought could help her, "from surgery to God," and had her draw pictures, "which showed unconscious positive attitudes toward radiation and chemotherapy, although consciously she resisted both at first. Several months later she called to tell me that she had started chemotherapy and the tumor had melted away. Her response was so dramatic that her oncologist didn't even think she would need radiation. My acceptance of Bridget's condition had enabled her to accept what the medical profession had to offer."

To illustrate the importance of positive personal attitudes, Siegel cited the work of Dr. Caroline Bedell Thomas of John Hopkins University Medical School. Beginning in 1946, Thomas began personality profiles of 1,337 medical students, then surveyed their mental and physical health every year for decades after graduation. She was searching for psychological antecedents of heart disease, high blood pressure, mental illness and suicide, but included cancer in the study "for the sake of comparison, because she originally thought it would have no psychological component. However, the data showed a 'striking and unexpected' result: the traits of those who developed cancer were almost identical to those of the students who later committed suicide. Almost all the cancer patients had throughout their lives been restricted in expressing emotion, especially aggressive emotions related to their own needs. She also found that, using only the drawings they made as one of the tests, she could predict what parts of their bodies would develop cancer."

Another advocate of the connection between health and a healthy attitude was Virginia Dell Kelley, the mother of U.S. President Bill Clinton. Kelley, 71, died of breast cancer January 6, 1994, after a long bout with the disease. A month before her death, she told a Breast Cancer Awareness Evening audience in Ottawa that a positive attitude had helped in her fight against breast cancer. "I have always believed that attitude controls a lot of our feelings, a lot of our well-being. Attitude helps in the survival of breast cancer."

The medical establishment has been slow to recognize the validity of any of this, but as the weight of evidence mounts, there has been at least a grudging acceptance by some. In June 1991, for example, the National Institutes of Health opened an Office for the Study of Unconventional Medical Practices directed by Joe Jacobs, a medical doctor who is also a Native American trained in traditional healing techniques. Two years later it began dispensing modest research grants of about $30,000 each to 30 groups, chosen from more than 800 applicants, investigating alternative methods of healing. The initial grants, awarded in November 1993, covered a broad range of investigations from visualization to the power of prayer, electrochemical treatments (widely used in China) for shrinking tumors or boosting the immune system, yogic breathing technique, high doses of antioxidant vitamins, macrobiotic diet in cancer treatment to hypnotic guided imagery enhancing the mood and immune function in breast-cancer patients.

A *Washington Post* story paraphrases Jacobs saying that his office wanted to be open to the widest possible spectrum of alternative medical regimens. At the same time, however, there was a need to make sure funded studies used scientifically valid methods, to avoid criticism that the office was being used by quacks and charlatans hoping to gain validity for their favorite brand of snake oil.

Normal NIH studies use expert panels called study sections to judge research proposals in a given field. Instead of study sections on precise categories, Jacobs' office used a panel of 15 reviewers, each of whom focused on one of several broad topic headings — such as mind-body cures, bioelectric methods and traditional and ethnomedical healing. Each proposal was discussed and then scored by secret ballot.

John Spencer, an analyst at the alternative medicine office who helped oversee the three-day judging marathon, told the *Post* that the pressure to succeed was great. "You've got to understand the enormity of what we're trying to do here. Alternative medicine doesn't get many opportunities to really prove itself, and we wanted to do it right. It was an experimental marriage, and in the end there was not a lot of heated debate. In fact, each learned a lot about the other's point of view."

And Jacobs said, "The point is not whether we believe in these things or not, but whether we are willing to investigate them fairly. One of the major failings of conventional medicine is its refusal to take into account cultural and religious belief systems. People can lose sight of the human dimension of medicine, which is much more art than science. . . . Somebody has to study these dimensions."

In the past, conventional practitioners have not been willing to do even that much.

In April 1994, *Life* magazine ran a cover picture of celebrities Phyllis Newman, Jill Eikenberry, Shirley Temple Black, Marcia Wallace and Linda Ellerbee and nine other breast-cancer survivors from the Cedars-Sinai Comprehensive Cancer Center. The photo heralded a feature story on immunologist Georg Springer, whose first experimental patient, his wife Heather, died of breast cancer in 1980 — six years after she was given a year to live. Springer, like other maverick researchers, was long ostracized by the establishment, but Edward Sondik, deputy director of the National Cancer Institute, concedes that "as far as bottom-line statistics, nothing looks very good. We have made no major break-throughs in terms of a cure." He says there is growing interest in therapies that muster the body's immune defenses against cancer.

"Springer's results are startling," wrote *Life*. "All 19 women from his first study group survived for five years and 16 are still alive — 11 after a decade or more. However, prominent scientists say too few women have been tested with his vaccine for results to be meaningful, pointing out that interesting data often doesn't stand up in large-scale, random-ized trials."

Springer invented an early-detection cancer test more than 20 years ago. Isolating antigens that occur on the surface of cancerous cells, he devised a simple skin test using similar antigens made from healthy cells, which is 90 percent accurate and "can detect cancer years before it shows up on a mammogram." His vaccine — which cost him $1,500 a year per patient to produce, and is not covered by insurance — uses injections of the antigens to stimulate the immune system. He also recommends several vitamins: 4,000 mg of Vitamin C; 20,000 units of betacarotene; 800 units of Vitamin E; and a multiple vitamin daily. Another vaccine, similar to Springer's, developed by Biomira Inc., a Canadian company, showed some early success, and the University of Pittsburgh is also experimenting with a cancer vaccine. Immunologist Olivera Finn told *Life*, "I would be incredibly surprised if the vaccine approach failed." Michael Sporn, director of a new NCI lab designed to intervene in precancerous stages of the disease using a combination of new therapies, went even further — likely too far — when he predicted, "Over the next twenty-five years breast cancer will disappear like the Cheshire cat."

Another factor forcing the U.S. establishment to take a harder look at new and/or unconventional methods is the growing threat of legal action if they don't. In December 1993, for example, a California jury awarded $89.3 million to the family of a woman whose health maintenance organization (HMO) refused to pay for a bone-marrow transplant — an expensive, experimental procedure — to treat her advanced breast cancer. A mother of three young children, Nelene Fox, who developed breast cancer in 1991 at age 38, died in April 1993, eight months after receiving the therapy thanks to $212,000 in cash and donated drugs raised through public appeals.

Dr. David Eddy, a health economist with Duke University who has advised the White House and served as a consultant to insurance companies, told the *New York Times* that it was crucial to distinguish between issues of contractual obligations and scientific evidence on marrow transplants.

"If the message here is that health care organizations should be more precise in their definitions and procedures, and more consistent in applying them, then over the long run that's fine. . . . But if this is interpreted to mean that investigational procedures should be covered, that is a disaster, not just for the cost of health care but also for the quality of health care." Insurance coverage, he said, is a major barrier preventing wide use of unproved, possibly harmful treatments.

Horror stories about lack of insurance coverage abound in the United States, of course, but even in Canada, which likes to boast that its national health-care plan is the envy of the world, most forms of alternative medicine and many of the emerging, hi-tech cancer-fighting methods are not covered.

Sylvia Morrison, a member of the Burlington Breast Cancer Support Services Inc., one of the original and most effective patient activist organizations in Canada, testified October 22, 1991, before a Special Subcommittee on Breast Cancer of the Standing Committee on Health and Welfare, Social Affairs, Seniors and the Status of Women. Morrison had been diagnosed with advanced breast cancer in February 1991. Speaking in a voice made barely audible by radiation treatment, Morrison told the committee how she needed a bone marrow transplant but only 15 were allowed each year in Hamilton, where she lived, and these were reserved for young adults with lymphomas and leukemia. Morrison pointed out that she was in a more fortunate position than many women. She and her husband, a university professor, were relatively comfortable financially and she had access to the best medical advice because her daughter was a final-year medical student at the University of Calgary and her son was a resident in internal medicine at the Cornell Medical Center at New York Hospital. Her son arranged an appointment for her with New York surgeon Dr. Mitchell Gaynor, who recommended immediate high-dose chemotherapy plus an alternative to bone marrow transplantation, a procedure being used in the United States using granulocyte colony stimulating factors (GCSF) with the trade name of Neupogen. It stimulates the bone marrow to produce white blood cells, and another drug, Epogen, stimulates it to produce red blood cells. The treatment was not only unavailable in Canada, but Morrison's oncologist had never heard of it. And the drugs, Neupogen and Epogen, were not licensed in Canada.

Morrison opted for bone marrow transplant in New York. Even though Ontario's medical plan pays 75 percent of hospital costs, the remaining 25 percent is formidable. Calculating costs of $900 a day in hospital for 90 days, Morrison said her share of the cost was $20,250, "and this does not include drugs, the IV therapy and anything else above and beyond that."

After a modified radical mastectomy in New York Hospital, and more treatment at the Roswell Park Memorial Institute in Buffalo, New York, Morrison again tried to get the treatment she needed, radiation therapy, in Hamilton, only to learn there would be a 10-day delay to get an appointment and, even if she were accepted into the program, a three-week delay before treatment began. "Remember, we are discussing a tumor that had been growing at the rate of one centimetre a week," she said. Morrison then learned that the Ontario Health Insurance Plan (OHIP) would not cover the treatment for two reasons: prior consent was needed, not always practical in emergency situations, and even though the treatment was widely used in the United States, it was considered experimental in Canada and not eligible for funding. For the first three months, Morrison submitted a bill for U.S. $25,000. OHIP paid $3,900 (Canadian).

Morrison's testimony underscored three main points: there is a lack of information available to women; a lack of facilities for treatment, especially for advanced breast cancer; and a lack of medical research that can delay new methods of treatments for years even after they have been proven effective elsewhere."

Two months later, Sylvia Morrison died.

Insurance coverage, or lack of it, is also sometimes a major weapon used by particular self-interest groups to wage war against methods that could directly affect their profit margins. A case in point is the long and ultimately successful fight by the powerful radiologist lobby, the medical equivalent of the National Rifle Association, to have thermography de-listed as an insurable procedure.

The thermography apparatus looks like a large TV camera with a separate monitor and a series of controls. The person being scanned acts as the sole energy source in a completely darkened room, and the screen detects emitted energy from the patient. Then the various levels of heat emitted are read by the thermographers. Practitioners argue it is potentially one of the more useful weapons in early breast-cancer detection, but pressure from radiologists has kept it from full and proper recognition.

Dr. Harold Isard, himself a radiologist at Albert Einstein Medical Center in Philadelphia, and one of the first in the United States to use breast thermography, says the American Medical Association and the American College of Radiology "have long objected to thermography. They say it's not a real technological tool, that it's experimental. . . . The bad part of all this is the political stuff. It's like batting your head against a brick wall. We think our patients get better care because we use thermography."

In fact, Isard's clinical study of 10,000 women published in the August 1, 1988, edition of *Cancer*, found that about 75 percent of women who showed an abnormal thermogram did, in fact, end up with breast cancer. He says the procedure, which measures infrared heat from tumors, does not replace mammography but is a helpful diagnostic tool. "It can be a marker for high-risk women. If a woman has an abnormal thermographic study, that patient is at higher risk of the possibility of getting breast cancer." Although France has been using thermography for years, he says, in the United States, although it was part of the massive 1973 Breast Cancer Detection Demonstration Projects (BCDDP), it created some early excitement but "unfortunately, few people were really interested in it. They [radiologists] felt it was a nuisance. We already had mammography, so why bother?" (The technique is only used sparingly in Canada, with a few machines concentrated in the major cities.)

For one thing, thermography, unlike mammography, is absolutely harmless. It's noninvasive, the woman having it is not touched, so there is no danger of internal tumors being broken as there is during the squeezing process in mammography. It's also cheaper and faster.

The obvious question then is that if thermography works, why isn't there more of it? To answer that, you have to understand the political history of the device.

It didn't begin as a healing mechanism. Quite the opposite. Its early history is as an instrument of the Cold War. When the Soviets shot down Gary Power's U.S. spy plane in 1960, the Americans decided they couldn't risk flying over Soviet territory, so they poured billions of dollars into a crash program to develop thermography for satellite spying. Dr. Phil Hoekstra, head of Therma-Scan Inc. of Huntington Woods, Michigan, who has been working with thermography for 22 years, has a personal understanding of its history. His father, an optical engineer, was project director of the thermography project. "In the Cold War mentality, everything was top secret," says Hoekstra. "My father took components around the country literally handcuffed to him and to an FBI agent. The Cancer Society had a program giving preferential treatment to certain women, and when [Lyndon] Johnson was president, my father flew down to Texas and gave thermography to the whole first family. It was all very much top security."

The first medical application, however, belongs to Ray Lawson, a Quebec doctor and fishing buddy of R. Bowling Barnes, a manufacturer in Stanford, Connecticut, who had a contract to develop a prototype. Barnes, a former infrared physicist at Princeton University, caught some of his staff aiming the machine at a woman's washroom, where they could tell if a woman was wearing a padded bra or not by the amount of heat generated. Hoekstra says that after giving them a stern lecture on trivializing such top-secret equipment, Barnes thought more about its nonmilitary possibilities, and after discussing it while on a fly fishing trip with Lawson in the late 1950s or early 1960s, in violation of all types of national security laws, Barnes put a thermography machine in a van and shipped it to Lawson.

The first application Lawson made was in breast cancer. With the help of a printed guide Barnes had sent him, Lawson fired up the machine, found some hot spots in women's breasts and wrote a paper arguing that a breast tumor was associated with a small increase in skin temperature above the affected part. The paper caused considerable security problems. Still, as a result, Barnes manufactured one of the earliest medical thermography machines, and soon several commercial models were available from Barnes Engineering, Smiths Industries of the United Kingdom and two Swedish companies, AGA and Bofors, both with major military interests.

In an abstract on thermography published in the *International Journal of Technology Assessment in Health Care* in 1993, the University of Amsterdam's Stuart S. Blume writes that in the early days, "radiologists never had any doubt that any possible utility of thermography would be in the area of breast cancer screening. By the time the first prototypes were available, Gershon Cohen had already created a thermographic division within his radiology department, thereby setting an example of the incorporation of thermography into radiological practice."

But not all radiologists were as enthusiastic. "To secure the place of thermography within radiological practice," writes Blume, "it was not enough merely to show that a breast containing a malignancy produced a distinctive thermogram, as Gershon Cohen had done at . . . [a] 1963 conference. Radiologists wanted to assess the value of the technique more precisely by comparing its accuracy with the accuracy of existing techniques." Used alone, thermography could not distinguish benign from malignant disease, but used in combination with mammography, the rate of detection could be raised significantly above that offered by either technology.

The real split with radiologists, however, came over a highly technical point — a kind of medical theology over the difference between process and structures. "Structures, of course, are the very essence of radiological practice," writes Blume. "It is highly significant that Lawson initially had justified the interest of thermography precisely in terms of its representation not of structures but of process." In short, radiologists preferred to stick with what they knew, and when thermography couldn't be suitably adapted for their purposes, they not only abandoned it, but waged a campaign against it.

Hoekstra argues that thermography is "as good as if not better than mammography" in terms of accuracy, but "the problem is that thermography is in a competitive situation with mammography. Radiologists are a powerful lobby group. Thermography is used extensively in Europe and Asia where the influence of radiologists is not so great. Radiologists seem to covet mammography. I don't know why. It's really a piss poor technique."

Between 1973 and 1977, Hoekstra and his father rented community rooms in shopping malls around Detroit, where they did group screenings. Two hundred and fifty women could be examined in one day for $20 each, more than ten times the number of screenings mammography is capable of, and at only a fraction of the cost for each. "It was causing a lot of ire among physicians who didn't want tests done that they didn't order, so we had to discontinue that sort of thing. But we found many breast cancers in women who had no idea they had anything wrong with them. We still hold the record for detecting the smallest breast cancer in this state (Michigan). It was described as the size of a grain of rice back in 1975.

"Thermographers don't have a position of strength," says Hoekstra. "This helps radiologists, but it also does very much to harm women with breast cancer. Radiologists maintained a constant and sometimes vehement opposition to thermography based on some very poor NCI studies in the mid-70s."

Another problem, says Hoekstra, is that because no major corporations manufacture thermography machines — only small, high-tech companies — this has a major impact on what is taught in the medical schools. "The big companies direct a lot of education of professors," he says. "Basically they buy professors by buying a chair, or paying people at the university to do the work. That's why there's such miserable education on nutrition. No major company is buying nutritionists. There are some professors doing thermography . . . but in most universities it is not taught at all.

"When studies are well done, thermography shines through every time. You know, the medical and cancer establishment say they're making progress against breast cancer. It's bullshit. The fact is, incidence is going up. No matter what combination of treatment, it's not working. Breast cancer is being detected too late and is occurring in younger and younger women. The death rate is either unchanged or getting worse. Women are being strongarmed by bullshit, getting unnecessary surgery . . . the establishment does a fine job of espousing all the dogma, strictly cookbook medicine. Theirs is state of the art. We're just technicians. In the meantime, the bodies are piling up."

Under pressure from the medical establishment, the Health Care Financing Administration (HCFA) first withdrew medical coverage for thermography and breast disease in 1984, then for all other uses of thermography in 1993. Citing the lack of sufficient scientific evidence and dismissing studies as containing serious methodological flaws, some scientists called thermography "not only unreliable but dangerous." The HCFA report in 1992 also claimed that "the use of thermography for diagnosing breast disease has been universally discredited." This is not true. It is used successfully in other parts of the world, and studies in the States have shown it can be helpful. In addition, techniques have improved since studies were done in the 1970s — just as they have improved for mammography. But the plain fact is that there is more money to be made in mammography and the interests of radiologists superceded those of thermographers.

As Blume concluded in his abstract on the subject, "The history of thermography shows how the process of continuous assessment through which a new medical technology takes shape is necessarily dominated by certain values, priorities, and assumptions and not by other equally valid ones. Certain participants in the process have the ability to impose their definitions, their criteria, and their agendas. We cannot understand the career of medical thermography other than in terms of social processes such as these."

Thermography, of course, is far from the only technique victimized by the medical establishment. As Ralph Moss writes in Part Two of his landmark book, *The Cancer Industry*, "The 'proven' methods of treating cancer are in a state of crisis. Clearly, the cancer problem cannot be solved in any ultimate sense by sticking to today's 'safe and sound' methods. Something radically new is needed — approaches that are fresh and daring."

The one constant in all of these cases, and many others, is the active hostility toward anything new, even in the face of legitimate clinical evidence, by the medical establishment, the American Cancer Society and such government organizations as the Food and Drug Administration and the National Cancer Institute. You might think such organizations, while legitimately concerned about quackery, would at least be open-minded about unorthodoxies that show promise in fighting cancer or easing the suffering of cancer patients. But that is not the way it is. Quite the opposite.

In his book *Vital Choices: Life, Death and the Health Care Crisis*, Dr. William Molloy, associate professor of medicine and director of research in the Division of Geriatric Medicine at Hamilton, Ontario's, McMaster University, wrote: "The cancer establishment represents an enormous industry. It has intensive propaganda, slick media relations, political lobbying and powerful fund-raising."

Until the 1950s, the American Cancer Society had a Committee on Quackery, but it subsequently changed its name to the Committee on Unproven Methods of Cancer Management. But, as Moss points out, its view that anything outside the norm is quackery hasn't changed much. He cites in *The Cancer Industry* an ACS claim that "proponents of new or unproven methods of cancer management range from ignorant, uneducated, misguided persons, to highly educated scientists with advanced degrees who are out of their area of competence in supporting a particular form of treatment. A few hold Ph.D. or M.D. degrees . . ."

Of the 70 advocates of unorthodox therapies listed by the ACS, however, Moss points out that 41 held bona fide medical degrees from such universities as Harvard, Illinois, Northwestern, Yale, Dublin, Oxford or Toronto. Two more were osteopaths who became medical doctors and only one held a medical degree from what the ACS described as a "class C institution which went out of existence." While the ACS claimed that only "a few" held Ph.D. or medical degrees, in fact, 77 percent of them did. But because they opted to pursue research outside the established norm, they were essentially dismissed as quacks by the ultraconservative ACS.

This is not to say there are not some quacks out there, only that everybody who pursues something different isn't necessarily a quack. As Moss underscores, many widely accepted treatments came from rather bizarre sources to begin with. The drug Premarin, used by millions of women to relieve the effects of menopause, is derived from pregnant mares' urine. Penicillin comes from mold. The orthodox anti-cancer agent Mustargen is a form of poisonous mustard gas, and another anti-cancer agent comes from the periwinkle plant.

Moss traces the history of Coley's toxins, or "mixed bacterial vaccine," discovered by Harvard Medical School graduate Dr. William B. Coley late in the last century. "His discovery was first tolerated, then ridiculed, and finally suppressed. Today, although given lip service by some doctors, its potential is still largely unexplored." In 1893, of 17 cases of advanced carcinoma treated with his vaccine, 4 were permanently cured, 10 showed improvement that added years to their lives and 3 showed no improvement. He at first used live erysipelas germs, but when that proved to be a terrible ordeal for patients — nearly 6 percent of his first group died of streptococcal infection as a result of the treatment — he devised a mixture of toxins. In a later test on breast-cancer patients, 13 of the 20 with inoperable cancer, or 65 percent, and all 13 with the operable type were alive after five years. Despite this success, many surgeons were suspicious of Coley's methods and, by the time of his death in 1936, chemotherapy and the new, high-voltage X-ray machines were grabbing all the medical attention and financial support. While some toxins were still being produced commercially, that too ended in 1953.

Even so, thanks to the efforts of Coley's daughter, Helen Coley Nauts, a clinical test was performed at New York University–Bellevue Hospital, one of the few double-blind clinical studies ever held on an unproven method. The authors concluded that "Coley's toxins has definite oncologytic (tumor-destroying) properties and is useful in the treatment of certain types of malignant disease." Yet the American Cancer Society included Coley's toxins in its 1965 "Unproven Methods" and wrote: "There was little objective basis offered for believing that bacterial toxin therapy had significantly altered the course of disease in any of the treated cancer patients." Moss concludes that "the fact is, a century after Coley's initial success, it still remains nearly impossible for a patient to opt for this extraordinary therapy in any form."

Moss also traces the controversies surrounding laetrile; the chemotherapy drug hydrazine sulfate; Dr. Lawrence Burton's immunological therapy; Dr. Stanislaw Burzynski's antieoplastons chemotherapy; and the work that two-time Nobel Prize winner Dr. Linus Pauling did with Vitamin C and other nutritional approaches. Pauling, incidentally, called the fight against cancer a "fraud," because in his view it is fueled by politics, not science.

The lack of cooperation by the medical establishment is particularly unfortunate since most "alternative" practitioners are only too willing to cooperate in the interest of improved health care.

Seattle's Dr. Jeff Bland, a nutritional biochemist who operates Healthcomm, a leading American researcher into vegetarian diets and the use of plants to improve the immune system, says most people in alternative medicine are not opposed to traditional chemotherapy and surgery, "but simply recognize the adjunctive method can help prevention and rehabilitation and lower the side effects of treatment."

Bland, whose clinic employs 30 full-time researchers, says "the information is there, but much of it is lying dormant. The consumers don't know about it. It's not just a bunch of mumbo-jumbo. There's a lot of good basic science being done in this area."

For example, says Bland, studies show that if a woman gets on a regimen of vitamin E before starting her chemotherapy, "it will significantly reduce her hair loss. One study showed women going all the way through chemotherapy with only minimal hair loss. There are actually studies done, but they haven't gotten into the general medical community. This is important psychologically, not only for making the woman feel better about herself, but it helps in her recovery. There are studies which show that."

So why don't doctors tell their patients about it? "It's partly a turf war," says Bland. "It's also not taught in medical schools. The pharmaceutical companies have a significant bias against nutrients because nutrients are nonpatentable. There just aren't the profits to be made in them."

Despite the history, however, Bland believes the worm is beginning to turn. "I believe medicine is going to change dramatically over the next decade. The data to support this is irrefutable. Over 6,000 articles every month are published in medical journals devoted to nutrition. That's a big body of evidence which is hard to ignore.

"Another factor, given the cost of health care; so-called alternative medicine is cheaper. What may have been dismissed a few years ago as unnecessary or strange will be looked at as a cost-effective way and found to be both cost-saving and effective.

"What we have now is a two-tiered system; the traditional, reimbursed system, and the other system beneath it which is self-reimbursed, called alternative medicine," says Bland. "We're going to see that change too thanks largely to citizen advocacy. If citizens demand certain things, believe it or not, things will happen . . . there definitely is a move toward increased advocacy, particularly toward women-centered health care . . ."

Support for unorthodox therapies, it seems, is not only growing among grassroots organizations, but has its champions in the British Royal Family. Queen Elizabeth has her own personal homeopathic physician, and Prince Charles has been a long-time supporter of the Bristol Cancer Health Centre, which he formally opened when it expanded in 1983.

Writing about the Bristol centre in a 1990 *Canadian Medical Association Journal,* London writer and editor Caroline Richmond explained that the Bristol treatment "is based on the belief that the body needs to be 'detoxified' by a strict vegan diet augmented with carrot juice and vitamin tablets, that patients might have developed cancer to satisfy a deep psychological need that can be expurgated, and that the immune system can be strengthened by an act of will. Thus, cancer can be fought by diet, meditation, counselling, the laying on of hands, and by patients visualizing their immune system killing their cancer cells."

Therapy, which includes meals but not accommodation, costs £100 a day, or £600 a week. One of the strengths of the center for patients is that it restores their "sense of being in control of their bodies, which patients had felt were under the control of either their doctor or the cancer," writes Richmond. "Another attractive feature may be that it is refreshingly free in its use of the word cancer — there is no mention of the lumps and other euphemisms preferred by so many mealymouthed surgeons."

But does it work? Not too well, judging by a study published in *The Lancet* in 1990. The study involved about 300 Bristol patients, all of whom had taken conventional therapy as well, matched against 200 controls from a center of excellence and another 200 from three district general hospitals. The study found that Bristol women had nearly twice the death rate and three times the metastasis of women who received the same treatment but did not go to Bristol.

Penny Brohn, the center's founder and then 11-year survivor of breast cancer, "was unembarrassed by the results and denied that they were a reflection on the centre's treatment," wrote Richmond. "Her response was to place the blame firmly back on the patients. She offered the 'cancer personality' argument; if they fare badly it is because of their innate mental or physical state, or the virulence of their cancer, or because they didn't follow the regimen strictly enough, or even because they followed it too strictly. She also says that the findings cannot be extrapolated to cancers other than of the breast and that the vegan diet is healthy. The centre is now suggesting, with the same confidence that it once predicted improved survival, that research now in progress is likely to show that Bristol patients have a better quality of life.'"

Despite the poor results of the Bristol method, however, there is a growing body of science that shows that diet does indeed make a difference in cancer and other diseases, such as heart disease.

In a study by Japanese scientists, Suketami Tominaga and Kuko Kato, published in 1990 on changing patterns of cancer and diet in Japan, the two epidemiologists argue there is a correlation between the western-ization of Japanese diets and the increased incidence of various cancers, including breast cancer. Fortunately, the Japanese government had conducted the National Nutritional Survey every year since 1946 to estimate the nutritional status of the Japanese, making comparisons in dietary change easier to track. In addition, studies on Japanese migrants to the United States have also shown an increased incidence of breast and other cancers that could be tied to diet. When they compared 1987 with 1950, they found that the intake of milk and milk products, meat, eggs, oils and fats, and fruits all increased in Japan, while the intake of cereals, pickles and potatoes dropped. Fish and shellfish and beans remained relatively constant. Among the nutrients, the largest increase was in fat, followed by animal protein, calcium and Vitamins A and B2.

During this period, several cancers increased substantially, including breast cancer, which began to rise after 1960.

They concluded that "chronological correlations between foods/nutrients intake and cancer mortalities in Japan showed strong positive correlations between westernized dietary habits and the mortalities of cancers of the colon, breast, ovary and prostate. . . . However, the correlations do not necessarily suggest a causal relationship."

Intrigued by the potential of diet playing a role in the development of cancer, however, the National Cancer Institute of Canada, supported by the Canadian Cancer Society, began a massive cohort study in 1992 for which they hope to recruit 100,000 men and 100,000 women over the age of 30, and 20,000 girls aged 7 to 12, in a passive look at their dietary habits. Participants are asked to complete two questionnaires: one, a food-frequency survey dealing with dietary intake in the year before recruitment; the second, probing other lifestyle factors, such as types and frequency of exercise, occupation and smoking habits. They were also asked for a brief medical history, and women were asked about their reproductive history and use of oral contraceptives and hormone-replacement therapy. Then, four and eight years after enrolment, they'll be given follow-up questionnaires.

A commentary in the April 1992 issue of the *Canadian Medical Association Journal* said, "Diet is believed to play a role in the promotion or prevention of some cancers, most notably ones involving the colon, breast, pancreas and lung. A high fat intake is postulated to be a risk factor for the development of colon and breast cancer. On the other hand, a diet high in fibre, especially from fruits and vegetables, is thought to reduce the risk of colon cancer. In addition, high intakes of vitamins A and C may protect against cancers of the colon and lung. The CCS [Canadian Cancer Society] recommends that Canadians lower their fat intake and increase their fibre intake."

In the October 1992 issue of *Vogue* magazine, John Glaspy, director of the Bowyer Oncology Center at the UCLA School of Medicine says, "Studying nutritional factors is going to yield pay dirt." At about the same time, the National Institutes of Health, under its new director Bernadine Healy, was launching a 60,000-patient long-term study of low-fat diets and cancer prevention. The first phase consisted of a three-year Women's Health Trial Initiative aimed at testing the feasibility of encouraging 2,250 women from different cultural and economic backgrounds to change their diets to include less fat.

At the same time, a major study led by Dr. Walter Willett of Brigham and Women's Hospital in Boston published in the *Journal of the American Medical Association* found no evidence that a link exists between dietary fat and breast cancer. Willett and his research team charted the health of 89,000 nurses for eight years, paying particular attention to their diets. About 1,400 of the women developed cancer — 600 of them breast cancer — but the researchers said they could not draw any link between that and the women's diets. (Willett's study relied on the women's memories of what they'd eaten, which would inevitably lead to error and bias in the results.)

Several recent studies, however, have drawn a connection between diet and cancer, particularly the value of certain fruits and vegetables such as broccoli. Not everybody agrees with that. During one state dinner, then President George Bush announced that "I am rebelling against broccoli and I refuse to give ground. I'm president of the United States, and I'm not going to eat any more broccoli."

Maybe not. But in March 1992 researchers at Johns Hopkins University led by molecular pharmacologist Paul Talalay discovered that broccoli contains sulforaphane, a superactive mustard oil found in other greens as well, which helps fight carcinogens by prodding the body into making enzymes known to enhance the process by which noxious chemicals are neutralized and flushed out by our kidneys. According to a January 1993 story in *Discover* magazine, the researchers tested a series of vegetable extracts — broccoli, scallions, carrots and others — growing mouse cells in plates, squirting the extracts on them, then measuring the protective enzyme levels produced by the cells 48 hours later. "What we've found," said Talalay, "is a chemically well-defined mechanism for mobilizing our own defenses against cancer."

The January 9, 1993, edition of *Science News* reported on the results of a Swedish study by epidemiologist Lars-Erik Holm, then at Stockholm's Karolinska Hospital, of 220 women who had had surgery to remove a malignant breast tumor. After the surgery, the women received adjuvant therapy, such as radiation, chemotherapy or hormonal treatment with tamoxifen, then researchers sent a nutritionist to each woman's home to investigate diet and food preparation during the year prior to the patient's diagnosis. The team then monitored the women for at least four years and the subsequent statistical analysis revealed that fat intake did influence the outcome of breast-cancer treatment, but only in women who had tumors with lots of estrogen receptors. Women in the group who ate the most saturated fat ran a 20 percent higher risk of recurring cancer than those whose diets contained the least saturated fat.

In November 1993, the $625 million Women's Health Initiative launched by Dr. Bernadine Healy during her two-year tenure as the first woman director of the National Institutes of Health, came under heavy fire from a committee of the Institute of Medicine. The committee was an independent body of experts that advised the government, but was chaired by Dr. Marion J. Finkel, a vice-president of Sandoz Pharmaceuticals, and included 6 other women among its 11 members. This trial, the largest ever funded by the NIH, involved 14 years of research and more than 160,000 women and began recruiting in September 1993. It was designed to assess whether a low-fat diet could reduce the risk of breast and colon cancer, whether hormone-replacement therapy reduces the risk of heart disease and whether calcium and Vitamin D supplements cut the risk of osteoporosis.

The committee said that "if low-fat diet in adulthood affects breast cancer risk, most epidemiologists agree that its effect is likely to be small. Thus, the diet-breast-cancer hypothesis is considered to be quite weak." It recommended that the study's primary focus be shifted to the prevention of cardiovascular disease rather than breast cancer. But the NIH replied that the project "has the clear potential to produce much-needed information about the role of diet in preventing breast cancer." As Healy put it, "Billions of dollars have been spent to do research in men, and now a relatively modest study comes along to do studies in women, and it is subject to this kind of scrutiny. However, when the study is over, we will know a lot more about women's health than we do today."

Dr. Venket Rao, a University of Toronto professor of nutritional sciences, told the April 1994 *Chatelaine* magazine that naturally occurring chemicals in food, in addition to playing a role in cancer prevention, may someday be used in cancer treatment. While still mainly at the laboratory and animal research stage, he said test-tube trials indicate that genistein, for example, blocks the growth of blood vessels in newly born malignant tumors, stopping them from becoming large enough to cause harm. In addition, anti-oxidants, which neutralize and clean up free radicals — harmful molecules that occur naturally in the body but can also be caused by exposure to sunlight, X-rays and environmental pollutants — can alter the DNA of normal cells, causing them to become malignant. Like Vitamins C and E, some food chemicals are anti-oxidants. One of those, carotenoids, required for the formation of Vitamin A in the body, may inhibit the growth of lung, colon and breast cancers. Carotenoids are found in crucifers, such as broccoli and cauliflower and cabbage, and deep-orange and yellow vegetables, and fruits, such as carrots, sweet potatoes and cantaloupes. Rao says that flavonoids, chemicals that accelerate the metabolism of the female hormone estrogen and speed its exit from the body, may reduce the risk of hormone-dependent malignancies in some women, including many breast cancers. Flavonoids are found in most fruits and vegetables, particularly the cruciferous groups.

Also, some naturally occuring chemicals in foods may stimulate the production of cancer-fighting enzymes in the body. Indoles, for example, present in broccoli and other cruciferous vegetables, may trigger enzymes that reduce the estrogen blood level, helping inihibit the growth of hormone-dependent breast tumors. And sulfur compounds in garlic, onions and scallions appear to protect against cancer by encouraging enzymes that strengthen the immune system. Other animal research links garlic with a reduced risk for breast cancer.

Despite the contradictory evidence and quarrels among scientists, it seems the public was buying into the notion that diet and more natural foods are better for your health.

An April 11, 1994, *New York Times* story from Paris reported that sales of medicinal herbs in that country had doubled in less than ten years and pharmacies have even joined the new trend by selling capsules and infusions filled with natural plant powders. "For the last 30 years the chemical drugs had made such great progress that people had forgotten about plants," said Jean Gaulin, president of the National Association of Pharmacists. "Now there's a return to plants because we remember that they act gently and may be less invasive than chemically based medicines."

The annual Fair of Alternative Medicine in Paris, the largest exhibition of its kind in Europe, drew 50,000 visitors a month earlier. Still, France's powerful medical association has managed to block recognition even of therapists now widely licensed in the West, such as chiropractors, osteopaths and acupuncturists, and proposals to change this have been held back by the Parliament, where 62 of the 577 deputies are medical doctors. But a recent survey found that one in five Paris households was using herbal remedies of some type. Regine Simonet, editor of the 100,000-circulation magazine *Médicine Douce*, told the *Times* that the growing interest in natural health care is linked to people's fears — fear of dependency on and the side effects of synthetic drugs, fear of too many chemicals in the environment and in one's own body, fear of losing even more contact with nature.

Dr. Paul Talalay, Dr. Gary Posner and their colleagues at Johns Hopkins University added to the evidence, reporting new proof in the April 12, 1994, issue of *The Proceedings of the National Academy of Sciences* of the protective benefits of chemicals found in many plant foods — including the cancer-fighting sulforaphane. But at the same time, another major study published in the *New England Journal of Medicine* found no evidence that vitamins can protect against cancer and heart disease — and may even do actual harm. That study, sponsored by the National Cancer Institute and the National Public Health Institute in Finland, was designed to discover whether Vitamins A and E reduce the incidence of heart disease and lung and other cancers. It studied 29,000 Finnish men aged 50 and over, all of them long-term smokers. Even so, experts involved in the study said it was possible that a benefit in eating fruits and vegetables might merge as the study continued. They concluded that people should continue to eat a lot of fresh fruit and vegetables, since the benefits seen in earlier studies may have come from something other than the vitamins in those foods.

The fight over the relationship between foods and cancer has also spilled over into the farms, where many argue that the pesticides used in food are at the root of the growing incidence of cancers and other diseases. In April 1994, the Clinton administration offered a proposal to rewrite two laws controlling the use of pesticides in food, but neither environmentalists nor the industry supported his approach. Since 1958, any residues of cancer-causing substances, no matter how small, were prohibited in food processed in the United States, but that law remains largely unenforced. The issue also sparked a controversy over genetically engineered food and in particular about the use of synthetic bovine somatotropin (rbST) to increase a cow's milk production by up to 15 percent.

As a result of all this, the National Cancer Institute, the U.S. Environmental Protection Agency and the National Institutes of Environmental Health Sciences announced a massive, 10-year Agriculture Health Study in early 1994 under the direction of Dr. Charles Lynch of the University of Iowa's Department of Preventive Medicine and Dr. Margaret Pennybacker of Survey Research Associates, Inc., Durham, North Carolina. The goal is to study some 112,000 farmers, their spouses (about 37,000 spouses), dependents and commercial pesticide applicators to discover why, despite a low mortality overall, farmers appear to experience an excess of several cancers. These excesses have been observed in epidemiological studies among agriculture workers in several countries, among them the United States, Canada, Sweden, Denmark, Finland, the United Kingdom, Spain, the Netherlands, Australia and New Zealand.

"The study will also provide an opportunity to assess the role that diet, various cooking methods, and other lifetyle factors have on the etiology of cancers and other diseases," according to a summary released by the study. "This is important not only to be able to disentangle the effects of lifestyle factors from those of agricultural exposures on disease risk, but also to evaluate risks from non-agricultural exposures experienced by rural populations."

The study sees a need to identify and clarify the occurrence of cancer excesses among farmers in several developed countries; an excess cancer incidence among other occupations involved with pesticide exposures; a rising incidence for several of these same tumors in the general population; and a growing concern regarding nonmalignant diseases in agricultural populations.

And so it goes. Despite continued opposition from the medical fraternity, pharmaceutical and chemical companies and many of the more traditional cancer organizations, the notions about holistic medicine, low-fat diets and other nontraditional approaches are slowly gaining a place in modern society.

For many people, however, this grudging acceptance is not happening swiftly enough. James S. Gordon, a psychiatrist, director of the Center for Mind-Body Studies in Washington and clinical professor in the departments of Psychiatry and Community and Family Medicine at Georgetown Medical School, wrote a persuasive article published in the August 29, 1993, *Washington Post*, arguing that the time has come to bring holistic medicine in from the therapy fringes. Given the Clinton administration's emphasis on health-care reform, and the prohibitive costs associated with health care, Gordon says the entire system "requires a profound shift in emphasis from authoritarian medical intervention to authoritative self-care.

"Much of what we have tended to regard as peripheral or trivial must become central; the therapeutic use of nutrition, exercise and relaxation; the mobilization of the mind to alter and transform itself and the body; group support. Techniques that are fundamental to the healing systems of other cultures — like acupuncture and yoga — should be fully integrated into our own. Alternative approaches, nourished on our own soil yet largely scorned by the medical establishment — herbalism, chiropractic and prayer among them — should once again be considered as members of the family of official medicine."

Gordon says the current surgical and pharmacological remedies "are potent and effective in emergencies, but for most chronic illness they are little more than palliative. And all too often, both surgical and pharmacological treatments are used inappropriately, produce significant deleterious side effects and are overpriced."

A 1991 American Medical Association survey found 69 percent of those polled believed that "people are beginning to lose faith in doctors," and 63 percent felt "doctors are too interested in making money." It's not just the patients who are unhappy with the status quo, however. A

1989 American Medical Association poll found that one-quarter of those in current practice "probably would not go" to medical school if they had to do it over again.

So what's the solution? According to Gordon, the system should create healing partnerships between patients and doctors, make self-care primary care, examine alternative medicines, restructure health financing, reallocate research priorities and understand illness "as a transformative process and the healer's work as a sacred trust.

"Our current reimbursement system rewards diagnostic and surgical procedures at 10, 20 — even 50 — times the rate of equivalent amounts of time spent listening to, educating and counselling patients. To redress this imbalance, we should give talking, teaching and prevention as high an economic priority as technological treatment."

Finally, Gordon argues that many indigenous cultures understand illness "as a sign of imbalance between the individual and the social, natural and spiritual world as well as imbalance within the individual. This understanding helps makes illness intelligible to the patient, gives larger meaning to his or her suffering. It also provides the rationale for future changes in behavior and attitude.

"If we modern healers wish to perform the same service for our patients, we must first explore our own blind spots. We must fashion a new kind — and also a very old kind — of deeply personal medical education for ourselves and for those who come after us.

"Only those who are exposed to the healing systems of other cultures and times will have a critical perspective on our own medicine. Only physicians who are taught to temper the arrogance that inevitably comes with status and expertise with the humbling power of self-awareness can heal themselves and teach others to do likewise."

Barry Norton, a chiropractor who operates a large holistic practice in Ottawa, believes that shift in perspective is already underway.

The paradigm shift has already occurred in the public, but the medical profession had to be pushed by the public as usual. The profession is always way behind. It took the public in England storming Parliament to get the medical profession to recognize public vaccinations. . . . It has been difficult to get funding for alternative research. . . . Most research in cancer has been directed to viral causes of cancer because they want a pharmaceutical cure. There's really not a whole lot of profit in terms of manufacturing herbal or nutritional approaches . . . although pharmaceutical companies bought the four major nutritional companies in the U.S. who work with holistic medicine.

There has been a movement in the U.S. to have all nutrition done by doctors, even though they don't get it in medical school. There's even an attempt to have nutrition prescribed in the drug stores, pretty scary stuff. There is still an awful lot of antagonism which seems to be originating from the medical profession . . . they use the phrase 'consensus of medical opinion,' and if something doesn't agree with that, then it is not approved.

But it is my feeling that people are tired of invasive drugs and the guts-out philosophy of medicine. . . . There is an extraordinary growth in public interest in diet and other approaches to health. . . . People are beginning to realize that something that would make a healthy person sick isn't going to make a sick person healthy. There is just too much public awareness out there now for the old system to continue.

And given the phenomenal growth in health food stores and holistic medicine, it's hard to argue. Despite the continued opposition of much of the traditional medical establishment, people, it seems, are voting with their feet.

12 Taking Charge

O N APRIL 10, 1993, COLUMNIST STEPHEN Strauss in *The Globe and Mail*, Canada's self-declared "national newspaper," pointed out that during the previous two years his newspaper had published 600 stories, letters, editorials and announcements specifically relating to AIDS. The *New York Times* published 1,182 AIDS-related stories during that time, the *Washington Post*, around 1,000, and the weekly British science magazine, *New Scientist*, 172 AIDS stories.

"Concurrent with this outpouring of media reportage, stories have continued to appear saying AIDS is being ignored," he wrote. "In February, the National Research Council in the United States issued a report suggesting that the disease 'will disappear,' not because it is cured but because those who are afflicted are 'socially invisible.' The same thesis underlay a recent book suggesting there has been a systematic lack of attention paid to women with acquired immune deficiency syndrome.

"We have printed only 25 articles about women and AIDS. However, to put that in context, the LCDC [Laboratory Centre for Disease Control/in Ottawa] says its figures suggest that fewer than 200 women in Canada likely died of the disease between 1990 and 1992.

"At the same time, around 10,000 women died of breast cancer, an issue we wrote about 39 times. (Just 11 stories about breast cancer appeared in the *New York Times* during a similar period.)"

Strauss, of course, was not arguing that newspapers shouldn't write about AIDS, or that it's not a serious problem, only that the attention given to AIDS is out of proportion with that afforded other diseases.

But it wasn't just in the media that AIDS enjoyed a massive edge in official interests. It was also in government funding for research.

During the mid-1980s, Dr. Alastair Clayton, then director-general of the LCDC, predicted there would be 20,000 cases of AIDS in Canada by 1990. In fact, between 1981 and the end of 1990 there were 4,193 reported cases in Canada.

Even so, for the 1990/91 fiscal year, Ottawa committed $38 million toward AIDS education and prevention, but less than $500,000 to breast cancer. In March 1993, when Health Minister Benoit Bouchard announced Canada would spend $42.2 million a year over the next five years to fight the disease, activists and opposition critics alike were outraged. Liberal health critic Rey Pagtakhan, now a junior minister in the Liberal government, called the decision "a serious setback" for AIDS. And New Democratic Party MP Svend Robinson, then the only declared homosexual in the House of Commons, called it a "shameful abdication of responsibility."

Yet three months earlier, when Bouchard had ventured to Toronto and announced $20 million would be channelled into breast-cancer research over the next five years — plus $5 million into other breast-cancer support activities — the announcement was nearly universally applauded.

And when Bouchard himself made the connection between funding for AIDS and for breast cancer, again he was widely attacked. "In breast cancer," Bouchard said in February 1993, "there are about 1 million women who face the problem and we spend about $25 million. There are about 30,000 people with HIV in Canada and we are spending between $35 and $37 million a year. We need to keep perspective." The Canadian

AIDS Society immediately attacked Bouchard for making "misleading and harmful" funding comparisons and announced it would be presenting a brief to Bouchard recommending a minimum funding hike to $55.35 million a year for AIDS.

But Bouchard was merely arguing that there was only a certain amount of public money to go around. He wasn't suggesting one disease is more or less deserving, although many AIDS activists claim that. In an article in the Spring 1993 edition of the *Globe and Mail*'s *Body & Soul* magazine, well-known homosexual activist Gerald Hannon cited a fictitious pamphlet arguing that heart disease, for example, is killing "fat white straight guys in bad suits. There is not exactly a shortage of fat white straight guys in bad suits. AIDS, on the other hand, is killing our Nureyevs, our Keith Harings, our Michel Foucaults." While Hannon tells readers there is "no need to panic," because the pamphlet isn't real, he concludes his piece by saying he longs for such an organization to make such arguments. "In my bitterness, and the misanthropy that attends it, I think I do not care about the victims of heart disease or cancer or any other affliction," he writes. "I become glib and ridiculous — I tell myself that those other illnesses are decimating the ranks of the boring and badly dressed, but that AIDS is cutting the heart out of Western culture," although he softens the blow slightly by saying that "I know, when I feel those things, that I am wrong."

While breast-cancer research enjoys relatively more funding in the United States than in Canada and elsewhere, there is still the same kind of overemphasis on AIDS to the exclusion of other diseases, largely as a result of the strength of the AIDS lobby campaign. The October 3, 1992, *Economist* reports, for example, on a 20-member Hollywood elite called ANGLE (Access Now for Gay and Lesbian Equality). It identified 172,000 homosexual voters in Los Angeles County alone, sponsored a $125,000 fund-raiser for Bill Clinton and launched a campaign to raise $1.5 million for the Clinton campaign. It was joined by the Human Rights Campaign Fund, a Washington-based political action committee working on homosexual issues, which donated $518,000 to various Congressional candidates in 1990 and was expecting to double that in 1992. The Gay and Lesbian Victory Fund, with a $100 entrance fee and a minimum of $200 annual membership dues, also hoped to distribute $250,000 in that campaign. Most of these funds went to Democrats.

The Truth About Breast Cancer

It was no accident that Clinton allowed a homosexual man infected with the AIDS virus to address the Democratic Convention or that one of his earliest moves as president was to lift the ban on homosexuals in the military and to give more money to AIDS research. Even so, AIDS activists attacked him for not doing enough. When Clinton responded during an international World AIDS Day event on December 1, 1993, the *New York Times* ran the story on the front page, and excerpts of his speech, along with other stories on the day, inside. When Clinton pledged three weeks earlier that he would increase breast-cancer research at the NIH by 44 percent under his budget, to almost $300 million from $208 million, the same newspaper buried a four-paragraph story about the announcement in the bottom left-hand corner of page A27.

Author Michael Fumento, writing in the October 1990 issue of *Commentary*, pointed out that the federal Centers for Disease Control, the Public Health Service and the World Health Organization all dramatically lowered their original estimates of AIDS cases and former Surgeon General C. Everett Koop, thought to have coined the expression "heterosexual AIDS explosion," now claims he knew "from the very beginning" that such a thing would not happen. Despite this, Fumento writes, funding for AIDS continues to skyrocket, arguing that "concentration on AIDS has in general prompted a de-emphais of other medical diseases." For those who argue AIDS deserves more funding because it's contagious, while heart disease and cancer are not, he writes, "In fact, AIDS is contagious almost exclusively through behavior, and modification of that behavior could in theory reduce AIDS cases virtually to zero without another penny spent on research and without a single medical breakthrough."

To those who argue that research into AIDS will result in positive spin-offs for other diseases, Fumento points out that so far, just the opposite is true. "As it happens, increasing spending on cancer at the expense of spending on AIDS might do more for both diseases: of the first three drugs approved for treatment of AIDS or its conditions, two — AZT and alpha interferon — were spin-offs of cancer research."

Fumento, author of *The Myth of Heterosexual AIDS*, writes that the "most vocal opposition to spiraling federal AIDS expenditures has probably come from women concerned about breast cancer, which kills about 44,000 a year; every two years as many women die of breast cancer alone as the number of men and women who have died of AIDS over the course of the entire epidemic. . . .

"The blunt fact is, then, that a great many people will die of other diseases because of the overemphasis on AIDS. We will never know their names and those names will never be sewn into a giant quilt. We will never know their exact numbers. But they will die nonetheless."

Another media phenomenon has been the number of stories playing down the seriousness of breast cancer, a stark contrast to the number of stories elevating the risk of AIDS. Even though predictions of AIDS cases and deaths in North America have been consistently overstated, and the risk to women and heterosexual men is regularly overblown, AIDS is routinely called an "epidemic," but breast cancer rarely is. AIDS certainly reaches epidemic proportions in some parts of the world, Africa in particular, but ranks far behind other diseases in North America. While governments run advertising campaigns arguing that everybody is at risk of AIDS, examples abound of the media arguing that women are being unnecessarily frightened by breast-cancer statistics. The March 15, 1993, *U.S. News and World Report*, in a story headed, "The breast cancer scare," argues that women in their 30s and even 20s are increasingly fearful, but "most of them needn't be." Statistically, that's true. The problem is, unlike AIDS, breast cancer is not attached to a particular lifestyle, such as homosexual sex or intravenous needles, and while it won't hit all women, all women are, in fact, at some risk. It is true that the widely quoted 1-in-8 statistic for U.S. women is often not presented as a lifetime risk — at age 25, for example, the odds of a woman getting breast cancer are just 1 in 19,608. But like a lottery, where everybody has a ticket but only one will hit the jackpot, women have no way of knowing precisely when, or if, their number will come up, so it's not surprising the disease makes them nervous. After all, some 80 percent of breast-cancer victims have none of the known "risk factors," apart from being a woman. What's more, while most younger women perhaps needn't worry, they are worrying because even in the under 40 group, incidents jumped to about 12,000 in 1993, up from about 10,000 in 1980. Granted, that reflects the growing ranks of baby boomers now in their 30s, and while the magazine reassuringly points out that "only about 6.5 percent of the 182,000 new breast cancer cases in the United States this year will be in women under 40, and less than 1 percent in women under 30," for those thousands of women whose ticket is drawn, this is small consolation. According to Bonnie Courte, a nursing co-ordinator at the Cedars Breast Clinic, quoted in the October 25, 1993, Montreal *Gazette*, "Breast cancer remains the disease women fear the most." No wonder.

Even the major women's organizations — such as the National Organization of Women (NOW) in the States and the National Action Committee on the Status of Women (NAC) in Canada — didn't champion the disease that was killing so many of their own sisters, mothers and aunts. They were constantly organizing marches and rallies and write-in campaigns for equal pay, lesbian rights and abortion, but they virtually ignored breast cancer.

American-born Judy Rebick, a former NAC president, whose own family has a long history of breast-cancer deaths, says, "We were all caught up in other issues and we just didn't realize how political the treatment and handling of breast cancer was. We saw it strictly as a medical problem, not a feminist issue.

"It was a mistake, clearly. That's all I can say. And until the AIDS thing happened and we saw how a disease can be dealt with in a politicized way, we just didn't get involved in breast cancer. It was the breast cancer victims themselves who started the movement. Now we're getting involved, but we should have begun a lot earlier."

In the United States, while the media bias favoring AIDS is pretty much the same, the funding differentials are not quite as stark. (Ironically, the media bias is most pronounced in Hollywood circles, where many big-name stars are recovering alcoholics and/or drug users, both of which problems have killed thousands of their colleagues with little public recognition about them from anybody.) Still, the Public Health Service spent $1.878 billion on all types of cancer in fiscal 1992, and $1.262 billion on AIDS/HIV research. Yet, since 1980, 194,000 Americans died of AIDS, while 450,000 died of breast cancer alone.

In fiscal 1993, the federal Public Health Service AIDS budget was about $2.1 billion, while the non-AIDS portion of the National Cancer Institute budget was $1.8 billion. Put another way, the research dollars invested per death for AIDS in 1989 alone ($66,792) were almost 30 times the total spent for cancer ($2,520) and about 200 times the amount spent for heart disease ($299).

It is, in fact, the AIDS experience that finally fueled a revolution in breast-cancer advocacy. While it's true that breast cancer received national attention long before AIDS came on the scene, particularly in the United States, women with the disease tended to withdraw into the privacy of their homes rather than organize and demand action.

Indeed, the traditional cancer societies have seemed more in tune with the needs of the medical and research establishments over the years, not to mention their historical ties to drug companies through their boards of directors. In his book, *The Cancer Industry*, Ralph W. Moss points out that the American Cancer Society was married to the establishment since its beginning as the American Society for the Control of Cancer (ASCC) at the New York Harvard Club in 1913 funded by John D. Rockefeller, Jr. During the 1930s a spin-off organization called the Women's Field Army sprung up and was remarkably successful in raising funds for impoverished patients — in the midst of the war in 1943, for example, it raised $356,270. At its peak it had over a million members, compared to 986 in the ASCC, and was poised to replace the establishment-oriented organization, so in 1944 a group of self-described "benevolent plotters" took over the ASCC, changed its name to the American Cancer Society (ACS), abolished the Women's Field Army and instituted a top-down control of all branches from its New York headquarters. The key figure in the ACS was Elmer Bobst, president of the U.S. branch of Hoffmann-La Roche and later of the Warner-Lambert pharmaceutical company, described by Moss as basically "a drug salesman, with close connections to the medical profession and to politicians, such as Richard Nixon." Other leaders all had close ties to major corporate interests, including leading advertising executive Albert Lasker (whose slogan for the American Tobacco Company, "Reach for a Lucky instead of a sweet," convinced thousands of women to start smoking in the 1930s and 1940s) and his philanthropist wife Mary Lasker. Their public relations efforts were so successful, writes Moss, that Associated Press once ran an ACS publicity piece as a ten-part "objective" news series on cancer without acknowledging it came from the society. Asked about the propriety of this, a senior Associated Press executive replied: "I never considered the ACS to be a political organization. . . . That's just like saying that God is political."

The ACS derives much of its power through its control of considerable research funds across the country, which means, says Moss, that scientists "must be responsive to the goals and thinking of the Society if they expect to be funded. . . ." The result has been that most funding goes to established universities and, more to the point, established treatment methods. Moss documents how the ACS has not only encouraged the standard approach, but has actively discouraged innovation in science. "The Society now has tens of millions of dollars to distribute to those who favor its hegemony," he writes, "and many powerful connections to disconcert those who oppose it."

A study released in September 1974 by the National Cancer Institute, reporting the results of various studies involving 1,700 women at 37 U.S. hospitals since 1971, concluded that radical mastectomies, which often produced lifelong pain, weakness and periodic swelling of the arm, were not required for patients whose lymph nodes were cancer-free. They said the less traumatic simple mastectomy — amputation of the breast but not the lymph nodes — was often just as effective for more than half the patients. Typically, the American Cancer Society took a cautious view of the study, saying it would continue to recommend radical mastectomy for most cases of breast cancer. At that time, 95 percent of women requiring surgery received radical mastectomies. It would be many studies and more than a decade later before the radical mastectomy stopped being the operation of choice by surgeons. Although even today, it's performed in disproportionate numbers in various U.S. states and Canadian provinces, particularly in smaller towns or rural areas.

Most cancer research money in Canada comes from donations to the Canadian Cancer Society, roughly $50 million a year. The National Cancer Institute of Canada, however, is fully funded by the federal government. Canada has two federally funded agencies that do cancer research — the National Health Research and Development Program (NHRDP) and the Medical Research Council of Canada (MRC). In addition, Canadian scientists and physicians often receive money from U.S. sources for research.

Canadian cancer agencies remain unenthusiastic about public involvement in their funding decisions. They believe scientists are in the best position to determine where research should be conducted. An article in the June/July 1992 edition of *This Magazine* cites David Beatty, the National Cancer Institute of Canada's executive director, telling an Ottawa committee that genetic research into a rare childhood eye cancer could be significant for breast cancer. He said directing research funds to specific areas might "stifle the creativity of investigators." He also said in a CBC radio documentary that he could see no reason for targeting breast cancer over lung cancer, which kills more people, prompting breast-cancer survivor Paula McPherson to point out that we already know the causes of lung cancer, but not breast cancer. The article added that like most disciplines, cancer research too has its old-boys' network, where researchers have been doing the same research for decades with limited success but are reluctant to try anything new.

Canadian activist Sharon Batt, testifying in November 1991 before a special parliamentary committee on breast cancer, conceded that the Canadian Cancer Society does do some good work, but she was sharply critical of parts of its much-ballyhooed Reach for Recovery program. Batt told the story of Darlene Betteley, working as a volunteer for the program, which involves visiting cancer patients, who had had a double mastectomy and had chosen not to wear a prosthesis. She "was told on that basis that she could not work as a Reach for Recovery volunteer. That bothered me. I have talked to people about that, and they say that this is consistent with the approach of the Cancer Society." (It wasn't until September 1994, when Betteley told her story at a breast-cancer forum in Toronto, that a Society spokeswoman stood up in the audience and apologized to Betteley.) Batt met another woman in Denver who had undergone a mastectomy and had a condition called milk arm, where the lymph fluid flows into your hand. "She was wearing a sleeve, and she was asked not to wear it when she was meeting with cancer patients, with women who were about to have an operation, because it would scare them."

Canadian Cancer Society official Joan Loveridge, however, told the committee that the program, which began in the United States, is now available to women in France, the U.K., Italy, Ireland, several Scandinavian countries, Mexico, the Latin American countries and — she hoped — Leningrad (now St. Petersburg). Under the program, volunteer drivers take patients to and from the clinics for treatment and often act as sources of information "as well as acceptance, understanding and encouragement for people who are in active treatment for a disease shrouded by secrecy and fear."

The Society also sponsors a CanSurmount program, a one-to-one visiting program that links the newly diagnosed cancer patient to the volunteer whose life has been affected by cancer, although not necessarily breast cancer. Indeed, one Ottawa woman found herself meeting a 70-year-old man who had had prostate cancer. "He may have been a very nice man, but what were we going to discuss? I just couldn't believe it when he showed up."

It's no wonder then that advocacy groups, looking for people to promote their interests as opposed to the corporate interests, haven't exactly embraced the Cancer Society. In the United States, for example, the Breast Cancer Coalition convinced Iowa Sen. Tom Harkin to lead efforts to divert $210 million in Defense Department funds to breast-cancer research, and various groups were also instrumental in increases in allocations to the National Cancer Institute.

It wasn't until AIDS activists showed what could be done through political, social and economic action, that women who had long suffered in silence realized that if they organized they, too, could mobilize political support and public research funding.

Dr. Susan Love, surgeon, author and one of the founders of the Washington-based National Breast Cancer Coalition in 1991, argues that political pressure is mandatory to force politicians into funding more breast-cancer research. Even though there is more information available now, much of it is confusing. She told a Knight-Ridder reporter that "doctors tell women to do [self-exams] because there is nothing better. I say run your hand over your breast every few months when you're in the shower and get a good clinical exam once a year." She says by the time a lump is palpable it has probably been there eight to ten years and is about the size of a grape. What's more — contrary to what many doctors say — it's not an emergency. "We make it sound like every breast cancer starts the size of a grain of sand, goes to the size of a BB and then a grape, and if you catch it as a BB your chances are better. In fact, that just isn't true. All this theory does is put the blame on the patient."

Love said she got involved politically because she got "so frustrated telling patients the same thing every year and watching them die. There is nothing magical you can do to protect yourself," she said, but even Love gets into this things-aren't-as-bleak-as-you-think routine, arguing that the more you know the less frightened you will be, comparing breast cancer to earthquake preparedness. "Women worry that if they think about it they'll get it . . . it's not as scary as you think."

Cancer societies too like the more upbeat approach, better to show they're actually making progress with the millions they get in public and private funds. The emphasis on early detection and slogans such as "cancer can be beaten," aren't particularly wrong, but they aren't necessarily right either. Some forms of breast cancer can't be beaten no matter when they're discovered. Others can be. The problem for the cancer establishment is that the angrier women become over the lack of real progress in the field, the more headaches they're going to make for them by demanding changes in current approaches.

In the United States, the so-called "War on Cancer" dates to January 22, 1971, when then President Richard Nixon said in his State of the Union message that he planned an all-out drive to conquer the disease. "The time has come in America when the same kind of concentrated effort that split the atom and took man to the moon should be turned toward conquering this dread disease."

A few weeks later, Nixon's chief science adviser, Dr. Edward E. David, Jr., announced details of the Administration's cancer strategy in a speech in Chicago to the Association of American Medical Colleges, saying stewardship of the program would be given to the National Institutes of Health, despite considerable Congressional pressure for the establishment of a new, separate agency to head the effort. Nixon had asked for $100 million, of which about $30 million would be used to launch the program. In addition, the National Cancer Institute was receiving $232 million for its efforts to fight cancer.

As Nixon himself had said, the belief at the time was that if Americans could put men on the moon and split the atom, surely they could defeat cancer.

With that in mind, and striking a military-like pose, Nixon on May 11 announced he would assume "personal command" of his administration's cancer war, planning to defeat this dreaded enemy by 1976, so America could celebrate its 200th anniversary as a cancer-free nation. Nixon said that "success will test the very limits of our imagination and our resourcefulness. It will require a high sense of purpose and a strong sense of discipline."

The Truth About Breast Cancer

In December, after months of bickering over whether it should be controlled by the National Institutes of Health or a new institution, the House and Senate compromised (both had passed different versions of the bill) and authorized a $1.6 billion fund to conquer cancer. The main thrust of the bill was directed at cancer research, including setting up of 15 centers for clinical research and patient treatment.

Dr. Susan Love explained on a 1993 television special hosted by broadcaster and breast-cancer activist Linda Ellerbee that women want "a national strategy for breast cancer. We want it proclaimed an epidemic. And we want a strategy to solve this disease.

"We have a blood test for prostate cancer. For breast cancer, we don't have a clue. I think the reason more is not known about this disease is because, in part, it's a woman's disease, and women have been well socialized to be good little girls and not to demand more attention.

"What's happened more recently is women have started to see with the AIDS movement that here was a group of people who took it into their own hands, who said 'we're going to yell and scream until you give us enough research money and we start to solve this disease.' Women with breast cancer are now saying, 'Hey, we can do that too.' And all of a sudden there was a channel for all of this anger and they really started to act."

And the results have been dramatic.

Federal funding for breast-cancer research in the United States jumped from $92.7 million in 1991 to $421 million in 1993, largely due to the efforts of Love and a growing band of activists who are tirelessly touring the country delivering speeches, organizing rallies, and instigating write-ins and phone-ins to politicians to push their point.

In Canada, much the same sort of thing has happened.

While the initial burst of interest in the mid-1970s after the Temple/Ford/Rockefeller revelations resulted in considerably more activity in the medical community in Canada as well, women themselves remained unorganized, each facing her ordeal by herself, or with her family, and pretty much relying completely on the expertise of the physicians in determining her course of action.

Then along came AIDS, and all that began to change.

After a 1989 international AIDS conference in Montreal, where people with the syndrome captured as much media attention as scientists presenting papers, Montreal *Gazette* reporter Kate Dunn wrote: "It will be interesting to see if people with cancer, Alzheimer's disease or Parkinson's start pushing for the same presence at their doctors' annual high-sci conflabs."

Women did not immediately convince the politicians to invest more money in breast-cancer research, but when Health Minister Benoit Bouchard finally did announce significant increases in December 1992 he said breast cancer "is seen by women, themselves, as the most important health issue. So [I] have to give it the attention, accordingly."

Such attention is due in no small measure to the work of Pat Kelly, president of the Burlington Breast Cancer Support Services Group and, along with Sharon Batt, one of the key pioneers in breast-cancer activism in the country, who criticized traditional cancer organizations for not being aggressive enough in representing women's interests in the past.

In conjunction with Bouchard's announcement, Dr. Jacques Cantin, president of the Canadian Cancer Society, acknowledged that without the "incessant lobbying" of breast-cancer action groups, "I don't think this cause would have gone as far as it has. I salute you."

But the Society itself, and the National Cancer Institute of Canada, which receives the bulk of its funds from the Society (it spent $35 million on cancer research in 1992, at most $2.8 million on breast cancer) has never been known to rock the boat, something Kelly, who lost a breast to the disease seven years ago, made crystal clear.

"The Canadian Cancer Society has not done the work of championing the cause of breast cancer," said Kelly. "I'm uncertain at this point," about Bouchard's announcement. "It's going to take much more than glib assurances. If it's a token gesture, it's meaningless."

Kelly, working to build a national network of survivor groups, called the 1991 all-party Commons committee investigation into breast cancer, and its subsequent report entitled "Breast Cancer: Unanswered Questions," a "watershed event" for breast-cancer activists. She said it gave them a voice and the strength to fight for their place on the national agenda. "Once you've had cancer," she told Southam News columnist Ken MacQueen, "there are very few things you're afraid of."

Kelly says that Canada's nationwide medicare system explains why Canadian women were slower in getting organized than American women in the fight against breast cancer. "The Americans are still fighting to get basic human health care," she said. "That can be a more compelling issue to rally around."

Nancy Paul, founder of the Canadian Breast Cancer Foundation, said, "I think there is a place and a time for lobbying. This [breast cancer] is a national health concern that affects women and it is of interest to men as well."

Paul, whose foundation was set up in 1986 to raise money for breast-cancer research in cooperation with the corporate and media sectors, said, "At that time, no one could tell us how much was spent on breast cancer research — and we still don't know the actual amount."

Indeed, the Canadian Cancer Society's claim of $2.8 million on breast-cancer research seems dubious. Officials appearing before a Commons committee on breast cancer earlier in 1992, grilled at length by women politicians (some of whom had suffered breast cancer themselves), were unable to say how much they spent on breast-cancer research, but their ballpark figures were about half that stated amount.

With such a conservative medical-cancer establishment, many women decided to take some initiative themselves. One woman who typifies this entrepreneurial spirit is Janice Guthrie of Hope, Arkansas, whose story was told in the June 21, 1993, *Forbes* magazine. Guthrie, 50, was diagnosed a decade ago with a rare type of ovarian cancer, granulosa cell tumor, for which the suggested treatment after emergency surgery was radiation therapy. So Guthrie headed directly to the University of Arkansas medical school library in Little Rock only to discover that radiation therapy didn't keep granulosa patients alive any longer than those who opted for regular checkups after surgery. Her oncologist warned her, "You can know too much," an attitude, says Guthrie, that "really made me angry." After more research, she found a Houston doctor who'd successfully treated granulosa, but since another operation meant giving up her $12,000-a-year job as a university administrator, she borrowed $2,700 from her family, bought a computer and printer, set up shop in her garage and announced in a classified ad in the *Arkansas Democrat* that the Health Resource was open for business.

The service she offers is research. A client calls or writes with a diagnosis and she researches and writes a 50 to 150-page report on all the treatment options, including lists of books, specialists, self-help measures and organizations. The first year, she earned $693, but by year three revenues hit $12,300, and in 1992 grossed $184,486. She has 5,000 clients in her file. Her whole philosophy is that doctor doesn't always know best. An educated consumer is the best patient. "Patients can be active participants in their treatment decisions and in their healing."

The fact is, despite billions spent on cancer research in the United States during the 1970s, there is little tangible evidence of progress beyond the fact that some women are surviving slightly longer and mastectomies were no longer automatic. Cancer officials favor using a five-year survival rate. To say the rate has improved is misleading since much of the "improvement" comes from cancers having been found earlier through mammography, so the five years comes earlier. But in that scenario, a woman who dies after seven years is counted a survivor, hardly an accurate picture of the disease.

Linda Reyes, a San Francisco editor and mother of five, suffered through months of debilitating chemotherapy to fight tumors that had spread to her bones and lungs. In a May 1992 *U.S. News and World Report* article, Reyes says she was just another angry breast-cancer victim until a potluck cancer patients' dinner in 1979 when she saw a 32-year-old woman, a scarf hiding her baldness, an infant on her lap and a toddler by her side. "The sight of that young mother with breast cancer was unbearable," she said.

Then 52, and in remission, Reyes turned activist. She and three members of her group decided to learn more about the disease, beginning what became Breast Cancer Action, which blossomed in just two years from a 12-woman circle into a nationwide network, complete with its own 2,000-subscriber newsletter, that Reyes, as secretary, assembled on her dining room table.

Also in 1979, two women with breast cancer organized an informal support group for a dozen women in a Chicago suburb. By 1991, Y-ME had become the largest consumer-based support program for breast cancer in the States. What began as an answering machine in somebody's home has expanded to a nationwide, 800-number hotline, with 200 women specifically trained in the work of answering the 1,000 calls a month. In addition, it has a 24-hour emergency hotline, not an 800 number, staffed by about eight volunteers. Y-ME bills itself as a "support, referral, and information program." Everyone who calls gets a customized set of pamphlets to her particular needs.

The Truth About Breast Cancer

In December 1990, Susan Love (a lesbian herself) met with Susan Hester, director of the Mary-Helen Mautner Project for Lesbians with Cancer, to discuss the possibilities of forming a national breast-cancer lobby. Next, they contacted Amy S. Langer, executive director of the National Alliance of Breast Cancer Organizations, and launched the national coalition. Within a year, it had 150 member groups.

In 1991, receiving tactical guidance from local AIDS activists, Cancer Patients' Action Alliance (CAN ACT), a New York-based cancer patients' advocacy group, picketed Blue Cross/Blue Shield's Manhattan officers to protest the company's refusal to cover experimental cancer treatments.

In 1987, Fran Visco, a commercial trial lawyer, wife and mother, was advised by her doctor to have a baseline mammogram, although her family had no history of breast cancer. As a result, Visco discovered she had the disease and, after recovering, decided to devote her energies to help the survival of millions of other women.

A November 23, 1992, editorial by *U.S. News and World Report* editor-in-chief Mortimer B. Zuckerman on Visco pointed out there were 2.8 million breast-cancer victims in the United States then, costing the country over $6 billion a year in medical costs and lost productivity, and that the disease is the leading cause of death for women aged between 32 and 52.

Visco joined the Linda Creed Foundation, named after the 37-year-old songwriter victim and dedicated to the early detection and treatment of breast cancer, and in 1991 she became the first elected president of the National Breast Cancer Coalition, which Zuckerman calls "a model of the American gift for association in action."

In 1991, the group decided to collect 175,000 letters — the number of women who would be diagnosed that year with breast cancer — but within six weeks had collected more than 600,000 letters. Next, they organized a conference of leading scientists "and concluded that an additional $300 million could realistically be spent annually on breast cancer research."

Their next move was to march to Capitol Hill. They arrived by the busloads, setting up a vigil on the Senate steps, and eventually convinced Congress, and finally President George Bush, to approve spending of $400 million, nearly triple the previous budget, what Zuckerman calls, "the first meaningful increase in appropriations for the disease. . . .

No longer would women have to pay for breast cancer research with brownie sales and chili cook-offs."

Zuckerman concludes that the National Breast Cancer Coalition "deserves credit for refusing to fight with other medical centers for what little funds were available for medical research and for fighting instead for new money altogether. But where would we be if Fran Visco, and women like her, had not taken up the cause? Their efforts demonstrate how individual enterprise can reawaken a proper sense of national priority."

For her efforts, President Bill Clinton subsequently appointed Visco to his national cancer panel.

Another major U.S. player in breast-cancer advocacy is the National Alliance of Breast Cancer Organizations (NABCO), which aims to provide unity among the various organizations. It has also established a Research Task Force, organized a series of inter-disciplinary hearings and acted as a watchdog on cancer spending, criticizing the NCI for not seeking outside input on how to allocate cancer research funds.

The National Cancer Survivorship Organization, with its headquarters in Washington, is an umbrella organization of cancer survivor groups and publishes a monthly *Health Letter*. It works on such issues as retention of medical insurance after a cancer diagnosis, job-related discrimination of cancer patients, information networks for newly diagnosed patients, support groups and services for patients and families. It also operates one of the largest clearing houses on breast implants in the United States.

The National Women's Health Network, one of the most widely quoted groups in the field, began in 1975 as a watchdog on the promotion of high dose birth control pills (those containing high levels of estrogen), but quickly expanded its interests to the Dalkon Shield, DES and the growing incidents of cesarean births. The Network launched The Breast Cancer Project to advocate patient involvement in research, access to accurate information and the best treatment options, but really made a national name for itself with its strong, and effective, opposition to the tamoxifen trials on healthy women.

The April 21, 1993, *Journal of the National Cancer Institute* carried yet another story on the growth of patient advocacy groups in the United States, pointing out how they were now setting the cancer agenda, making regular appearances in the media, routinely solicited for Congressional testimony and increasingly represented on a variety of advisory panels. "Activists attribute the rising tide of cancer-patient advocacy to a variety of converging factors: the success of AIDS activists in rallying support, frustration with a perceived inaction among older and more traditional cancer advocacy groups, and what they term an "ivory tower" mentality in the medical and research communities, which they feel has marginalized their participation."

"The political, medical, and research establishments are learning that we are a force to be reckoned with," said Beverly Zakarian, president of CAN ACT. And Gertrude Swerdlow, executive director of Families Against Cancer Terror, DeWitt, New York, said membership in her organization had grown by "the thousands" over the previous two years. "The need for us was never more visible than it is now. People hear of us and want to get involved. We've had nothing but strong support from the clinical oncology community and we're on a first-name basis with Congressional Appropriations Committee staff."

A February 7, 1993, report in the *New York Times* explored the questions of AIDS money versus spending on other diseases that kill people. It pointed out that AIDS-related research accounted for almost 10 percent of the NIH budget — $858 million of $9.2 billion. By contrast, federal spending on military research and development exceeded $37 billion. The United States spent $25 billion on funding for cancer since Nixon's 1971 "war" was announced — but with smaller sources of research money drying up (like state funding, which gave $27.2 million for AIDS in 1988 to just $5.3 million in 1991) — and more pressure from other disease activists. The *Times* predicted the problem would get worse.

"AIDS competes with many other diseases, including breast cancer," it said. It quoted an unnamed Senate staff member saying, "Women's health issues seem to have eclipsed AIDS as one of those political forces that cannot be resisted." Despite an expanded definition of AIDS, which the Centers for Disease Control and Prevention in Atlanta predicted would add an extra 100,000 or so new diagnoses of the disease in the United States in 1993, AIDS still fell behind seven other diseases as the nation's biggest killer overall since 1981.

Even the American Cancer Society, which many activists accuse of lack of responsiveness and "lethargy," has been kick-started by the groups, joining the National Breast Cancer Coalition and offering the use of its Washington facilities to them when they hold demonstrations and deliver letters to Congress. "If we can't be specifically behind every kind of cancer," said Alan C. Davis, vice president for public affairs, "there is certainly a role for people who are involved in a particular kind of cancer to move that one to the top of the list. If they find the resources and funds to do it, that's fine with us. We're not the gatekeepers."

In Ontario, while the provincial government was subsidizing privately operated abortion clinics in Toronto with millions each year — despite the easy access to abortions in several publicly funded hospitals in that city — Toronto breast-cancer patients beginning in 1989 were being shipped hundreds of miles north to Sudbury and Thunder Bay, far away from the support of their friends and families, for their radiation treatment. Because of a 14-week waiting list caused by shortages of radiation machines, oncologists and therapists, 228 breast-cancer patients between June and January alone were referred from Toronto to other centers. In fairness, Princess Margaret Hospital was rebuilding and the Toronto Bayview Regional Cancer Centre was doubling its size, but still women who needed radiation treatments after their surgery were being forced into unfamiliar surroundings in order to get the medical attention they needed.

Worse, the Ontario Cancer Treatment and Research Foundation knew for more than two years that it was not providing "timely and adequate" radiation treatment. One 14-week backlog culminated in the Bayview centre briefly stopping accepting patients for radiation treatment who had already undergone breast surgery. On March 19, 1994, *The Toronto Star* reported that doctors, fearing the long wait for radiation could cost patient lives, "performed disfiguring mastectomies, instead of breast-conserving lumpectomies on some patients."

While the breast-cancer story hasn't always received adequate media coverage, one area where the media is regularly enthusiastic is in the reportage of new high-tech treatments, or supposedly important research discoveries.

The Truth About Breast Cancer

Canadian activist Sharon Batt, writing in the June/July 1992 edition of *This Magazine,* makes the point:

As taxpayers and citizens, we all have a stake in the outcome of cancer research, even if we never get cancer, yet public discussion of cancer research is almost non-existent.

Those of us living with cancer have an even greater stake in keeping our comprehensive medical system intact as we will be especially vulnerable if we lose it. Like AIDS activists, we need to voice our concerns about new treatment directions. Media reports frequently give uncritical play to high-tech treatments that are lucrative and challenging for the doctors who do them, but costly for the public and of dubious benefit for patients.

An example is the complicated reconstructive breast surgery known as the tram-flap. Plastic surgeons are touting this procedure, which uses skin, muscle and fat from the woman's own abdomen, as an attractive alternative to silicone implants. This year, a March 7 Globe and Mail article on this surgery said nothing about either costs (up to $18,000) or long-term effects such as herniation, poor tissue transfer and compromised stomach muscles that can cause the stomach to sag and prevent future childbearing. A huge best-case photo accompanied enthusiastic quotes from a doctor who performs the operation.

Batt, a Montreal writer and researcher, was diagnosed with breast cancer in November 1988. In July 1989 she wrote an inspirational, bellwether piece for the *Gazette,* arguing that cancer victims can indeed learn from AIDS sufferers. Batt subsequently helped start Breast Cancer Action Montreal, one of the first breast-cancer activist groups in the country. Her article, accompanied by a picture of Batt showing her hair-loss from chemotherapy, wrote that "stoic optimism, a stance common among breast cancer patients these days, is a step away from silence, a sideways step."

Pointing out the odds of surviving breast cancer "have scarcely improved in 50 years," in 1987, 4,350 Canadian women and 31 men died of breast cancer, compared to 417 from AIDS. "By force of numbers, breast cancer patients might be expected to wield even more political clout than those with AIDS. This simply hasn't happened. In fact, women in Canada have shown little inclination to speak openly about breast cancer. . . . And no one, on either side of the border, has organized a project to stitch the names of breast cancer mortalities into a quilt for posterity, as the AIDS community has done for its dead.

"Instead, the current vogue is to be hopeful, even chipper, about breast cancer . . . ," she wrote, referring to a mid-June NBC broadcast entitled "Destined to Live," which, she wrote, "illustrated this upbeat perspective. . . . Pithy, bright messages dotted the testimonials. . . . Everyone felt [and looked] great. They had chosen the treatments that were 'right' for them. Husbands were supportive, friends were loving, careers flourished as never before.

"All had total faith in their doctors. One young woman was shown yachting with her oncologist. Several other women had given birth to healthy children since their diagnosis.

"Courage is all very well, but the picture was one-sided to the extreme. Patients who felt sick were not heard from, and those who have died were not mourned. Missing from the broadcast was any hint that the public should be concerned about breast cancer."

Arguing that women with breast cancer should be "furious about the scam surrounding breast implants of dubious safety," Batt added that "like the AIDS activists, we should dare to be outrageous to make a point. As American writer Audre Lorde put it, 'What would happen if an army of one-breasted women descended upon Congress and demand that the use of carcinogenic fat-stored hormones in beef-feed cattle be outlawed?'

"Breast cancer patients can't afford to be complacent. We should drop the pose that we're one happy, beautiful bunch of survivors."

Three years earlier, Toronto interior decorator Nancy Paul was asked by Shari Creed, then co-owner of a high-end Toronto fashion boutique, to host a fund-raising dinner with Italian designer Valentino as guest of honor. Paul, whose close friend had just been diagnosed with breast cancer, agreed on the condition that they donate the $13,653 raised at the dinner toward fighting the disease. The Canadian Cancer Society, however, did not allow donors to designate how their contribution could be spent, so Paul and nine other people formed a committee, wrote directly to breast-cancer researchers in Ontario asking them to submit proposals for funding, and dedicated themselves to raising funds and promoting awareness of the disease.

Subsequently forming the Canadian Breast Cancer Foundation, its 600 members have raised more than $500,000 for breast-cancer research, helping researchers in four provinces initiate 14 new studies, and sparking four national public education campaigns to alert women to the importance of early detection, including a deal with Kellogg Canada Inc. where the food company agreed to print information on breast cancer on packages of a new breakfast cereal called Nutrific. It also cut a deal with the C.E. Jamieson Company for a body awareness lotion that has a little neck collar on it, the "how to" breast self-examination. They also produced a breast self-examination video. The body lotion sells for $5.99, with the Canadian Breast Cancer Foundation getting 50 cents for each bottle sold. In addition, Shoppers Drug Mart, with LA Law stars Michael Tucker and Jill Eikenberry — herself a breast-cancer survivor — as their spokesmen, committed $1 million to the foundation with education and awareness breast self-examination shower cards.

While the organization clearly has done good work, it is more closely tied to the establishment than other activist groups, with two doctors from the National Cancer Institute of Canada on its medical advisory board.

Canadian activist Pat Kelly says that breast self-examination is "a tactile skill. Trying to teach women breast self-examination through shower cards or through provision of pamphlets is not going to be successful. . . . The only way women can actually learn the skill is through guided instruction on their own breasts where they have an opportunity to recognize what is normal for them, because women's breasts change from month to month. . . . Ninety percent of lumps, and I am talking about lumps that ultimately turn out to be breast cancer, are detected by women, so although it is a very poor early detection method and very primitive, it is one that obviously many women use as their first line of self-defence." Kelly says that in her group, about 25 percent were initially advised by their doctor that it was "probably not serious. . . . These were women who went to a doctor for medical diagnosis, not glib assurances. Yet these women were observed for periods ranging from three months to one year before a pathologic finding confirmed breast cancer in all of them. Some have since died of metastatic cancer. It is probable that some would still be alive had their cancers been detected earlier.

"Women talk about the need to change the future legacy of this disease, because today the best treatments available still fail thousands of women every year. Prevention is just a dream," Kelly told a parliamentary committee in November 1991. "We believe women must assume individual and collective responsibility for their own health. Despite decades of research, experts still don't know why we get breast cancer and there is only a vague notion of who is at risk."

Another major player in the breast-cancer field is the YWCA, which, over the past decade, has devised a myriad of programs aimed at women in general and breast-cancer patients in particular. In Canada, for example, the YWCA and the federal government produced an extensive five-booklet series covering all aspects of the disease. It also sponsors the Encore Program, first developed by the U.S. YWCA, which provides education, support and physical activity to women who have or had breast cancer.

Even so, parts of corporate Canada were happily jumping onto the breast-cancer bandwagon. In mid-November, 1991, on the eve of a highly publicized, federally organized National Forum on Breast Cancer in Montreal, Avon Canada's 55,000 representatives were dispatched door-to-door selling small, gold-colored pins in the shape of a flame for $2 each, $1.12 destined to go to the Breast Cancer International Centre, set up as a professional fund-raiser to run the campaign to solicit corporate donations and finance research. That campaign was aiming to raise $1 million, with another directed at corporate funding hoping to raise $10 million a year for five years. The question, wrote *The Globe and Mail*'s Vivian Smith, "is whether the company and the breast cancer centre are creating wonderful opportunities or being opportunistic." Many activists in the field assumed the latter. "My main objection is that they are circumventing what breast cancer patients want," said Mona Cedolia, a volunteer with the Burlington Breast Cancer Support Services Inc. in Burlington, Ontario. "It is as if they are jumping on the breast cancer bandwagon, but not for our benefit."

Ms. Cedolia said Avon, by recruiting corporations into its fund, is ignoring hard-won government efforts to tap into corporate donations to a new fund supporting Canadian scientists. Pat Robinson, a Toronto lawyer and board member of Avon's international center, says she is upset by such criticisms, since "it is not our intention to go out and 'cut their grass,'" although she did concede that "obviously, no company does something for purely altruistic reasons. Breast cancer would fit in to its [Avon's] corporate commitment to women." A few days after the initial news stories, after the three-day national forum in Montreal, Avon Canada Inc. public relations and advertising manager Denis Gallienne said some of the money raised could go to breast-cancer support groups. But pioneer activist Pat Kelly, who also attended the forum, said the Avon campaign may split fund-raising efforts in the country. "Everyone's wondering why we need another one. I'm suspicious of any agency that promotes itself as an innovative fund-raising partner. Maybe it's an altruistic attempt, but they certainly haven't indicated that to us. They haven't involved [breast-cancer] survivors in any capacity."

Then there was the "Look Good . . . Feel Better" campaign from the Canadian Cosmetic, Toiletry and Fragrance Association Foundation, which included a glossy magazine with a series of stories essentially saying that with a dab of lipstick here and a touch of rouge there, breast-cancer victims will not only look better, they'll feel better too. It's not that this isn't true, it's just that the blatant self-serving commercialization of the subject is, well, tacky.

At the same time, the American Cancer Society, along with the National Cosmetology Association and the U.S. Cosmetic, Toiletry and Fragrance Association, began running large, full-page advertisements featuring a smiling, made-up woman under the heading: "Karen Campbell has cancer, but she doesn't look it." Again the message was clear: buy our cosmetics and you'll look good and feel good. Even the *New York Times* got in on the act, saluting the Cosmetic, Toiletry and Fragrance Association on its centennial "and its success in securing the industry's future since 1894."

European women have been much slower to organize than their North American counterparts. And groups that have sprung up tend for the most part to remain more closely associated with the existing cancer establishment, a kind of "official activism," rather than taking the more independent North American approach of using activism to force the establishment to change its approach.

A March 3, 1993, issue of the *Journal of the National Cancer Institute*, for example, announced that a "breast cancer advocacy movement" called Europa Donna — meaning "Women of Europe" in Italian — was launched in Paris at a meeting of representatives from cancer societies and women's support groups in France, Austria, Germany, Hungary, Italy, Luxembourg, Norway, Poland, Portugal, Spain, Switzerland and the United Kingdom. The group was headed by Dr. Umberto Veronesi, scientific chairman of the European School of Oncology, Milan, aimed at gathering 1 million signatures to support the group's charter, which calls for approaching European parliaments for support of better screening, education and treatment for breast cancer (which kills about 52,000 European Community women each year). According to the NCI journal, the charter asks women "to commit themselves to making other women aware of the problem of breast cancer, educating themselves about their breasts, increasing their requests for medical checkups as they get older, having a mammogram every two years after age 50, and supporting the development of breast cancer prevention studies." In addition, it also involved family doctors and specialists in promoting treatment and rehabilitation options along with randomized controlled clinical trials. This is a perfectly reasonable position for Veronesi, one of the leaders of the tamoxifen trial in Italy, but the conduct of clinical trials has been a major area of concern to activists in the United States, demonstrating the natural conflicts that often arise between the medical establishment and patient rights groups.

Not everybody is happy with the new activism. As that March issue of the NCI journal pointed out, the National Breast Cancer Coalition wants a seat on the organization's National Cancer Advisory Board and wants formation of an NCAB Breast Cancer Subcommittee, along with a direct channel to the NCI directors and active participation on NCI peer-review panels. "The more direct approach has raised the eyebrows of many in the research community who feel that basic biomedical research will suffer at the expense of 'cancer-of-the-month' funding that is driven more by political pressure than by scientific merit."

Showing that when it comes down to supporting the new activism or the established conservatism, there's no doubt which side the American Cancer Society is on. The Society's public relations boss Alan C. Davis told the NCI journal, "There's a risk in balkanizing the research process by having the group with the most political clout at that moment diverting funds to the issue it is most particularly interested in. It takes away a lot of flexibility."

It also takes power away from the Society and the other established organizations, which, until the last few years, have pretty much had their way with research funds.

There are some legitimate concerns, however, over the tendency of single-disease groups gaining a larger share of the research pie at the expense of other diseases. Writing a June 22, 1993, opinion column in the *Washington Post*, Dr. Anna Marie Skalka, scientific director of the Institute for Cancer Research, Fox Chase Cancer Center, Philadelphia, argued that while breast-cancer activism has its good points, it also creates problems. "Many of us who are both women and scientists have watched the effects of women's activism in this arena with much sympathy, pride and concern. We share the goal of improving the prevention, diagnosis and treatment of breast cancer. We applaud their success in ensuring that women are not left out of these efforts. Our concern, however, arises from the fact that some of the demands of breast cancer activists, as well as their single-mindedness, threaten to defeat the goals they are intended to serve.

"That's because — from the point of view of a basic researcher — the increasing tendency to earmark funds is an alarming one. . . . As more money is directed into specific disease-related efforts, the funds available for broad-ranging basic research are diminished.

"The reality is that the only real hope for improved cancer prevention, diagnosis and treatment comes from a better understanding of the fundamental, molecular causes of all cancer. To fragment existing resources reduces the possibility that a key discovery will come from a completely unexpected source. It is possible, even likely, that the next advance will come from studies using simple organisms to answer seemingly unrelated questions. It is equally likely that the study of some rare or unusual malignancy will provide the fastest route to a better understanding of all cancers." To illustrate the point,

Skalka wrote that the current model for researchers studying cancer genes, including breast cancer, came from the study 20 years ago by Alfred G. Knudson into a rare children's cancer of the eye, called retinoblastoma.

"Cancer survivors and patients should take an active, involved role as advocates for cancer research," she wrote. "The problem arises when the advocates pursue a single issue, a position that serves to fragment and politicize scientific efforts. If we hear more from breast cancer representatives, shouldn't we give equal time to survivors of lung, prostate or colon cancer? Who will speak for basic research, or other less politically important cancers?

"There seems to be an underlying implication that being a scientist somehow impairs our ability to see the human dimensions of the disease. In truth," wrote Skalka, "there are few of us who have not been touched personally by cancer."

Fran Visco, president of the National Breast Cancer Coalition, responds to such charges by saying the coalition doesn't want a bigger piece of the pie for breast cancer, "We want a bigger pie." She told the *New York Times Magazine* in August 1993 that research funding has always been political because there has never been enough money for research. "Someone has been making the decision to fund 'X' at the expense of 'Y.' For too long those decisions have been made at the expense of women's lives. We've come along and we've said enough, stop: you have to start spending more of that money on breast cancer."

Dr. Susan Love says the National Breast Cancer Coalition does not have an adversarial relationship with the NCI, for example, but wants some say in setting research priorities. "The misconception is that grassroots people are stupid, when in fact many of our members are health professionals and researchers. Even those that are not well versed in the science of breast cancer research can learn it and help set the agenda — the AIDS movement has shown that."

While breast-cancer advocacy groups have picked up pointers from the AIDS activists, most have remained less confrontational than AIDS activists in demanding more medical research. Some women think that too should stop. New York artist Matuschka, for example, churns out her posters showing the mastectomy scar to demonstrate graphically what cancer does to women.

The Truth About Breast Cancer

Her self-portrait on the *New York Times Magazine* cover on August 15, 1993, generated much publicity, but Barbara Balaban, a Long Island breast-cancer activist said, "Some people are upset by that cover, but let me tell you, it's not as upsetting as having breast cancer." And Elin Greenberg, head of the Komen Breast Cancer Foundation, said, "This is what it looks like when a part of your body is removed. I was afraid people would be horrified, but several said, 'It doesn't look as frightening as I thought.' It demystifies mastectomy. Here is a person who had breast cancer and lived."

As women stepped up their breast-cancer activism, the media too began to pay considerably more attention. The September 20, 1993, *People* magazine, for example, ran a full-length feature on New York NBC correspondent Linda Ellerbee on her ABC special, "The Other Epidemic: What Every Woman Needs to Know About Breast Cancer." Ellerbee said the show was about survivors, "but also about anger. We say, 'Look, most of us live, so get that lump checked.' But we also say, 'Look how many of us are dying. Raise your voice.'"

The same edition ran a feature on Matuschka, who says, "I am obsessed with documenting my body. I'm driven by wanting other people to see the truth." Her truth is shown in two plaster casts of her own torso sitting on some kitchen cabinets. One torso, with two breasts, was made in June 1991, a few days before her mastectomy. The other, with the right breast gone, was made several months later. Matuschka, who dropped her given name Joanne years earlier, was just 11 when her mother, Helen, was diagnosed. She died 18 months later, leaving behind her husband, a policeman, and four children. "The doctors told her she would live to see her children have children," said Matuschka. "They should have said that if she lived, she would live to see her children have cancer." After a wild, teenage bout with heavy drugs, including four years as a ward of the state, she was taken under the wing of foster parents, Anton and Maureen Marcos, and eventually ended up studying art at Prescott College in Arizona, moving back to New York City as a model and beginning her self-portraits in 1983.

After her mastectomy — which she had a film crew in the operating room recording, and now believes the operation was not necessary — she said her life was "governed by fear at first. I thought I would be dead in a year and a half, like my mother." But she began to follow a strict macrobiotic diet and her prognosis is now good. "Meeting men is no more difficult now," she says. "My first love is my artwork, and it's hard to find a man who can deal with that."

Other artists have also used their talents to demonstrate the devastation of breast cancer. Nancy Fried, a New York sculptor, underwent a mastectomy in December 1987 and has since made many pieces on the topic. She told the *Washington Post* in August 1993 that one of her favorites is a piece called "The Unkept Secret," a torso pulling (its) breast back, and under the breast is a scar. "I made it about the secret I was supposed to keep but couldn't keep; breast cancer and a mastectomy. Hopefully, it's a universal piece. It's about all those secrets — rape, incest, homosexuality, cancer." She says a rewarding side effect of her work "has been the women who thank me, women with mastectomies who have never seen their image in art, especially in such a proud, positive way. Perhaps my work is successful because it never asks for pity."

And dancer Faye Kahn, who had a lumpectomy for her breast cancer in 1990, followed by chemotherapy and radiation, worked for 18 months to record a 36-minute piece called, "If My Breasts Could Talk," featuring the voices of three women talking about discovering the disease, making decisions, remembering their youthful development of breasts and finally, surviving the disease and carrying on with their lives. While the piece plays, Kahn and two other dancers perform and act out the scenes. One of the women in the piece asks, "What did I get from having breast cancer?" Then different voices chip in: "I got a lot of attention." "I started to dream bigger." "I think I just punished myself for so many years." "I didn't fight back." "The cancer made me strong."

Audre Lorde, the official State Poet of New York in 1991 — who lost her breast in 1978 and died in 1992 — refused to wear a prosthesis, arguing, "When other one-breast women hide behind the mask of prosthesis or the dangerous fantasy of reconstruction, I find little support in the broader female environment for my rejection of what feels like a cosmetic sham. But I believe that socially sanctioned prosthesis is merely another way of keeping women with breast cancer silent and separate from each other."

In September 1993 the National Museum of Women in the Arts in Washington featured a 14-painting exhibition by Chicago artist Hollis Sigler, herself a breast-cancer victim, entitled "Breast Cancer Journal:

Walking With the Ghosts of My Grandmothers." Lee Fleming in the *Washington Post* wrote: "Bringing her deceptively delicate fauxnaif style to bear on enduring questions about life, dying and death, she [Sigler] taps the range of emotions: rage, joy, frustration, sorrow, acceptance and transcendence. Ultimately, these paintings are the moving chronicle of a human spirit struggling toward acceptance of death — and achieving a fragile peace along her painted way."

On October 18, 1993, the *Washington Post* ran a front page picture of Syracuse, New York, utility company dispatcher Fred Miccio, a chunky, balding man, standing off by himself clutching a picture of his wife of 20 years, Maria. She would have been 45 that day had she not died of breast cancer a month earlier. "I felt perhaps I could do something," he said. "Somebody has to speak out."

Well, somebody did. In fact, more than 1,000 demonstrators walked from the National Museum of Women in the Arts to the Ellipse in Washington, while in the White House East Room, leaders of the National Breast Cancer Coalition met with Clinton and his wife, Hillary, and presented them a petition with 2.6 million signatures collected in every state over the previous six months, intended to represent the number of women in the United States who have breast cancer, both those who know and those who don't. Clinton promised Secretary of Health and Human Services Donna E. Shalala would convene a meeting the next month to begin drafting a "national action plan" for preventing, diagnosing and treating breast cancer. He also signed a proclamation making it National Mammography Day. Matilda Cuomo, wife of New York Governor Mario Cuomo, and a part of the delegation meeting the Clintons, said, "If we can send a woman to the moon, we can surely find a cure for breast cancer," an oft-used line that is catchy enough, but doesn't make much sense and harkens all the way back to Richard Nixon's war on cancer when Americans believed they could solve anything if only they spent enough money.

Later that same month, Clinton's Special Commission on Breast Cancer chaired by Nancy Brinker said federal agencies needed to spend a least $500 million a year to make substantial progress against the disease. It said almost half a million American women will die of it in this decade while research projects that offer hope of better treatment are delayed for lack of money.

"There are two things we don't know about breast cancer," said Brinker. "We don't know the cause, and we don't know the cure. Until we make such a commitment, we're not going to know either one."

Brinker said since 1950 the incidence of breast cancer had increased by 53 percent in the United States, one of the fastest growing major diseases in the country. Harmon J. Eyre, a vice president of the American Cancer Society and member of the panel, said the National Cancer Institute had identified about $1 billion worth of promising cancer research projects that have not been funded. "Breast cancer would be a very high part of that," he said. "There are at least $200 million worth of additional opportunities that should be funded."

Not everybody accepts the notion that the problem is strictly a shortage of money — a notion that conveniently sidesteps the issue of studying how most of the current money is being spent. Ann Flood, a sociologist at Dartmouth Medical School, told *Time* in November that nobody can guarantee more money will bring a quicker cure. "People say that the money will save lives, but that's not necessarily true. It's not like we are close to brand-new information that would benefit from such funds." Indeed, while nobody is going to oppose more money, it could simply end up raising unrealistic expectations.

In the meantime the message about breast cancer appears to be getting through. In the United States, calls to the NCI's 17-year-old cancer hot line skyrocketed to 600,000 calls a year from 120,000 in 1980. And thousands of women are tapping into CompuServe or Internet, getting directly into Physicians Data Query (PDQ) through their computers. PDQ alone receives about 40,000 queries a month from various sources on all types of cancer. NCI's Cancerfax system also gets thousands of requests for information each month.

On May 8, 1994, Dr. Michael Friedman, associate director of the NCI's cancer-therapy evaluation program, told the *Wall Street Journal* that the rising activism of breast-cancer patients reflects the fact that today "there are more treatments available, from the drug Taxol to (bone-marrow) transplantation," so women have more decisions to make.

That may be, but so far at least, those treatment options haven't proven to be helpful in the vast majority of cancer cases.

And the activists, despite their phenomenal successes, are not about to rest. Fran Visco, for example, told a Congressional subcommittee on the subject that the experience with fraudulent data in Montreal and the University of Pittsburgh showed that women need to be more involved in breast-cancer issues.

"We must make it a matter of policy that consumers.. . . are involved at every stage of the research process," she said, including helping decide the awarding of grants.

That won't please the scientific community, but they had better get used to it.

Women who just a few years ago dared not speak about the disease now won't stop talking about it.

Epilogue

THE TINY PINE TREE WE PLANTED NEXT to Beverley's grave is big now, giving her the shade she always craved in life and requested in impending death.

The children too are grown, adults now, although I worry about our daughter Kathy, given the family history.

That's the thing about breast cancer. There's not much more you can do than worry about it.

Other diseases have more obvious cautions. Lifestyle decisions, really. Lung cancer? Don't smoke. AIDS? Practice safe sex or don't share needles. Heart? Moderate your diet.

Sure, women can — and should — practice breast self-examination and have an annual breast examination by a professional. Women over 50 and some at particularly high risk should also have mammograms.

And the growing evidence linking fat — or perhaps the pollutants in fat — to breast cancer should act as an incentive to govern your diet accordingly.

But beyond that, it's pretty much a mug's game, a deadly lottery that, when your number is drawn, means death about one-third of the time, and pain, trauma, mutilation and fear for the rest.

When I think of Beverley dying just when her life was really beginning, I also think of all the other families I know who have been struck by this disease.

Few families have escaped. Look at your own acquaintances. How many breast-cancer victims do you know?

True, there are some bigger killers. But science has made greater progress in understanding and combatting heart disease. And lung cancer — tragically skyrocketing in women — can be, for the most part, directly traced to smoking.

But breast cancer goes marching on.

It is not that scientists don't want to stop it. Of course they do. But we have to ask, in the wake of billions of dollars spent on breast-cancer research for such little real return, is it being spent wisely?

The results say "no."

The vast bulk of this spending is on the so-called "proven" methods of cancer fighting.

Proven? To do what? In many cases these methods fail altogether. In others, they stave off death for a few more years. They don't actually cure. The cause isn't even known yet, let alone the cure.

It is likely there is not a single cause, since, of course, breast cancer is not a single disease. There are numerous types of breast cancer. Nor is there likely to be a single cure.

The scientific-medical establishment has to begin to open its minds — and its grant system — to new, innovative approaches simply because what they're doing now, while comforting to those making a living from it, simply isn't working very well.

Never mind the concentration on a magic cure, the moon-landing equivalent that Richard Nixon evoked 20 years ago when he launched his so-called war on the disease.

Forget all those happy-face Cancer Society slogans that imply all you need to do is have regular checkups, find cancer early and believe you can beat it, and everything will be fine.

Well, everything isn't fine.

More than 1 million women worldwide, and a few thousand men, will die of the disease this year. How many children will that be without mothers; men and women without sisters; uncles without aunts; and so on?

Millions more will get the disease. All of them also mothers, daughters, aunts, sisters, cousins: real people, real life, real suffering.

Things are not fine. This is an epidemic of staggering proportions, and so far, the combined weight of government, industry, science and medicine has failed even to curtail it, let alone stop it.

Yet the cancer establishment won't acknowledge it's an epidemic.

Let's quit kidding ourselves. Breast cancer kills and maims. It can strike anywhere at anyone. Sometimes it's stopped. Often it isn't.

Now we have read about a major scientific breakthrough — the discovery of the specific breast-cancer gene.

Beyond the massive headlines and scientific awards, however, what does it really mean? Not much, alas.

It might ultimately advance the understanding of the hereditary type of breast cancer — which represents somewhere between 5 and 10 percent of all breast cancers — but it won't, by itself at least, put an end even to that.

It could, in fact, make things worse if women discover they have the gene — or if their employers and/or insurance companies find out. It could traumatize them, imposing lifelong mental suffering on women who know they have the gene, but also know they can't do anything about it.

So what to do?

There is no easy answer to that except to say that much of what governments and medical institutions are spending money and time on now — the questionable high-tech solution — is being wasted right along with the millons of productive, loving lives lost to this disease.

These efforts have become misdirected not just because it's a woman's disease, although science only recently has begun to give women their fair share as subjects of research projects, something long reserved for men.

Rather, it's a question of built-in interests protecting their own turf.

The whole system militates against change — grants, often backed by drug companies; peer reviews, often by specialists unwilling to look beyond their own narrow field of expertise; the direct relationship between publishing and prestige, technology and tenure; and the unseemly hostility toward those outside the loop who want to try different approaches.

It all practically guarantees that most of the effort will be directed to those areas already accepted by the establishment.

That's what has to change. Attitudes. Economic and academic inertia.

Women know that, which is why, finally, they've begun to mobilize and pressure the establishment to change the way things are.

Yes, they've had some marked successes. Yes, research into breast cancer has increased substantially.

But most of it still goes to the same old "proven" methods, the same old "proven" technologies, all of which — as the incidence and mortality figures show us — have really only been shown to be ineffective.

The whole system itself needs radical surgery.

This is too bleak, you say? Too morbid? Surely there is good news?

Yes, there is. Every woman who survives breast cancer is good news. Even those who live a year or two longer than they would have thanks to chemotherapy or radiation is good news. But even those women are never really cured, never relieved from the pressure of knowing that it's there, maybe sleeping, maybe not.

And there are still far too many unhappy endings.

Just before Christmas 1993, Bill Clinton's mother, Virginia Dell Kelley, came to speak to a breast-cancer forum in Ottawa.

A cheerful, gutsy, inspirational woman, she ended her short speech by telling her audience, "I'll be back to see you next year."

She didn't make it.

Too many women don't.

Index

Abrams, Jeffrey, 23
Access to Effective Cancer Care in Ontario, 25
Adey, Christopher, 128
Africa, 58, 62
Ageless Body, Timeless Mind, 238
Agricultural Health Study, 261–262
AIDS, funding/media attention for, vs. breast cancer, 265–269, 270–271, 276–277, 281, 284
Alberta Cancer Board, 98, 104
American Academy of Family Practice, 149
American Cancer Society (ACS)
    and breast-cancer activism, 283, 290
    and breast-cancer incidence, 64
    on breast-cancer risk, 74–75, 77, 210
    and environmental health hazards, 202–203
    and mammography, 123, 126, 129, 131, 140–141, 145, 149, 150, 151
    and mastectomy, 272
    and medical/research establishments, 271–272
    and non-conventional treatments, 251–252, 253

    and prostate cancer, 160–161, 166
American Chemical Society, 183
American College of Obstetricians and Gynecologists, 149–150
American College of Physicians, 148
American College of Radiology, 98, 140–141, 145, 150, 246
American College of Rheumatology, 98, 109
American College of Surgeons, 98
American Holistic Medical Association, 240
American Industrial Health Council, 181
American Medical Association, 98, 110, 246, 262–263
American Medical Women's Association, 150
American Public Health Association, 204
American Society for the Control of Cancer (ASCC), 271
American Society of Plastic and Reconstructive Surgeons Inc., 85, 98, 106, 117
Andersen, Aafe, 158–159
Angell, Marcia, 117–118

Arnold, Andrew, 41
Asia, 62, 181
Atlas of Cancer Mortality in the European Economic Community, 59–60
Australia, 3, 20–22, 59, 100, 113, 142
Austria, 289
Avon Canada, 287–288

Bailar, John C., III, 48–49, 173
Baines, Cornelia, 102, 122, 146–147
Barish, Geri, 177
Basinski, Antoni, 127–128
Batish, Chris, 87
Batt, Sharon, 144, 273, 277, 284–285
Baum, Michael, 131–132
Baxter Healthcare Corp., 111, 112
BCDDP. *See* Breast Cancer Detection Demonstration Project
BCPT. *See* Breast Cancer Prevention Trial
Beatty, Perrin, 89, 92
Beral, Valerie, 69–70
Berkel, Hans, 97–98, 99, 104
Berkelman, Ruth, 141
Bertazzi, Pier Alberto, 204–205
Bertell, Rosalie, 143–144, 184–185
Biomira Inc., 244
Birdsell, Dale, 97, 98
Black, David, 95
Black, Shirley Temple, 7
Blais, Pierre, 86, 88, 89–90, 92, 93, 97, 102–103, 106–107
Bland, Jeff, 253–254
Blumberg, Barbara, 78
Boley, Bill, 102
Botstein, David, 228
Bouchard, Benoit
    and breast-cancer research, 266–267, 277
    and breast implants, 95, 100, 102, 104–105, 107
Boucher, Sylvain, 87
Boyes, David A., 96, 99
BPCO Inc., 202
Brady, Judy, 173
Bragg, David G., 149
BRCA1 (Breast Cancer 1), 159, 213, 228–229
BRCA2 (Breast Cancer 2), 215
"Breast Cancer: Unanswered Questions," 277
Breast Cancer Action, 279, 284
Breast Cancer Coalition, 274
Breast Cancer Detection Demonstration Project (BCDDP), 138–139, 247

Breast Cancer HELP (Healthy Environment for a Living Planet), 174, 175
Breast Cancer International Centre, 287
Breast Cancer Prevention Trial (BCPT), 11, 12, 13, 16, 23, 25–26, 3541. *See also* tamoxifen trials
Breast Cancer Project, 281
Breysse, Patrick N., 158
Brinker, Nancy, 294, 295
Bristol Cancer Health Centre (U.K.), 254–255
Bristol-Myers Squibb Co., 84, 92, 95, 96, 111, 112, 218–219
Britain. *See* United Kingdom
British Columbia, 128–129, 181
British Medical Research Council (MRC), 27–28
Broder, Samuel, 52, 55
Brown, Robert S., 211–212
Bryant, Heather, 98, 146
Bryant Medical Products, 86–87
Bureau of Medical Devices (Canada), 84
Burlington (Ont.) Breast Cancer Support Services, 63, 245, 277, 287
Burton, Lawrence, 253
Burzynski, Stanislaw, 253
Bush, Trudy, 13–14

California Medical Association (CMA), 134–137
Calle, Eugenia, 75
Canada
    breast-cancer death rates in, 3, 4, 12, 154
    breast-cancer incidence in, 3, 8, 12, 154, 181
    breast-cancer risk in, 58, 59
    and funding for breast-cancer research, 266–267, 276
    male breast cancer in, 154
    prostate-cancer deaths in, 162
Canadian Breast Cancer Foundation, 278, 286
Canadian Cancer Society (CCS)
    and breast-cancer activism, 277, 278
    and breast-cancer research, 278, 285–286
    on breast-cancer risk, 76, 256
    and CanSurmount program, 274
    funding for, 272
    and mammography, 131, 142
    and Reach for Recovery program, 273
Canadian Cosmetic, Toiletry and Fragrance Association, 288